I DANCE THEREFORE I AM

A MEMOIR OF SCOTLAND, AMERICA AND DANCING

ROBIN EDWARD POULTON

I Dance

THEREFORE

I Am

A MEMOIR OF SCOTLAND, AMERICA
AND DANCING

ROBIN EDWARD POULTON

*Stories for Isabelle, Liam and Roisín to share the wonders of
Scotland: so they may love their Celtic heritage and discover the joy
of dancing in beautiful St Andrews, Scotland, in Europe, Africa
and America with beautiful and intelligent women.*

Cover photographs are from the family's collection.

Front cover: the author's children Catherine Leïla and Edward dancing the Gay Gordons at a family ceilidh in 1988, with brother Rory, his wife Maureen and our parents Teddie and Delicia dancing in the background.

Back cover: the author wearing the Maclean of Duart dress tartan. He received this kilt for his 21st birthday (the reverse pleat has been let out!) proving that a good kilt lasts a lifetime. He is wearing the RSCDS tie, and medals awarded for his work on peace and disarmament in West Africa (Mali), Afghanistan (UN), and Cambodia.

All profits from the sale of this book will be shared by the Royal Scottish Country Dance Society (RSCDS), 12 Coates Crescent, Edinburgh EH3 7AF, and the Music Department of St Andrews University, Fife, KY16 9AJ, to develop Scottish dance and music in celebration of the university's 600th anniversary and 100 years of partnership with the RSCDS in the university's Younger Hall.

Designed by Madeline Farlow

Printed by Kindle Direct Publishing

ISBN: 9781729316009

Imprint: Independently Published

KEYWORDS:

Scotland — dancing — music — happiness — healthy life — keeping fit — St Andrews — Royal Scottish Country Dance Society — Edinburgh — Glasgow — Scottish dance — Contra dance — Irish dance — German dance — American dance — English dance — Colonial dance — Celtic heritage — Joie de Vivre — France — Brittany — Virginia — Richmond — Charlottesville — Washington — New York — talented women — beautiful women — reels — jigs — strathspeys — waltz — minuet — moonwalking — gender stereotypes — leadership.

ABOUT THE AUTHOR

Robin Edward Poulton danced his first highland fling at the age of six. He danced at and graduated from St Andrews University in 1969, going on to study rural economics and development anthropology at Balliol College, Oxford and the Collège Coopératif in Paris (France). Following an overseas career in humanitarian and peace work, he divides his time between teaching in Richmond, Virginia and writing in Brittany, France. He dances in both places and wherever he can.

Robin is passionate about Scotland and St Andrews – which he says is the most beautiful city in the world—and about Scotland's dancing heritage. He had two Scottish grandparents, two dancing parents and is a proud Life Member of the Royal Scottish Country Dance Society (RSCDS), one of the world's great international friendship networks. He is also passionate about dancing with beautiful, intelligent women and promoting equal opportunities for women's education and careers. Each chapter of this book recognizes at least one brilliant woman, her gifts to life and to dancing.

This book visits many types of dance (American Contra, English, African, Irish, German, French, Scandinavian, Flamenco, Salsa, Ballet, Waltzing, Hip-hop and Moon-Walking, Morris, Medieval, Renaissance ....) but focuses especially on Scottish Dancing and on the cultural importance of dancing for mental, physical and spiritual health. Dr Poulton explains to his grandchildren why every child should learn some form of dance, and describes lots of interesting dances for them to try. The book promotes laughter for healthy living, and the values of "the greatest happiness of the greatest number" as a philosophy for life. The final message of this entertaining book: "**I dance, therefore I am .... fit and healthy at the age of 70**" which is a valuable message for everyone.

Contactable through: poultonrobin@gmail.com
and at the website: DanceFitandHealthyat70.blogspot.com

ALSO BY ROBIN EDWARD POULTON

Popular Social Books

Sister Cities: A story of friendship from Virginia to Mali. Edwards, Ana and Poulton, Robin Edward, with a preface by the Vice-President of Sister Cities International. (Brandylane Editions: Richmond 2019.)

Villes Jumelées: Ségou (Mali) et Richmond (Virginie): 10 années de jumelage et 400 années d'histoire. Edwards, Ana and Poulton, Robin Edward. (Editions La Sahélienne: Bamako 2019.)

Sunjata—Children of the Mali Empire ~ Then and Now. Stories about Malian Children (some of whom grow up) for Teachers and Students of Africa and America's West African Heritage. (Kindle 2017.)

Djita, a Malian girl from Virginia French/English for teachers and students (AuthorHouse: Bloomington 2011.)

Peace and development books:

The Limits of Democracy and the Postcolonial Nation State: Mali's democratic experiment falters, while jihad and terrorism grow in the Sahara. Poulton, Robin Edward and Rafaella Greco Tonegutti, with a preface by Professor Christopher A. Brooks. (Mellen: Lewiston NY & Lampeter, UK. 2016.)

Bound to cooperate—Conflict, Peace and People in Sierra Leone. (UNIDIR: Geneva 2006.),

A Peace of Timbuktu: democratic governance, development and African peacemaking. Poulton, Robin Edward and Ibrahim ag Youssouf, with a preface by Kofi Annan. (UNIDIR: Geneva 1998.)

Putting people first: voluntary organisations and third world development. (Macmillan: London 1988.)

ACKNOWLEDGMENTS

No book is produced without support from others. I must thank all the people who have danced with me over many decades and in many countries, as well as the teachers and musicians who have brought us joy: writing these memories has caused me to remember all of you with great pleasure, whether in Europe, in Africa or in North America. My first teachers were my parents, who both loved dancing and who passed on this love to me. I hope to pass it on to my grandchildren, and the grandchildren of anyone else who reads this book and shares it. The texts have been read, proofed and enriched by several dance friends whom I want to thank: Elisabeth Drumm, Maddie Farlow, Sandy Miller, Audrey Briand, Penny Gibbs, Moira Turner, Caroline Morgan-Smith, my brother Rory and his wife Maureen ... and Professor Michael Newton ... each of whom has been kind enough to make corrections, to suggest additions and improvements. Any bits that have not been improved are my own fault. I have also had encouragement from leaders of the Royal Scottish Country Dance Society (RSCDS) who are cited in the text and whose skills and dedication I salute and admire. Without the RSCDS there would be no Scottish country dancing. The RSCDS is a great and precious worldwide friendship network.

They say that a clear conscience is the sign of a bad memory. My conscience is far from clear: I know that I have forgotten people and events meriting thanks and gratitude. Did I leave out some great stories? Yes. In some cases I have spared people from embarrassment by leaving out their stories, and those people owe me gratitude. Above all I thank my wife and kids, and the grandchildren whose evident love of dancing inspired me to describe for them my own dancing passions.

WOMEN I HONOR BY CITING THEM ADMIRINGLY IN THIS BOOK:

Abigael, Aelyn, Agnès, Alana, Albane, Alice, Aline, Alexandra, Alison, Allison, Andrea, Angela, Anna, Anne, Annie, Atsuko, Audrey, Awa, Beate, Becky, Bess, Beyoncé, Billie-Jean, Brigitte, Carol, Caroline, Carrie, Catherine, Catherine Leïla, Cathy, Catriona, Cécile, Celia, Céline, Charity, Chatty, Chimamanda, Chrissie, Christiane, Christina, Christine, Claudine, Dale, Darlene, Debbie, Delicia, Diana, Djita, Dolly, Doris, Effie, Elfrida, Elke, Eleanor, Elisabeth, Elizabeth, Ellen, Emily, Emma, Eowyn, Eva, Fatou, Fiona, Françoise, Frida, Gaye, Grace, Hanneke, Helen, Holly, Huguette, Isabelle, Janet, Jean, Jennifer, Jo, Joanna, Julie, Kate, Laura, Laurel, Leah, Leïla, Lesley, Linda, Liz, Louise, Lucie, Ludmila, Mabel, Maike, Margaret, Marian, Marie-Françoise, Marie-Jo, Marie-Laure, Marie-Madeleine, Marie-Pierre, Marilyn, Marion, Marjorie, Martine, Mary, Marya, Maureen, Melissa, Michelle, Mo, Moira, Muriel, Nicola, Noëlle, Nelly, Olive, Orlane, Pam, Pat, Paula, Paulette, Pauline, Patricia, Peg, Peggy, Penny, Rachel, Raphaëlle, Rebie, Riekje, Rochelle, Roísín, Rosy, Ruby, Ruth, Sally, Sandy, Serena, Sherry, Soizic, Sonya, Sophie, Stephanie, Stella, Su, Susan, Susie, Sylvie, Talia, Tatania, Tessa, Tikki, Tina, Tor, Trish, Ugly Nun, Valerie, Venus, Victoria, Virginia, Viviana, Wendy, Yolanda, Ysobel, Zélie .... Alas! I have had to leave out so many other beautiful dancers whose praises I wanted to sing. I would need to write a second book to include them all. Perhaps I will. I will sing the praises of courageous women and their #MeToo movement bringing hope, support and pride to ladies who take control of their lives and become leaders in their communities.

DEDICATION

First I salute two dear departed Scottish dancers whom I miss: Trish Nunley and Jim Washington. We had so much fun together on the dance floor. I hope you are dancing together with angels.

This book was written for my lovely dancing grandchildren Liam Edward and Isabelle Yvonne Poulton (their birth certificates mention other names celebrating other ancestors, but this is not an official government form and I do not need to cite every detail including their blood group) and their lovely parents Edward and Louise. Liam and Isa gave me the idea for this book. It is mainly for them.

I wish to add to this dedication the lovely Roísín Newton of Chapel Hill, North Carolina, an honorary granddaughter. Her talented parents Michael and Stephanie will give her music, poetry, dancing and laughter throughout her life. I arrived in Roísín's home in 2016 for her fourth birthday party, wearing the Maclean dress tartan kilt and my St Andrews scarlet gown. Small children gazed up at me in amazement. Many Americans walk around dressed in under garments (just shorts and T-shirt) so a properly dressed Scotsman made a big impression. Roísín immediately took charge of me, saying "Come here, Robin Hood," and "Have some cake, Robin Hood," and "Do up my shoes, Robin Hood"—and I fell in love with her. Roísín is bilingual in English and Gaelic: her lovely mother Stephanie leads a Gaelic choir, while her brilliant father Michael is the leading Scottish Gaelic scholar of his generation.

THIS BOOK, CHILDREN, CELEBRATES YOUR CELTIC HERITAGE. Liam and Isabelle have Irish, Scottish, Breton and Welsh ancestry as well as English, French and Quebecois. With Irish, Scottish and English ancestry, you probably also have Scandinavian ancestors: your delightful maternal grandmother Patricia from East Anglia must have some Danish DNA. During the Middle Ages the Danes occupied East and Northern England, while many of the Scottish and Irish Gaelic aristocracy are descended from Norwegian Vikings. Do you know how the thistle became the national flower of Scotland? It was those Vikings again. In the year 973 a nighttime Viking raiding party sailed up the Tay River to land at Luncarty, near Perth. They planned theft and pillage after killing the sleeping Scots. Taking off their boots to creep up in silence, the Viking assassins found themselves stepping onto a shore covered with spiny Scottish thistles. Their startled cries of pain awoke the Scottish sentries. Hurrah! Great Thistle!

Of course, William the Conqueror (1066 and all that) was a Norman: a Viking descendent, and most of the knights in his army were Normans or Bretons. I deplore the brutality of Normans and English in Scotland, and we must remember that the Normans first invaded Ireland in 1169. Subsequent English treatment of the Irish has been terrible for 800 years: various disputatious Irish chiefs invited the English in to fight against their Irish neighbors, and regretted it. If you sup with the Devil .... The Irish went to America because the English stole their land, destroyed their lives and undermined their traditions. The Irish are tough, and long-suffering. And they organize great parties.

So you are mongrels, my lovely grandchildren, descended from hereditary friends and hereditary enemies. I lived much of my life in West Africa and I married your grandmother in Central Asia. We are all cultural mongrels. There is no such thing as "ethnic purity" and we all have multiple identities. Some Northern Europeans have 5% Neanderthal DNA, and they look just like you and me. There is just one race: the wonderfully varied, incredibly complex and beautiful Human Race. Choose the identity you want, explore and develop the cultures that most appeal to your creative instincts, and make sure that music, poetry, dancing and laughter always occupy an important place in your lives.

CONTENTS

INTRODUCTION

"Cogito, ergo sum"—"I THINK, therefore I am," was the explanation offered by French philosopher-mathematician René Descartes for the nature of humanity. This, my darling grandchildren Liam and Isabelle, is the message that your French teachers will drum into you as you get older: "Je pense, donc je suis!" But beware! I am no fan of Descartes, a mathematician-philosopher whose rigidity of thought has distorted the French education system into a math-fanatic generator of elitism. As Roísín's father Michael would tell you, Descartes' ideas have been twisted by many false prophets and political movements. Instead I recommend you all to look at philosophical models promoting egalitarianism, human rights and social justice. Notably I recommend the Scottish Enlightenment ideas of Francis Hutcheson, and his admirer John Stuart Mill who believed that all human actions should aim to promote "the greatest happiness of the greatest number." This rule is known as "Utilitarianism" and it has guided me since my moral philosophy studies at St Andrews. Briefly: whatever you decide to do should not satisfy your immediate, short-term desires but should also take account of its impact on the happiness (or un-happiness) of yourself and of all those who are close to you. This is a non-egotistical philosophy of life, for it requires you to think of other people's happiness before you act. It begins with "Do No Harm" and ends with a commitment to caring for other people. Follow the rule, and you will avoid being dominated by your own ego while improving the lives of others. The word "happiness" (however you define it) leads inevitably to laughter and to dancing.

Malian philosophers and griots believe men are different from other animals thanks to KUMA, The WORD: the means of expressing thought, reason and emotion. St John the Evangelist agreed: "In the beginning was The Word," says St

John's Gospel. Scottish Enlightenment economist-philosopher David Hume had a different explanation: PASSION, said Hume, drives us. It is desire and not reason or thinking that governs human actions. "Reason is, and ought only to be the slave of the passions," wrote Hume, who was an empiricist: someone who looks at the world as it really is, and not—like many French philosophers—as they think it ought to be structured. I am an admirer of David Hume, whose work, like that of the Enlightenment economist Adam Smith, I studied as a student of political economy in St Andrews University. If passion guides us, then passion has guided me to be a dancer.

Most of all I try to follow the Utilitarian precepts of John Stuart Mill (1806–1873). "The greatest happiness of the greatest number" is a good rule for life, but Mill was good on other subjects as well. For example, he was the first man to introduce a debate in the House of Commons about votes for women. Like me, he believed in equality between men and women. J.S. Mill considered that women in his day were treated no better than slaves and he tried to improve their rights. A broader aspect of Utilitarianism was developed by the philosopher Jeremy Bentham (1748–1832) who influenced Mill's thinking. Bentham inspired the creation of London University, the first to open its doors to all regardless of race, class, creed, or political belief. This is celebrated by his "auto-icon" = a glass case in which you can meet Bentham in person in the entrance to University College London... or at least his mummified self, fully clothed and seated on a chair. Brilliant! Bentham rejoiced at the liberation of slaves by France in 1789, arguing that all "sentient beings" deserve to be treated properly ... including all human beings (male and female) and all other animals. Rather than considering animals as inferior because of their inability to reason, Bentham applied ethical utilitarianism to animals as well as humans. He said that because animals suffer, their happiness and wellbeing is relevant to "the greatest happiness of the greatest number." This is an ecologist's philosophical position that I share. I have tried to adopt this approach throughout my life in America, Europe and Africa.

West Africans dance and laugh to show they are happy. Me too. I love dance and laughter, and both are linked to music. Africans say that dancing is an ongoing conversation between dancers and musicians. West Africans dance to express happiness and celebration, but also for healing and restoration of the mind and body. Here are some Senegalese proverbs about dancing:

> *We dance, therefore we are.*
> *When the rhythm changes, so must the dance.*
> *To dance is to be healed, reconciled and restored.*

My own passions are DANCING and MUSIC. These skills set humans apart from the animals, every bit as much as thought or speech. Animals think and some animals dance: but they do not dance in the way that men and women dance.

Dancing adds cultural refinement to Hume's philosophical approach. In Scottish and Contra dance I try to maintain a conversation with the musicians, who need feedback from the dancers. Dancing also allows me to interact with beautiful, intelligent women - another of my passions—and this interaction adds greatly to the greatest happiness of the greatest number. How many women have I made happy? Masses, and they all made me happy as well. It is impossible to name all the beautiful women with whom I have danced, but I honor them all by dedicating the chapter headings of this book to some exceptional women.

Laughter is a key to happiness, so I have also tried to make this book amusing. One of our family passions is the limerick. My own father used to chant limericks, rather like Gregorian plainsong. It was less melodious than the monks in church, but a lot more amusing. So from time to time, I include a relevant (or irrelevant) limerick. Here is one of my father's favorites, related to the Highland cattle of Scotland with their beautiful long coats and gentle demeanor, which can change in the springtime:

> *Let X equal Cow.*
> *Then, if Y's a Bull,*
> *On meeting a Cow it's advisable*
> *To determine its sex*
> *Lest, what seems to be X,*
> *Should really turn out to comprise a Bull.*

Since your other grandfather is Irish, you have a genetic disposition to enjoy poems inspired from County Limerick. Your grandmother Mamie is Bretonne, but her paternal grandfather William George 'Bill' Elcoat claimed descent from the O'Neills of County Cork, next to County Limerick, saying they were the Royal Family of Ireland. You, our grandchildren, therefore have Irish, Scottish and Breton blood, as well as English and Welsh (the "pool-town" of your name was Welshpool, in Wales): so you are a Celtic Prince and Princess! Roísín is a Gaelic princess—a princess and a rose! Róisín Dubh, meaning *"Dark Little Rose"*, is the name of a famous medieval Gaelic song and a poet's name for Ireland.

I could write a joyful book about dancing in Africa with Fatou and Djita, in France with Françoise and Christiane, in Germany with Dale and Audrey, or I could take you Cajun dancing with Talia in Louisiana, Scandinavian dancing with Paula and Andrea, contra-dancing with Emily and Wendy, swing-dancing all over America, or dancing around Europe—maybe following music through the Renaissance which also had great dances. I could write you an entertaining chapter about Pordic's Town Twinning and dancing to the Glenn Miller Big Band Sound in Cornwall with Annie Danger, Agnès, Emma and Sonya; about late-night *Festnoz* Breton dancing with Soizic and Marie-Mad; or evenings of Arabesque and Latin dancing in Plérin with Noëlle et Olivier. I could write about Breton dancing at the annual St

Loup Festival in Guingamp, or the annual Celtic Festival in Lorient. I could write an exciting book about animal dances: not only the spectacle of peacocks or baboons trying to mate, or bonobos making peace, but also human dances that are based on animals. Highland dance—just one example—illustrates great stags like the one in Sir Edwin Landseer's famous painting *The Monarch of the Glen*. Highland dancers put their thumbs and their middle fingers together and hold their arms aloft just slightly in front of their ears, which imitates the antlers of a stag. Your Mamie and I have witnessed a mystical example of animal-inspired dance in Thaxted, Essex where Morris dancers come together for regular end-of-May ceremonies that involve beer and bells, fertility rights and eating fruit cake. The *Abbots Bromley Horn Dance* is a weird and wonderful procession of six dancers wearing or carrying deer antlers through the twilight to the haunting sound of a single fiddle: a pre-Christian Mercian ceremonial dance representing both the spirit of the hunt and an appeal to the spirit of the slaughtered stag to favor future hunting expeditions. Native American Indian dances sometimes worship and imitate the great buffalo herds of the plains. African dances often involve similar rites for similar hunting purposes: you should never kill an animal, children, without first begging its forgiveness and explaining to the animal's spirit that you need its flesh for food. The famous masked dancers of the Dogon cliffs in Mali imitate all the animals and birds of their environment. We are close to the animals that surround us. Often we eat them. We are also close to them because we are animals ourselves. Never forget that truth.

This book focuses on the culture of Scottish dance, which is of course related to and descended from other dance traditions. When I give you too many details about a dance, just skip it: I have described the way they are, and I include instructions in case you need them. I have written this book for you, my grandchildren Liam, Isabelle and Roísín, in order to share with you (and with other friends around the world) the joyous dancing and philosophy of life I have inherited from our Scottish ancestors and from my St Andrews university education; to celebrate my dancing friends; to share with you my passion for Scottish dancing and my proud membership of the Royal Scottish Dance Society.

Pordic, Brittany and Richmond, Virginia, Summer 2018
poultonrobin@gmail.com

1

DANCING A TIMELESS MINUET WITH ISABELLE POULTON, AGED FIVE

You will probably not remember, Dearest Sweet Isabelle, that when you were five years old you asked me one day, during a visit to you and your parents: "Papy, why do you always wear the same thing?"

The short answer could have been: "When I come for three nights, I travel with a small suitcase and two blue shirts: they may look the same but actually this is a clean shirt." That obviously is not what you wanted to hear, at the age of five. Instead, I replied: "I have my summer suit upstairs and I will wear it for you."

I pulled on my light seersucker suit in blue and white stripes, bought the year before for a peace conference in Belize, a small country in Central America with warm weather. It is wise, when you have reached grandfather age, to pack one smart outfit in your suitcase. With tightly rolled trousers and folded jacket, it fits even inside my small traveling case. Luckily, I was able to dress up smartly to please my fashion-conscious darling five-year-old granddaughter.

And when I came downstairs, Sweet Isabelle, you were wearing a princess dress and a million-dollar smile. Your father was grinning happily in the background, probably having bought you the princess dress for Hallowe'en. So I bowed low (very low, both because you were a princess, and also because you were only five years old and much shorter than me) and kissed your hand and asked: "Beautiful Princess, shall we dance?"

You smiled graciously, as befits a princess, and agreed that we should dance.

I taught you the Minuet. The step is quite simple, the timing is gentle but precise, and the movements are graceful. We bowed to each other, and then to the Presence (your father on this occasion, wearing shorts which is not how the Presence is usually attired) and we bowed to each other once more. Then we moved forward up the hall for four steps, turned for four steps, and moved forward down the hall for four steps before turning again, with you moving forwards and me moving backwards. After that, we repeated the movement all over again. Most elegant.

We could next have begun a Z pattern, meeting in the middle to turn with right hand, then with left hand, then with both hands ... perhaps we did some of that, but the whole thing is a bit long for a five-year-old. After all, you had not yet learned the A-Z alphabet! You were very pleased with what we achieved together. We bowed to each other and to the Presence three more times. Our dance was charming, graceful. For music I sang you Beethoven's Minuet in G: "tra la-la la-la la-la la-la la-laaa, tra-la-laaa, tra-la-laaa," etc. And why that tune? Because when I was six and my sister Alana was five years old, our mother taught us to dance the Minuet to the music of Beethoven's Minuet in G. She must have had a vinyl recording of Beethoven's music, which he composed 200 years ago.

That same year mother taught me the Highland Fling, which I first demonstrated on stage at the age of six at her dance-class concert in Byfleet village hall, with Mrs Gristock playing the piano. I am sure that Alana and I looked very sweet dancing the Minuet. I am sure the applause was sustained. Alana also sang very sweetly, in that same concert, the popular ballad: "Nobody loves me, everybody hates me, I'm going to the garden to eat worms: big fat juicy ones, long thin slimy ones—see how they wriggle and squirm." She received a huge ovation.

The Minuet was danced in aristocratic ballrooms throughout the 18th and 19th centuries. There was no television in the 18th century, so music, dance and poetry and story-telling were some of the ways that people entertained themselves in the evenings. Even when I was a child in the 1950s, there was no television in our house: our first TV experience was with elderly Mr and Mrs Pierce next door, who —like so many Brits—bought a TV set to watch the 1953 Coronation. We had radio, which had been popular since the early 1900s. Every afternoon after lunch, Alana and I would settle down to "Listen with Mother" recounted by Daphne Oxenford, and later at teatime we would hear a story told by "Uncle Mac" who finished every story with the words "Good night children everywhere." One day, thinking that the mike was switched off, we heard Uncle Mac say, "Well, that should keep the little buggers quiet for another day." Of course we did not understand what he had said, but it is a good lesson: never forget, children, and especially in this age of smart phones, that everything you say can be recorded. Anything you do could become an embarrassing photograph or video. Even as school children, you need to be conscious of managing your image in these days of instant messaging and permanent internet recording.

Before the Second World War, Europeans spent a lot of time creating their own entertainment. Nowadays most American and European entertainment is simply consumed: switch on, sit back, close down your brain, and watch TV. Few people know how to entertain themselves. Few people remember how to dance. Yet dancing is the best exercise you can find for the body and the brain. Medical research shows that dancing is the best recipe for maintaining alertness in old age and retarding senility—better than crosswords or playing chess. Dancing uses your whole body, teaching balance as well as memory. Dancing is also good exercise for the spirit.

There were no mobile phones when we were your age. I remember my Scottish grandmother Elfrida Maclean—Mrs Poulton who lived in St Helens Cottage on the Isle of Wight—had a black upright telephone with a separate earpiece. Your other great grandmother Delicia's dolls' house has one of these old telephones, with which you play sometimes and which dates from the 1920s. Granny's number was St Helens 22. St Helens lies just half an hour's walk up the coast from Ryde, where the Portsmouth ferry arrives. This provides me with a wonderful excuse, children, to tell you my favorite Isle of Wight limerick.

> *There was an old lady from Ryde*
> *Who ate some green apples, and died.*
> *The apples fermented*
> *Inside the Lamented,*
> *Made cider inside her inside.*

That old lady probably lived in the 19th century, before there were any telephones. When I made my first visit to Germany at age 15, I stayed in a lovely rambling 18th century wooden farmhouse with a family whose phone number was Laboe 321—a village that nowadays describes itself as "die Sonnenseite der Kieler Förde" trying to persuade tourists that life is sunnier on their side of the water! Living in Northern Europe, you need to accept that rain is a part of the beauty. Ireland is rich from "green gold"—the rain-fed grass that fattens lovely Irish livestock. In the Celtic lands there is no such thing as bad weather, children: only inadequate clothing.

Much later in 1981, when I was working to build farmer cooperatives in Timbuktu, my telephone number was 06. In 1981, the telephone in Timbuktu was an army wind-up field telephone left over from World War Two. I could not call Bamako, the capital city, from Timbuktu. Fifteen years later modern communications arrived, and I was able to call Wyoming, America from the Timbuktu Post Office. Life has changed so rapidly that every citizen in Timbuktu now uses a smart phone, just like you and your friends. So do the jihadists who claim they want to take Islam back to an imaginary "golden age" modeled on the 7th century. They want a 7th century dictatorship with 21st century conveniences, starting with smart phones and rocket-propelled grenades. But dancing never changes. Dancing is a part of the rootstock of our culture ... of every culture.

My sister Alana and I performed our Minuet in 1952, on a small stage in a church hall in Surrey where our mother was teaching dance shortly after the end of the second world war. The 1939–45 war dominated our young lives but you kids should not dwell on war: be happy, be filled with laughter, and dance! When you dance, dearest Isabelle, Liam and Roísín, always remember where dancing came from: from our ancestors who danced for joy. Africans dance for joy, and so do Europeans. Scottish dancing is joyous. The Minuet is elegant, beautiful, peaceful, timeless. The Minuet is a part of European culture.

Dancing is an exercise that you do in concert with friends and partners. Dance combines the blessings of friendship, music, and healthy exercise. People who dance have no time to make war. These stories will tell you how dancing has made me a multitude of my friends in the worldwide dance community, all fit and happy people. Medical research shows that collective activities like tennis and badminton, soccer and dancing produce better health effects than solitary sports like running or cycling. For the human body to receive overall health benefits, social and spiritual content are necessary to complete the purely physical effort.

One day in August 2018 as we sat lunching in the Brittany sunshine Isabelle, now aged seven, made this wonderful observation: "You cannot have too many Happy Trees." What a lovely sentiment to promote the greatest happiness of the greatest number: you are so right, my sweet!

2

DANCING THE MINUET WITH LINDA AND VISITING THE HEBRIDES

My first Minuet as an adult, Sweet Isabelle, took place in Richmond, the capital city of Virginia, at the turn of the millennium. I had recently arrived in America where your grandmother Michelle became head of programs for ChildFund International. While Mamie Michelle travelled the world looking after children, I became a university teacher and a dancer. I have been a Scottish country dancer and highland dancer since I was a child, but now in Virginia I explored new worlds of dancing: English, German, Spanish, Cuban, Mexican, Argentinian, African, Irish and American. One of my early new experiences was English country dancing, as enjoyed by George Washington, Thomas Jefferson and John Marshall during the 18th century in the American colonies. Trish Nunley, a wonderful dancer whom I met in the Scottish group, proposed that she and I should join the Colonial Dancers of Richmond. The Minuet is one of their dances. Linda MacDonald is the Colonial Dance Mistress, and a great historian of dance. Our first evening with the Colonial Dancers showed us that we were among their best dancers because Scottish dance had trained us so well. Linda invited us to join the Colonial Dance demo team and told us to be ready for the following week.

Trish took a day off work and drove me to Williamsburg, the old capital of Virginia, where we bought clothes: the sort of 18th century clothes that wealthy English settlers would have worn on their plantations in the 1770s. Mine included a three-pointed hat, while Trish chose a green bonnet trimmed with lace that matched her large skirts (there were three petticoats underneath, and bustles to enlarge the hips, but no hoops). When I was five years old, I already loved dressing up; my wardrobe of kilts, dance costumes and African robes shows that I have not changed. One of the old Poulton-Garnett family traditions is playing charades on long winter evenings. We also love amateur dramatics, including Gilbert & Sullivan operas: Mamie and I performed in *The Mikado*, *HMS Pinafore* and *The Gondoliers* (your father performed in this one as His Own Particular Drum, and—aged ten—raised the roof in his soldier's uniform by waving his cap to generate huge audience applause: he had great instinctive timing). We and the Hanlons also put on the Tim Rice and Andrew Lloyd-Webber musical *Joseph and his Amazing Techni-Colour Dreamcoat*. Once upon a time, at the British Council in Kabul, Afghanistan, I even choreographed the pseudo-Scottish musical *Brigadoon* and taught the lead actor the Sword Dance. As a small boy I was in pantomime (the page-boy in *Cinderella*: "Sire, it fits!") and innumerable Christmas shows as well as in many school plays. Dressing up is fun, and so is theater: I recommend them to you grandchildren. Choral singing as well: fantastic experience.

A few days after our shopping trip to Williamsburg, we were dancing the minuet in the magnificent atrium of Richmond's Twin Towers, wearing our elegant outfits of embroidered green (Trish) and Bordeaux red (Robin). Linda was dressed in elegant blue. She held my hand very tightly and guided me through the minuet. There are many types of minuet and plenty of variety in the steps, but the one we were doing is the one I taught you when you were five years old. It is simple and elegant. Later Linda would teach me a Baroque Minuet with more complicated steps and a much longer floor pattern, which we used for demonstrations of that period.

Like most dances with a partner, the minuet is very sensual. You barely touch your partner, but you look into their eyes the whole time (especially if, like me on that first adult-minuet occasion, you have almost no idea of what you are doing). So I gazed into Mrs MacDonald's eyes, touched her fingers for the bow and curtsey, held her hand for the turns, and realized that she is a very beautiful woman. Holding hands is powerful medicine! So is dancing, for it provides the excuse to hold hands and to gaze into each other's eyes at the same time. "Make eye contact!" say our Scottish dance teachers, trying to stop dancers looking at the floor .... And what they are inviting us to do is to flirt with our partner. That is fun. Never look down at the floor: you are dancing with your partner, not with the floor.

"Dancing is flirting" is something I read on one dancer's T-shirt at the Richmond Folk Festival, and that is a truth you should never forget. Dancing is healthy, and flirting is healthy: they are both part of normal human interaction. They are a part of joyfulness. Both dancing and flirting contribute to "the greatest happiness of the greatest number." Dancing also necessarily involves music, which is a balm for the human spirit. Nothing adds more to human enjoyment and happiness than music. I see you grandchildren dancing when the music inspires you, and I reckon —even at your young ages—that you are set on the right path to enjoy happy lives. I wish you this blessing: a life of laughter and dancing and happiness.

Minuet music is calm and melodious. Minuet dancing is elegant and smooth.

The minuet involves listening and moving, concentration and relaxation, individual enjoyment and gentle flirting with your partner. I was enjoying my first formal dance with Mrs MacDonald. But where, I wondered, was Mr MacDonald? It turns out that he was right behind me, dressed as Sa Gracieuse Majesté Le Roi Louis XVI—the well-meaning, well-educated but fatally indecisive King of France who went to the guillotine on 21ˢᵗ January 1793. Alasdair MacDonald, born on the Isle of Skye, was wearing a coat of elaborate yellow brocade, a white curled wig and an enormous tricorne hat that he waved to all-and-sundry with hugely exaggerated bows. Linda rolled her eyes, knowing that her husband had just completed nineteen holes of golf. Alasdair was hilarious and we have been firm friends for nearly 20 years.

Here is a limerick from the Inner Hebrides, of which both Skye (Alasdair's home island) and Mull (my Maclean grandmother's island) are a part.

> *There was an old man from the Isles*
> *Who suffered severely from piles.*
> *He couldn't sit down*
> *Without a deep frown,*
> *And he had to row standing for miles.*

Skye has a fine coastline, splendid castles and brutal midges, but you could visit other exciting places with strange names in the Inner and Outer Hebrides, such as the Butt of Lewis and the Cock of Arran. When you are older, you could visit Benbecula, Uist and Erinsay; or Rùm, Muck and Eigg which are not too far from Mull and Duart Castle (home of the Clan Maclean) and the Holy Isle of Iona where Scottish kings were buried and where St Columba arrived in a stone coracle to bring Christianity to Scotland. This really means he crossed the Irish Sea in a small wooden boat without a keel, carrying the Bible and a large piece of granite for ballast. From Mull you can reach Fingal's Cave on the spectacular, uninhabited Hebridean Island of Staffa, which inspired the music of composers as different as Felix Mendelssohn and Pink Floyd. Of course there is a strathspey called *Fingal's Cave*, but I have never danced it.

In the Southern Hebrides, the Island of Barra is exciting, home to the McNeills. My best friend from university, Professor David Williams, is married to a famous novelist in New Zealand called Helen McNeill. If they fly into Barra, they have to land on the only airstrip I know of that says "arrival is subject to tides"—because Loganair flights to Barra land on the beach. Helen's home island of Barra is the site of the hilarious black-and-white film *Whisky Galore* (1949): the original book was written by Compton MacKenzie, one of Scotland's wittiest writers. The story concerns a ship wrecked on the coast of Barra, which carries a cargo of whisky. The islanders help themselves and save the cargo; but the customs and excise men arrive and now the islanders must hide the hundreds of bottles of whisky in (of

course) the most unlikely and amusing places. I once hosted Sir Compton
Mackenzie to speak to the St Andrews University Celtic Society. He was hilarious.
Born in Hartlepool, he spoke like someone educated at St Paul's School in London
(which he was). But Mackenzie's heart was truly Scottish: a co-founder of the Scottish National Party and a great fan of Gaeldom.

RUFTY TUFTY, WALTZES AND POLKAS WITH TRISH

That evening in the atrium of Richmond's Twin Towers there was an orchestra of 40 musicians and they played for three hours. Our demonstration of colonial dances (including the minuet, *Rufty Tufty* and *La Belle Catherine*) lasted only ten minutes. Probably we repeated it a second time, but without the minuet. For the rest of the evening, we danced; and since the orchestra was playing a great deal of music written by the famous 19th century Viennese composer Johann Strauss II, we danced a lot of Viennese Waltz. I take my waltzing seriously, and I am not alone as this quote will show you:

> *"The waltz is a very serious dance....*
> *My mother lost all reason when she was waltzed."*
>
> — MISS FISHER (ESSIE DAVIS) IN "MISS FISHER'S MURDER
> MYSTERIES"

First I must share with you the steps of *Rufty Tufty*, a medieval dance that is fun and easy to dance with friends and family and which was danced long before the waltz. People in England have been dancing *Rufty Tufty* for 1000 years! The dance is recorded in John Playford's 1651 book of dances, but it had been around for centuries and there are regional variations. We dance the following version, in a square set of 2 couples facing each other, following a well-worn pattern in English dance of Stepping, Siding, Arming. Stepping means lilting towards the other couple, and back again. Siding means the man and woman step forward to brush right shoulders, step back, then step forward to brush left shoulders, and step back while smiling at your partner. Arming means placing your right hands lightly around each other's right elbow for half a turn, and coming back with left arms (NEVER grip the lady's arm with your thumb or you will leave an ugly bruise). After each of these verses, there is a chorus.

RUFTY TUFTY

Traditional English dance printed in Playford's book *The Dancing Master* of 1651.

The title meant "rough and tough" in late medieval English.

Verse 1 :

Bars 1- 4 : Double forward and back (one step towards the other couple, and one step back);

Bars 5- 8 : Repeat;

Chorus:

Bars 9-16 : Set and turn single, and repeat;

Bars 17-18 : Take partner's hand, double out, turn around, switch hands;

Bars 19-20 : Double back;

Bars 21-22 : Turn single;

Bars 23-28 : Take corner's hand, repeat bars 17-22;

Verse 2 :

Bars 1-8 : Siding.

Chorus repeat

Verse 3 :

Bars 1-8 : Arming.

Chorus repeat

These medieval dances are easy and fun to do, especially if you imagine that you are a knight in a baronial castle, a lady in sweeping velvet and silk scarves, or a miserable serf with bad teeth dancing in the fields after harvest time. In case you are a smelly serf with bad teeth, you should try not to breathe too close to your partner's nostrils. Far more satisfying, however, are the elegant dances of the ballroom, many of which evolved at the time of the Renaissance. I dance with enormous pleasure as one of the Richmond Renaissance Dancers, wearing magnificent costumes to present Italian and French dances of the 1500s. Linda MacDonald is our Queen Elizabeth I and—as you would expect—hers is the most extravagant costume. We each play a role at the English Court. I am Robert Dudley, Earl of Leicester, the childhood friend and 'Dear Robin' of Her Gracious Majesty Queen Elizabeth. I volunteered to be the executioner, but Linda chose my friend Mark Crean for that role. Probably he looks more villainous than me.

The Scottish ballroom dancing we enjoy goes back to the 1500s: to the time of Queen Elizabeth's cousin Mary Stuart, Queen of Scots. Waltzing is a ballroom dance that evolved during the 19th century, and it is one of the best. If you watch the videos of the Dutch impresario André Rieu's orchestra, you will see that he brings dozens of young Viennese couples to dance while he plays Strauss waltzes, and they dance in a very formal fashion: for twelve steps they turn to the right, and then they change with a quick running-step and turn twelve steps to the left, and so on. They dance almost elbow-to-elbow, so their steps have to be perfectly attuned in order not to knock each other over. All the men are elegantly dressed in black, all the women are beautiful in sparkling white gowns and the whole choreography is strict. Elegant it is; free-wheeling it is not. When I dance, I love the liberty of movement, of space and of variety. My version of Viennese Waltz is wilder than what they teach in Vienna. When you are old enough to enjoy the Viennese Waltz, children, I recommend the strict Austrian version for demonstrations, and my interpretation for fun.

Your grandmother Michelle and I had the opportunity to visit the city hall in Vienna, capital city of Austria and—in the 19th century—of the Austro-Hungarian Empire. The ballroom of Vienna's city hall is one of the finest rooms in Europe. It is so vast, that there are two platforms, one at each end of the ballroom, to allow for two different orchestras to play at the same time. Johann Strauss used to occupy one stage; one of his frustrated rivals would have his orchestra at the opposite end and the wealthy people of Vienna would dance to the music they chose. His rivals were frustrated, of course, because Strauss was the composer everyone preferred. His music flows with a smoothness and a vivacity that you otherwise find only in ballet, or in the Scottish strathspey.

Dancing in Vienna is constrained not only by the rigidity of the 12-step pattern, but also because often there are so many people on the dance floor that you can barely move. Watch a film of the Viennese New Year Ball and you will realize that people barely dance at all because they are all crushed together. You can see the beauty of this dance at the Stanford Viennese Ball: the 2013 internet choreography for their opening set pleases me particularly with its restrained and elegant twirls. In the atrium of Richmond's Twin Towers we had half-an-acre of space for three or four couples and we could do whatever we liked. Trish and I had our private orchestra of 40 musicians playing Strauss waltzes: elegant but not restrained, we let rip!

Sometimes the orchestra played a polka, and we tore the space apart with our energy and our whoops of delight. That evening Trish and I discovered that we both loved to waltz, that our polka was perfect, and it was the beginning of a wonderful 15-year dance partnership. Over the next few years we danced every type of dance you can imagine: Viennese, Bavarian, Irish, Balkan and Israeli, New England Swing, Scottish reels and strathspeys, English and Colonial dances, Quadrilles, Virginian reels, a bit of Tango, lots of Salsa, Cuban and Panamanian and Mexican dances, even Flamenco—which Trish and her friend Laurel did to perfection, and which I did simply to keep them company in the role of the aristocratic and arrogant Don Juan. Oh! Children! If only you could admire my haughty Spanish sneer!

Whatever the dance, usually Trish was better at it (except for Scottish), but I hung in there and kept her company. Trish was a scientist and a lawyer who never did anything without doing it perfectly. I generally do what I enjoy without worrying too much about over-rigid rules. Even Trish's death was perfect. These dance essays are both a salute to my lovely grandchildren and a tribute to the memory of my friend and dance-partner Trish Nunley, who died in her sleep on 26th June 2016, three days before her 61st birthday.

While her death left a lot of people devastated, Trish left us at the top of her game. She was so smart! Trish bowed out before the woes of arthritis, scoliosis, or bad knees-hips-ankles caused her too much pain and stopped her dancing. That elegant lady arranged an elegant exit. I do not know to what extent she planned it —probably not at all—but I know she was ready for it, calm and prepared, and I admired her ending as much as I admired her life lived in full control and achievement. The dancers of Virginia miss her, but death is not the tragedy that Americans sometimes believe. Death is a part of life. A good life is completed by a good death. My own father, when he felt that his end was near, told his friend George Swirles, "I have had a good innings and I think it is time to hang up my boots"—a cricketing metaphor that translates to baseball, and which shows perfect equanimity to the end of life. The family and the dancing will continue, whether we are there or not. Africans believe that we are reborn in our descendants, and science has proved it. My DNA continues in you: Africans are therefore correct. My generation hopes only that our children and grandchildren will remember us as kind people who did no harm, and who tried to leave the world a slightly better place by promoting the greatest happiness of the greatest number.

I have danced many other types of waltzes, and I should tell you about them: for example the New Waltz, which starts with the man moving backwards, doing a half-turn on every bar. The New Waltz was invented in the 1880s when ladies wore ball gowns that reached the floor: the man's first step backwards lifts the dress clear off the floor, and the constant turning keeps the hem of the dress flying inches above the surface of the dance floor. There is the Boston Slow Waltz using three equal steps: you exhale on the third (downward) step with a half-turn each time that is very elegant but demands tight control. Of all the waltzing I have done across the world, the relaxed Scottish and American waltzes are the ones that give me most pleasure, and the French *musette* waltz is far and away the most boring: the French turn without moving their heads, in a smooth and invariable path using tiny steps following the other couples around the edge of the floor and this gives me no pleasure at all.

My parents were good waltzers. My mother's favorite Scottish dance was the delightful *Waltz Country Dance*, an old Scottish waltz from RSCDS Book 4, known under various other names. The formal written instructions make the dance sound complicated, which it is not. As couples, you dance around the room facing other couples who progress in the opposite direction. You advance, retire and swap places four times, using gracious waltz steps. Then all four take hands and advance into the circle four times; each time as you dance back, the gentleman turns the lady on his left under his left arm so she passes gracefully across him to his right side and with a sweep of her long skirt. Finally, with eight bars of ballroom waltz, you and your partner dance on to find a new couple. So elegant!

WALTZ COUNTRY DANCE

Waltz n x 40 bars for 2 couples in a 2-couple set. Progressive around the room.

Start with 1s facing clockwise, 2s anticlockwise around the room, each M facing opposite L.

RSCDS records say this dance derived from a longer dance called *The Guaracha*, or *Spanish Waltz*.

Bars 1-2 : 1s 2s advance and retire;

Bars 3-4 : 1s and 2s pass opposites by the right, Man turning clockwise ¼, Ls ¾, to finish facing partners;

Bars 5-6 : 1s and 2s, facing partners, advance and retire;

Bars 7-8 : 1s and 2s pass partners (like bars 3-4), finishing facing opposites, 1s 2s now having exchanged places;

Bars 9-16 : Repeat bars 1-8 from new places, finishing in original places;

Bars 17-18 : 1s and 2s join hands in a circle and advance and retire;

Bars 19-20 : Men turn opposite Lady under the left arm so that Ls exchange places, finishing all facing partners with hands joined in a circle again;

Bars 21-22 : Repeat bars 17-18;

Bars 23-24 : Repeat bars 19-20, Men turning partners under the left arm;

Bars 25-32 : Repeat bars 17-24;

Bars 33-40 : Taking ballroom hold, 1s 2s waltz round to pass each other (giving left shoulders), finishing facing the original direction opposite new couples.

Most American waltzing is inspired by the Scottish waltz tradition, although German Waltzes and Ländlers are also popular. If you cross your hands with the right wrist on top, swing your hands left and right and turn the lady right round under your joined hands, you will find yourselves looking at each other through the "kissing window" or *kleines Fenster* which is fun—there is also a *grosses Fenster* where you are turning shoulder-to-shoulder. Making this Ländler kissing window is a great dance move to astonish and amuse a waltz partner, but don't overdo the kissing part, Liam, or you may get your face slapped!

In Richmond we have a tradition of waltzing sessions with CDs by great American dance bands, led by exciting dancers like Gaye Fifer, Catherine Farmer, Talia Moser, Linda Salter and Laura Duncan. I have many lovely dancing friends, some of whom use exciting, creative email names like 'WollesYarn' Elisabeth, 'Freckle-Beans' Sherry, 'Dancingscotty' Valerie, 'dancingdaughter' Michelle, 'WestBee' Darlene, 'ChippyChew' Rochelle—perhaps I should invent an exotic address for myself? Cathy Millar in Williamsburg uses her own name, but her ISP has the gloomy name of 'Widowmaker'—I think I will give than one a miss.

We waltz for two or three hours at a time, changing partners with each new tune. A lot of our waltz dancers come from the contra dance community, people who like to turn and spin: and so the leader will turn the follower under their arm, spin them in different directions, and generally introduce interesting variations as the waltz music takes them around the dance floor. If there is space, I love to stretch my partner out at full arm's length, then bring her across me to stretch out in the other direction, so we feel like a pair of swans floating across the surface of a great lake, then bringing her in again to ballroom hold in order to turn as a couple around and around and around again. With a light partner and a swift piece of music, such bliss! One year during the Springforth Ball Sunday Morning concert I had so much fun that I wrote a letter of thanks to the composer Owen Morrison who was also playing in the band.

Dear Owen Morrison

Today is Thanksgiving. Time to give thanks. For what? Well, in my case, it is time to say "Thanks for the dance."

Last 2016 Springforth Ball you played a concert on the Sunday morning, and during the concert your band played two waltzes composed by you. They were wonderful.

The first was advertised as great film music. I danced with Catherine Farmer at the back of the Ginter Park hall because such music is simply too good for listening. It enters my body through the ears, gets blocked in my emotions, and I have to let it out through my feet. Catherine Farmer is a wonderful dancer. We glided gently across the boards, me in the kilt, moving my body to your music while my lips described to Catherine the Scottish landscapes you were transcribing so vividly. I gave her a tour of the Scottish Highlands as we danced, passing shining lochs, traversing fields of purple heather, crossing gurgling streams of mountain water, climbing hillsides to see, across the glen, a glistening seascape with misty mountains and a beautiful glimpse of the Island of Mull just beyond the water. It was a wonderful journey, thank you. I thought of you frequently this past July, Owen, as I crossed the landscapes of your music, touring Perthshire and the castles of Royal Deeside during a break from dancing at the St Andrews RSCDS Annual Summer School.

Your second piece of music was quite different. Again, I was gliding gently at the back, alone with your music, when a tall lady whom I do not know stood up from the audience and came back to dance with me. She, too, must have found the emotional build-up more than her seat could support, and she needed to express—or expel—the emotion of your music. It was intense. I do not know her name, nor where she comes from (she does not normally dance in Richmond). We clung to each other for mutual support, and we danced with your tune. At one instant of intense emotion, I glanced at her face. Her eyes were shut and tears were coming from them. I felt the same. If I had known her name, I could not have pronounced it at that moment: I was completely choked up by the beauty and emotion of your waltz. Thank you.

Thanksgiving is not an American holiday I love. Our White ancestors immediately massacred the Native Americans who were hosting them, took their lands and reduced their descendants to poverty, refugees in their own land. So thank you for what? For being massacred? But giving thanks is something I prize. Today I am giving thanks—through your musical brilliance—for life and love and laughter, for beauty and music and dance. Please tell your band, and the rest of your family, that I am grateful they have all brought me joy through their music.

Best wishes to you

Robin

Owen was pleased to receive my "grateful dancer" letter. Musicians give enormous passion to their craft, and they get paid very little (unless they become world-famous stars like André Rieu). So I try to reward our dance musicians with heaps of praise, leading the applause, telling them how good they are, thanking them for their playing, and also by purchasing their CDs. Yes, children, what Mamie says is true: I do have a lot of CDs of dance music played by Scottish or Contra dance bands. The reason is not only that I enjoy their music, but also that I express my pleasure by buying their CDs.

LIAM EDWARD MOON-WALKING WITH MICHAEL JACKSON AND BEYONCÉ

My Dear Liam Edward, your sister has moved from minuet to ballet. I love the way she moves every time that ballet or other music plays in your home. I love the fact that your home is filled with music. And while Isabelle performs arabesques and pirouettes, I have also discovered that you are a very talented jazz dancer.

Your "take" on Michael Jackson is really exciting! Jackson was a very gifted musician and performer, from the age of seven when he was already the star personality of the Jackson Five. While his life was probably pretty unhappy (it is difficult to "live" when your life takes place on stage in front of fifty million people), Michael Jackson contributed a lot to the world of dance.

Jackson was already dead before you ever thought of dancing; and yet at the age of eight and nine years, you were dancing the steps and the style that Michael Jackson invented. Part of that can be explained by film, of course: you see him and you imitate him (and you imitate him very well). But more than the films of Jackson prancing, I think we should conclude that he was a great dance choreographer and performer, the inventor of a whole new mode of dancing that you have also seen through the performance of other dancers.

What could be more different than the revolutionary moves from *Thriller*, and the staid 18th century Minuet? Where did Michael Jackson's dance moves come from? What is the DNA of this type of dance, which is so different from the strict formality of European dance forms?

The answer is "Africa." African music crossed the Atlantic to the Americas, where it evolved into many different branches of music. From America, African music moved back across the Atlantic Ocean to Europe first as jazz, which is especially popular in Germany and Britain. African music means dance. Africans dance all the time. The roots of Jackson's dance and music are found in Africa. Africa is a part of Britain and America. Virginia's way of life is a fusion of Celtic and Anglo and African cultures. Virginia's music and cooking are mostly African, just as Indian curries have become the national dish of Britain and North African couscous has become a national dish of France. Did you know, children, that the famous "Indian" dish chicken tikka masala was invented in Glasgow? Chicken tikka masala was invented in 1971 by the chef Ali Ahmed Aslam, owner of the Punjabi Shish Mahal restaurant in Glasgow. He improvised a sauce using tomato sauce, yogurt, cream and spices to satisfy a customer who wanted a sauce on his grilled chicken. Maybe the Glaswegian was expecting some gravy. What he received was an innovation in Pakistani-Scottish fusion cooking that has become a national treasure.

The British Empire exploited many nations, but one hundred years ago it morphed into globalization through the Commonwealth's great spreading of African, Indian, Pakistani, Arab, Malaysian, Cantonese and British cultures. Globalization started with the vast and wonderful multi-culturalism created by the English language mixture of ideas and peoples—long before computers or the internet. Britain's culture and economy have been enriched by Africans, West Indians, Arabs, South Asians, people from Cyprus and Hong Kong, as well as Jewish, Huguenot, Dutch, Polish, Russian and other European migrations. Their legacy is your legacy. William Faulkner said, "The past is never dead. It's not even past." That is where Michael Jackson fits it: he is a part of this multi-cultural musical inheritance. We are all beneficiaries.

A retired English head teacher called David came to work as a volunteer in our ActionAid schools in The Gambia in 1986, helping our teachers to improve their performance in the classroom. David told me one day when he was chilling out in our home over the weekend, that he had attended a school dance somewhere along the banks of the Gambia River. How was it, I asked?

"I was rather disappointed," David replied. "The Gambian school kids all danced rather like the kids in our schools at home. I was hoping to see something more 'African' when they danced."

I laughed out loud. "But David, what do you think your English kids are dancing? Are they doing Minuets or Scottish or Morris Dances, or traditional European forms of round dancing? Not at all! What your English kids are doing is imitating African dance forms that accompany the African musical forms that are jazz and rap, reggae and swing music and pop music. In Africa, you will find the original dancing that your English kids are imitating."

So African culture, Liam, is where the Michael Jackson moves originate. He was an innovator, because Jackson took the dance form in new directions and contributed to the whole hip-hop movement. He joined West Coast street dancing to East Coast break dancing, and with the precision of his moves he linked

America back to the African dancers you see enlivening the concerts of major music performers like Salif Keita. Your father Edward can explain it better than me, for he is of the hip-hop generation, and he was raised in West Africa.

I remember one of the many occasions your father astonished me, when we spent New Year in the beautiful medieval city of Djenne, situated on an island in the Niger River. We attended the New Year Ball, organized by the local Malian youth association. The first dance was a Slow, danced by the two presidents (the male president and the female president) as a formal opening to the ball; and then everyone joined in. But at one moment the D.J. played some fast music, and suddenly your father Edward and his sister Catherine were performing dance steps I had never seen before. No one in Djenne (and that included your astonished grandparents) had ever seen hip-hop steps before. Quickly a space opened around my children as they demonstrated the latest hip dance moves from America (I suppose) and possibly they were learned from one of the videos made by Michael Jackson.

The other great American dance synthesizer of the current generation has been Beyoncé, an astonishing performer who has combined motherhood, business acumen and fashion leadership with dance and music stardom. Her *Run the World (Girls)* video is filled with stunning dance moves standing for a worldview that women can do and be anything. Beyoncé is a great leadership role model, who shows that women and mothers (of twins!) can keep fit. In her 2013 single *Flawless* Beyoncé quoted (with permission) from a TED talk given by award-winning Nigerian writer Chimamanda Ngozi Adichie (she calls herself "a happy feminist") entitled *We Should All Be Feminists*. Beyoncé uses Adichie's definition of a feminist as "a person who believes in the social, economic and political equality of the sexes." I share that view. I am a man and I am a feminist. Beyoncé Knowles like Michael Jackson is a star of the hip-hop generation, but Beyoncé offers the better role model. Hip-hop is not my sort of dance. I am mainly a country dancer. But if you decide to be a hip-hop dancer, or even a break-dancer, good luck to you. The main thing is TO DANCE!

When your great-grandmother Yvonne had a stroke, I went to Essex to look after her for three weeks while she recovered at home. Thaxted is a center of Morris Dancing in East Anglia, but I needed something different. So I looked to see what I could find, and signed up for a modern dance class in Saffron Walden, the local market town.

Of course I was the only man. I am usually one of very few male dancers. When I danced ballet with Tatiana, a Russian former ballerina who was living in Mali, I was the only man in that class as well: "The hippopotamus dancing with the gazelles" is how I described myself—which, if you think carefully, was a way for me to compliment the ladies in the class (even those who were not very good dancers). Because I was the only man, Tatiana cast me as The Prince in her annual dance gala, Scheherazade—the story of a princess who kept her prince enthralled by her late-night stories. Tatiana's annual ballet gala was a highlight of the cultural year in the Bamako of the 1980s. Tatiana was amazing as a teacher and as a dancer, bringing in people from age three to age seventy-three. Her costume-making team was especially impressive. Your aunt Catherine Leïla and her age group danced as flowers waving in the breeze during the Scheherazade gala, while I sat on my throne eating fruit, throwing grapes to the adolescent dancing girls. I left my throne only when the "new girl" Awa Beye, aged sixteen at the time, arrived in her veil as a gift to the Prince (that would be ME!). Together we danced a pas-de-deux using pas de basque, chosen because it was the only ballet step Tatiana and I were sure I would get right. But the audience never knew that.

Dancing is a form of sport and entertainment that attracts more women than men. I have never understood why. In earlier centuries, men were expected to be good swordsmen and good dancers, the two being very similar sports. A good dancer is an athlete. Before dancing, you must warm up properly. After highland dancing, especially, we sit on the floor and stretch every part of our body in the same way as any Olympian athlete after a race. You need to do the same in high-level modern dance, or if you dance for a long time. In the Saffron Walden class, for middle-aged adults and lasting 40 minutes, warm-ups and warm-downs were needed but I am not suggesting that any of us was dancing like an athlete. Even the dance teacher was not really exerting herself: let us call it "healthy exercise" and leave it at that.

After making sure that your great grandmother had eaten her supper and was ensconced in an armchair (or in her bed), I would slip out of the house twice a week and drive fifteen minutes to Saffron Walden (this means the "saffron woods" = the place where they grew and harvested crocuses during the Middle Ages to produce the expensive spice called saffron). You will be astonished to learn, Liam, that we danced steps invented by Michael Jackson. Yes, in the dance class in Saffron Walden, your grandfather was dancing the same steps that you dance: I was moon-walking, tipping my Michael Jackson hat, spinning and tap-dancing to a Thriller routine. Exciting moves, good exercise, and fun. But I must say, Liam, that you are better at moon-walking than I ever was.

ON LEADERS AND FOLLOWERS: THE EXAMPLE OF MICHELLE

D ance is about teamwork and partnership and this, my dear Liam, will be an important part of your education. Isabelle and Roísín too, of course. When I played tennis, which was my favorite sport as a young man, I always preferred doubles to singles because my pleasure is teamwork. My other sport was rugby football, where teamwork is the very essence of the game. Rugby is your inherited family sport: your father played for London Scottish youth; your grandfather played for St Andrews; your mother's father and grandfather played for Newcastle; your great-great-great uncle Ronald William Poulton-Palmer played for Harlequins and Liverpool and captained England's 1913 Grand Slam team. (Yes, it is a shame! the Scottish part of our family arrived in the next generation). RWPP was selected for England before he won an Oxford Blue. He still holds the record for the number of tries in a match (5 for Oxford against Cambridge, 4 for England against France). Ronnie's elder brother Edward (my grandfather EPP) played field hockey. Three generations of our family including Edward and Ronnie Poulton attended Rugby School and Balliol College, Oxford—the College that carries the name of the Scottish king John Balliol (reigned 1292–96), whose mother Queen Deborgail—or Devorgwilla of Galloway—founded the college in 1263.

Your maternal grandfather is Irish, so rugby football is in your blood— although I have noticed, Liam, playing in the garden, that you have increasingly good soccer skills. Soccer requires good teamwork and the feet of a dancer. At the international level, watching a soccer match is like watching ballet dancing with a ball. The inter-passing and reactive back-heeling to the teammate you know must be racing up behind you, require elegance and exquisite balance combined with instincts of partnership and teamwork.

When your father Edward was just a wee tot in 1981, we played a team game in the yard that I called "cooperatives" because at that time I was building farmer and herder and fishing and medical cooperatives in northern Mali after the Sahelian economy had been devastated by drought. Our game was this: with a bamboo cane and a piece of string, I would pretend to be landing a fish. Five-year-old Edward would have to catch the "fish" dangling on the end of the rope, and pull it into a basket. He loved trying to catch the fish, and I loved dangling the ? (was it a pair of socks?) in front of him and watching him try to grab it, improving his physical coordination as we played. Later we would play with balls, perfecting his catching skills.

One day when I was collecting him from nursery school, his teacher told me that Edward was one of the few children in his class who knew what his father did for a living. When asked this question in class, the children of teachers knew that their parents were teachers; the only child who had a different answer was Edward: "Mon père travaille dans les coopératives." So you see I was teaching him the value of teamwork from the very earliest days.

Teamwork is essential in dancing: you may be in a set of eight people, in which case the first couple acts as "leaders"; or if you waltz as a team of two, one of the two has to lead. This is normally the man. It is great training for life and for management to learn to lead in dancing. Being the "follower" also requires huge skill. Responding in exact time to the music and the leader requires sensitivity and agility. It is a matter of teamwork, which only works if the leader provides a clear lead.

Your grandmother was a very successful leader, promoted to Senior Vice-President of her development organization and elected to several international leadership positions in the UN and in Africa. She leads quietly. A leader who has to shout is probably a poor leader. Anyone who bullies is no leader at all. On a Harvard University leadership course, your Mamie Michelle discovered that Harvard identifies six styles of leadership. Successful leaders use at least four different styles at once. Michelle was the person in her course who best represented an understated model of leadership getting people to follow her by persuasion: a fusion of "coaching" and "affiliative" leadership models, while also being good in "democratic" leadership and at "vision setting"—showing people where they want to go.

I base my own leadership on the sports model: a team captain has to play harder than anyone else, inspiring others to follow; but if the goalkeeper (for example) is not playing well, a captain must be able and willing to assert authority and replace the goalie for the sake of the rest of the team. I earned respect by insisting on impeccable moral standards. Michelle led her teams, I think, by love: love of her job, love of the children she was protecting worldwide, love of the cultures she was sharing in many lands, love of the staff whom she was leading on their sensitive and often dangerous human rights missions.... And they loved her back. I never met someone who did not love your grandmother Michelle. She provides you children with a grand example of exceptional leadership, perhaps an inclusive and feminine style of outstanding leadership. You may learn—you MUST learn—from all the different leaders whom you will meet, but in the end each person has to develop his or her own leadership style.

Good teamwork and good leadership involve practice and planning, more than talent. Achieving success requires more perspiration than inspiration, including for dancers. Have you practiced your moves? Is the music perfect for what you need? Did you stretch your muscles before starting to dance? Have your dance shoes been worn into holes? Beware! If everything seems to be going well, you must have overlooked something. Early preparation is a good start, but careful preparation is the key to success. Remember that the early bird may get the worm, but it is the second mouse that gets the cheese. Obviously: the first mouse died, because he did not first check out the trap.

Your father Edward showed leadership skills at a young age. Like his sister Catherine Leïla, Edward was regularly elected class representative at the Lycée Liberté in Bamako. He said it was because he made people laugh, and he could do so in English, French, Bambara and Spanish. On one occasion when he was about thirteen, Ed's electronic calculator disappeared. I asked him if he wanted me to intervene, and he said no: he knew who had taken it and he would handle the issue in his own way. Back in school, Ed waited until the guilty party R had gone to the bathroom and then walked over to R's school bag and removed the *trousse* containing all his pens and writing equipment. He concealed R's *trousse* (what I used to call a pencil-case) in a friend's bag and cheerfully replied when accused of theft that R could have his stuff back when Ed had found his calculator. The exchange was duly made. I imagine that the whole class followed this transaction, watching the clash of wills and Edward's victory: impressive leadership.

My uncle John Garnett, head of the Industrial Society in Britain, was the nation's top trainer for business leadership. Yes, children, the advantage of a huge family network like ours is that you can find a specialist in nearly every domain. Teachers? We have them. Lawyers? We have plenty. Doctors or nurses or midwives? Whichever specialty you need, we have it! The first cousins of John Garnett and Teddie Poulton (my father) were the Symonds brothers. Ronald Symonds (whose great grandson Jack is now studying history and dancing at St Andrews University) was the head of both MI5 and MI6, and was our nation's chief spycatcher during the Cold War; his brother Richard was a United Nations peacemaker in Pakistan and Cyprus, and one of my role models. You probably will never need a spycatcher or a peacemaker: but if you do, we can supply the needful.

John Garnett argued that the greatest skill in management is persuading people in factories or on building sites (for example) to do the best job they can with the resources available: and this is achieved through good leadership. Leadership, he used to say, is best illustrated by sport.

"There is no team in sport larger than 11 people, except for rugby football," John would declaim with great eloquence and inimitable enthusiasm: "and in rugby football, which has a team of fifteen players, there are two captains: a leader of the forwards and a leader of the backs. This proves that the largest number of people who can be motivated by one person, is ten. In the army, they work on the basis of platoons, that are sub-divided into smaller groups of five or six soldiers— or 'sections'—led by a corporal."

Leading and following are therefore key components of life, and dancing is a good way for you, my dear Liam and Isabelle and Roísín, to learn both skills. Women need to learn to lead, just as men also need to learn how to follow. You must learn how to "manage up" as well as "manage down" because you will definitely all become leaders, and you may one day suffer from having a poor leader as your boss. Do not seek popularity in your career: if you are respected for your competence and your integrity and if you are also kind people, you will be popular. Compared to a couples dance like the waltz, the leadership role is less demanding in contra dance or in Scottish country dancing where there are set lines, and where the dancing partners are really equals—they are indeed equals, even though everything is written down, as a convention, using terms like "the gentleman leads his partner..." etc. Yet even in these group dance settings, the "leading" can become a necessity. There are plenty of times when I have found myself "leading" a whole set in order to get them through a dance. Leading is a valuable skill to learn. People who are followers—who include any dance partner who is uncertain of what to do —need a clear lead. To be indecisive is to be unfair to your follower: your lead should be simple, but clear.

Le Roi Louis XVI was indecisive, and look where that led him!

6

GOOD LEADERSHIP REQUIRES FIRM ARMS AND NO NOODLES—ASK J.LO

T alking of "indecisive" leads me to talk about "noodles" who are a menace to any leader. When you turn somebody in dance or when a couple give hands to turn, both dancers must offer a firm arm or the turn will fail: not a fist, but a firm arm starting at the shoulder. When somebody gives you a limp spaghetti arm with no force or weight behind it, the dance movement is spoiled. You cannot turn a noodle unless you have a fork in your hand. I sometimes say to women in desperation: "Imagine that you are lifting a saucepan of potatoes. You have a firm arm for the potatoes and I need the same firm arm for dancing." They still do not always remember, but you get fewer noodles if they are focused on lifting potatoes. Another recipe is to ask them to push. No one can push with a limp arm.

A good Scottish turn also requires eye contact—more than in waltzing, where the leader is also steering the couple to avoid hitting other dancers. The all-around diamond strathspey poussette, one of dancing's greatest joys, can be quite disappointing if both partners are not sharing their mutual pleasure. Eye contact is what does it. The shining of my partner's eyes as we turn, the feel of the firm arms as we guide each other along the sides of the diamond, the mutual appreciation of the perfect diagonal lines, of our perfect arm shape and impeccable timing .... Dancing the diamond poussette by yourself would be like eating French fries without salt... No! Worse, it would be like eating the salt without the fried potatoes. Sharing the enjoyment of dancing is important, and the sharing comes through the contact of the eyes. Oh yes, I think I mentioned that "dancing is flirting" and this is also important, passing through the eyes. Where is the beauty of a dancer? 1: her feet, 2: her posture and her firm arms, and 3: her eyes.

The rest of her body exists merely to join firm arms and supple feet to her shining eyes.

In Scotland, women have strong arms. There is a story told about a Russian and a Scotsman discussing their wives. The Russian advises his Scots friend to use firmness, to demand that his wife bring him breakfast in bed on Sunday morning. The Russian calls his friend the next week to ask how he is. "I'm doin' very well, thanks," says the Scot, with a lisp. "After I tried your idea of firmness on ma wife, she fetched me such a wallop that the doctor put me off work for two weeks: but noo I can see oot of ma left eye. I have stopped eating just soups. I'm back on porridge, an' I can move ma jaw a wee bit."

In ballroom dance the leader is the MAN—even when dancing with Scottish women. Leading is not about strength; it is about accuracy. I lead with my fingertips. If I am about to turn to the left, my right fingertips tighten slightly on the left side of my partner's back as I lift the fingers of my left hand so that she feels the direction of the turn. If I want to invite her to turn under my arm, my left hand raises the fingertips of her right hand, while my own right hand gently steers her body into the turn. If I want my elegant, athletic partner to turn three or four or five times, my fingertips turn hers and she spins around my middle finger until my fingers tighten on hers, and she stops facing me as I step into the next movement (usually backwards for her and forwards for me). It doesn't matter what you invite your partner to do, provided it is clear to her what move you are proposing.

This also means that your partner must be responsive. New dancers often clutch your hand so they cannot feel your finger tips, and they may turn any-which-way because they are too panicked to feel your lead. If your follower is not following, then you must relax and follow the direction of their turn. If you try to resist their movement, you may break their wrist.

It is advisable (and indeed courteous) to take the time to test out the skills of a new partner, and her willingness to spin (for example), before leading her into overcomplicated movements—especially in contra dance, but also in waltzes and other formats. Never, ever, try to force your partner to do something she doesn't like doing. Teamwork is about combining the skills of both partners—just like management in business. Don't assume anything. If in doubt, ask her: "Do you become dizzy when you spin?"

How would you feel, if you were to spin a lady and she collapsed onto the floor? You would not feel good! The leader must remain in control of the movement. I once lost my grip during a fast Tulloch turn when I was a student, sending my partner sliding across the floor into the next set where, inevitably, she knocked the legs out from under four other people. It was hilarious. We were all screaming with laughter. We were all young and fit, and no one was harmed. But really it was a shameful mistake on my part.

In the wonderful Jennifer Lopez and Richard Gere movie of 2004 *"Shall We Dance?"* (co-starring Susan Sarandon, and Stanley Tucci wearing a terrible wig) there is a classic line to guide dance leaders. This romantic comedy tells the story of a bored estate lawyer in New York called Mr Clark, who signs up for ballroom dancing lessons partly because he falls in love with the silhouette of a beautiful instructor. She (J.Lo who is extremely beautiful, as well as an exceptional actress and dancer) tells Mr Clark very firmly that dance is far too serious and too important to be confused with sex (which I agree with entirely): he must choose between dancing or leaving the studio. He falls in love with dancing (with which I also agree entirely). Once this is clear, Ms Lopez teaches him to dance.

"This, Mr Clark, is the FRAME," she explains as they take up ballroom dance position. "And the purpose of a frame is to make the picture more beautiful. You, Mr Clark, are the frame, and I am the picture."

It is a wonderful line, and a great lesson. I often tell this story to beginners. It is flattering for a lady to be told that she is a beautiful picture. I have never yet met a woman who was annoyed when I told her she was beautiful. When I dance, I ensure that my partner (the picture) is enhanced by my frame. My partner should appear to be the most elegant woman on the dance floor. That is my aim: and after many years of practice, I seldom miss my target. If my partner is dancing to her optimal capacity, then I shall enjoy the dance just as she does. Some ladies are tall, some are short; some women are older, or less stable or unable to spin without getting giddy; some dancers are light and others are heavy: even if they are all good dancers, they will not all be able to carry off the same moves with equal speed or facility. Many times I have danced with very elderly ladies in retirement homes (when we have been entertaining people with Scottish or German dancing, and I am wearing either the kilt or Lederhosen), and sometimes I have had to hold them close to stop them falling over. They love the fact that they are dancing again after many years, and that a man is holding them. They feel safe in the arms of a strong leader. After a few minutes old ladies are often out of breath, and they need to be seated gently in their place. In any case, I was taught very early that the man should always escort his partner back to her place, and I thank her (and her husband if he is present) for giving me the dance. The art of good and courteous leading on the dance floor is to appreciate what is possible, and to help the ladies to achieve it: to "make the picture more beautiful."

Beginners tend to grip my left hand—which is rather uncomfortable, especially if I have a sore thumb and they are hanging onto my thumb for dear life. If I didn't have a sore thumb before the dance, a tense and worried beginner can easily make my thumb sore. This also makes it difficult to lead because I cannot use my fingertips when my thumb is imprisoned. If I release my thumb and use the fingertips, a beginner probably cannot feel their guidance. In cases where you are leading a nervous beginner, talking about the dance can be helpful: tell her you are going to move right, or turn to the left. This gives confidence to your partner (who is desperately looking for it) and it helps her if you tell her clearly what she is expected to do next. She may even understand why you are desperately trying to get your thumb back.

Don't talk too much, though. I was chatting to Yolanda, a very skilled and beautiful dancer from Charlottesville, as we waltzed, when she said: "Robin, stop talking, and dance with me." She meant that I was not concentrating sufficiently on the dancing. Probably we were just chuntering around one-two-three, one-two-three, instead of swirling and turning with elegance through a skillful American Country Waltz. What I hope for, at the end of a waltz, is a "thank you" from my partner who has appreciated my "wonderful lead" that has turned her into a perfect picture.

7

CREATING WALTZ AND STRATHSPEY DEMOS WITH MOIRA

One evening in my kilt as I was putting on my black, lace-up dance shoes (my *ghillies*) at the Richmond Community School on the corner of Patterson and Libby Avenues in Richmond, two unknown ladies walked in, slipped on their ballet shoes, and began to dance around the stage using the traveling skip-change of step. One was wearing red shoes, the other black and their steps were divine. I was sitting on the steps of the stage, so they flashed past me at eye-level. One had blonde hair, one had dark hair and they danced like a pair of angels. I thought I had died and gone to heaven.

The angels were Allison Turner and her mother Moira. Allison came with us to St Andrews; her mother was already a fully qualified teacher with TAC, the RSCDS Teachers' Association of Canada. Moira soon created the Richmond demonstration team known as The Silver Thistle Dancers. She is our outstanding dancer. Dancing a strathspey with Moira is better than *Dancing with the Stars*. You can watch a dozen of our Scottish demonstration dances on YouTube, children, and you will see that we are really pretty good. You will easily recognize Moira by her footwork. Our other best dancer is Tina Mello, who—like Moira Turner—is a lovely step dancer. Tina's dance steps are strong and precise; Moira's are balletic and precise. Their contrasting styles were perfectly illustrated when they danced the three-person *Shepherd's Crook* together with my friend Bern Runk, another of our teachers (on YouTube you can also see me dancing *The Shepherd's Crook* between Valerie Brookeman and Allison Turner Garrison). We had been dancing Scottish together for some time before I invited Moira for a waltz during a Highland Ball, and there was a conflict.

What happens, my dearest children, is that the lady and her gentleman take up position (the "frame") and both listen for the beat of the music. You could try it together, Liam and Isa, and see how you each hear the music. Usually, after one or two bars, you feel the beat and you are off into the flow of the dance. Sometimes a band is slow to find its rhythm, or the beat is not yet clear, and you may wait for several bars until you "feel" the tune with your shoulders so that both partners are in sync. Then on the perfect beat, you lead off with your body and with a slight pressure of the fingertips: the man's left foot goes forwards as the lady's right foot steps backwards, and you are away. Except that this time, we were not away: Moira went in a different direction to my lead.

I stopped. "Moira, I asked, are you trying to lead me?"

"I always lead," she replied. Now Liam and Isabelle and Roísín, you have to remember that Moira is both a gifted dancer and a gifted dance teacher. She was probably used to leading: and indeed she was probably obliged to lead most of her partners. But I was an experienced waltzer in my fifties, older than beautiful Moira, and I was used to leading. There can only be one waltz leader, and I was deter-mined that was going to be me.

"You always lead?" I smiled. "Not with me, you don't!"

And with that I lifted my shoulders and elbows just enough to force Moira to raise herself onto her tiptoes and waltzed her straight back down the hall in time to the music, but with neery a turn. Perched on her very tippy toes, and with my firm strength moving her backwards, there was nothing Moira could do other than hang onto my arms and dance backwards under my momentum.

At the far end of the hall I stopped, turned my body just enough to keep Moira off balance, so that my partner was dependent on me to hold her or she would fall, and looked down into her eyes. "Moira," I asked with a wolfish smile, "who is leading?"

"You are," said Moira in a rather small voice.

From that moment onwards, we waltzed in perfect harmony, and Moira turned out—unsurprisingly—to be a wonderful partner. People stop to admire Moira waltzing. She is light and quick, beautiful to watch on her spins, and a dream to turn with arabesque swivels and swooshes. Wow! She has been my favorite waltz partner for years now. Moira has also devised some wonderful waltz and strathspey dances that we have used in demonstrations. We shall explore her very best strath-spey and waltz compositions.

Among many beautiful dances she has composed, Moira created a very delightful waltz-time English Country Dance called *Fifty Years On* (it could have been called "fifty years gone"!) for the golden wedding of our friends the Harkraders who live on a plantation in Louisa County, Virginia where they used for many years to host an annual eighteenth century dance for friends. Three generations of Harkraders and guests danced in 18th century costume: we elders danced on the terrace around the fountain, or sometimes on the balcony while the young ones leaped around at double speed on the lawns below. John Turner and

Friends provided the music. John is an exceptional musician and wit, and you can hear him fiddling with his friends in concerts or playing eighteenth century tunes in the taverns of Colonial Williamsburg. If you are lucky, his concert may include brilliant highland dancers like Melissa and Stephanie, who were youth members in our country dance group. John leads (with Moira) the Jink and Diddle School of Scottish Fiddling where he teaches young musicians, promotes new generations of fiddle music and has been boosting the Celtic cultural revival in America for the past 33 years.

Whenever I have been privileged to attend the Hardraker Ball in their gardens, I have had the delightful feeling of moving two centuries back in time. No, my lovely grandchildren, I am not saying that I wish that I lived in 1776: they had no dentists in those days. My nightmare worst possible way to die would be from a tooth abscess. Ow! In eighteenth century England, when death statistics were first collected, dental abscesses were a frequent cause of death, along with tuberculosis and small-pox infections, heart disease, and accidents mostly involving horse riding. But I am an historian, and history lives in my mind. At the Harkraders' home, much more than when I am visiting the artificial city of eighteenth century Williamsburg, I feel that I am living the physical experiences of Washington and Jefferson and Marshall and Munroe—I am talking only about their dance experiences, and I am not ignoring the fact that they were slave-owning aristocrats exploiting their fellow men and women in a time when most other people lived close to misery. We must see history as it was: the rich and the poor, the honest and the corrupt, the well-doers and the perpetrators of genocide were all a part of history ... a part of our history, for our ancestors made history. We must also see ourselves as we are: privileged members of an educated, white elite. But we can still dance, and encourage others to dance!

Moira's waltz is danced to music specially composed by her gifted musical husband John Turner, 10 times former National fiddle champion. John is so musical that Moira can show him a new dance after supper and he will sit down at the kitchen table and produce a fabulous composition before he goes to bed. The tune John composed on this occasion is called: *The Half-Century Waltz—Fifty Years Together*. Richmond dancers have sometimes presented this dance in Scottish demonstrations to add variety. It is a delightful dance with which to end any ball, helping the dancers' muscles warm down gently to waltz time.

FIFTY YEARS ON

A longwise duple minor in waltz time to celebrate the 50th wedding anniversary of Judge & Mrs. F. Ward Harkrader, Jr. Devisor: Moira J. Turner 2007, revised in 2008 and designed for as many as will—each iteration of the dance including both the '2s above' and the '2s below.'

Tune: *The Half Century Waltz ~ Fifty Years Together* by John Turner. Tempo: slow, stately, elegant.

A part

1-4 : 1st and 2nd couples join hands in a circle, balance into the center and back, and turn single one place to the right (W1, M2 into partners'places; M1, W2 into neighbors'places);

5-8 : 1st and 2nd couples repeat A, 1-4. (Progressed and improper);

9-12 : In long lines, 1s and 2s give right hand to partner and balance forward and back; change places—women turning under raised arms (as in Duke of Kent's Waltz)—then retain hands and face clockwise within the minor set. (Progressed and proper = on correct side of the set);

13-16 : 1st and 2nd couples star right once round. 1st couple face down, M1 taking partner's right hand in his left hand.

B part

1-8 : 1st couple lead down for four steps; gypsy with partner right shoulder once and a half to finish facing up, inside hands joined (improper);

9-12 : 1st couple lead up to 1st place (still improper) and face out. 2nd couple cast to 2nd place;

13-16 : 1st and 2nd couples gypsy with neighbor once and a half in opposite sideline –left shoulder on the men's side, right shoulder on the womens'side; 2nd couple finish facing out in 1st place.

C part

1-8 : 1st and 2nd couples double figure of eight—1s crossing up, 2s casting down to begin;

9-16 : 1st couple cross down between the 2s in the minor set below and cast up assisted by the 2s-below. Without dropping hands, 1s and 2s-below circle left once round. Retain hands to repeat the dance having progressed one place.

Dance Notes:

In a demonstration dance setting, I recommend sets of 4 couples or 5 couples. In the latter case, couples 1s & 2s and 4s & 5s can start. Second time through, couple 1 will dance with couple 3 while the others wait. In a 4C set, 1s & 2s and 3s & 4s can start all at once. On the second time through, the old 1s & 4s will dance in the middle position of the set while the original 2s and 3s wait one turn.

8

GENDER STEREOTYPES, POLITICAL CORRECTNESS AND THE POWER OF ELEANOR

A m I reinforcing the gender stereotypes in my description of "leaders and followers"? Are these roles natural or social? My first answer is that biological and emotional differences between men and women are real, and social differences have evolved from there. Simply watch the movements and actions of 7-year girls and 7-year old boys: they are different. In my opinion, dancing brings a perfect fusion of the male and female attributes. We have different strengths. A harmonious society needs the two genders to work together for the benefit of both, and for the greatest happiness of the greatest number. In that spirit we should strive to attain professional equality. The French have a proverb: *"L'homme propose, la femme dispose."* Each person may make a judgment concerning that balance.

In America the terms "leaders and followers" are often used by contra teachers and callers to avoid old-fashioned reference to ladies and gents. At Glen Echo and at contra festivals people are even avoiding the term "Gypsy" to describe the way that two dancers walk around each other with eyes locked. Why? Because we now call these nomads "Travellers"? Come on! "Gypsy" is the name of a dance move. Talk about gender-free contras can become absurd in its desire to avoid role designations. Leaders are leaders, followers are followers, and without leadership you can expect collisions.

I remember the delightful story of a woman who snorted: "You do not have to hold the door open for me because I am a lady."

"Madam, I am not holding the door open for you because you are a lady," smiled her partner, "but because I am a gentleman."

I am one of those who fear an obsession with "gender-neutral vocabulary" may damage the art form that we all enjoy. Too much political correctness creates its own tyranny. Every Scottish dance begins with straight lines and a chord with .... a bow and curtsey. As in judo, this courteous gesture is a sign of mutual respect. This show of admiration for our partner is a part of the dance. Times change and terms are always changing, kids. I have no idea how dancing will be described when you are adults, but courtesy will never go out of fashion. However I must warn you that —whatever the terminology—leading can be a high-risk game. I have been humiliated on the dance-floor, most recently by a very physically powerful Mexican woman I danced with in Juba, one Saturday evening in South Sudan. She told me I was an incompetent salsa dancer because I was unable to catch her. True: I could not anticipate her moves, she was extremely strong and Mexican salsa is not my dance. I sat out the rest of the evening, nursing my pride and watching people half my age having fun.

In medieval courtly love, which has strongly influenced our European culture and my own approach to women, Norman and Plantagenet and Angevin warriors used to put aristocratic women on a pedestal (metaphorically, not physically) and compose poems in their honor. Such women were perfect, beautiful, desirable and untouchable. Medieval and renaissance troubadours sang courtly love songs to praise the beauty of wealthy women like Eleanor of Aquitaine: wife of Henry II and mother of Richard Lionheart, she was a very powerful woman who was praised not just for her beauty, but also because she fed poets and offered them generous rewards. Our culture thus allowed—even encouraged—women to pass judgment on the men. Remember, children, Jean de La Fontaine's fable of the cunning fox and the foolish raven whose cheese was eaten by the fox: *Tout flatteur vit aux dépens de celui qui l'écoute. Cette leçon vaut bien un fromage, sans doute.* Do not be taken in by flattery: it will cost you more than a cheese if you are foolish enough to believe it. You can take it from me that Eleanor was not fooled by the flattery, but she loved the music and the poetry. It occurs to me that the influential wife of President Roosevelt, one of the authors of the 1948 Universal Declaration of Human Rights, was another Eleanor with little time for flattery.

The judgment of women terrified me when I was young; but with the confidence of age I find that it stimulates me. By the age of fifty I knew that I was a good waltzer. I cannot impress women with my jive or quickstep or the various Latin ballroom dances that are so popular; let alone Flamenco or Tango where my style is artificial and amateurish. In those dances I am not a confident leader. I am happy to lead beginners through some moves, but the idea of performing these dances with a strong and confident woman is emasculating.

There was a dreadful story told about a young woman at St Andrews University, who became annoyed that girls like her were sitting on chairs in long lines, being appraised by nervous young men around the entrance who were trying to pluck up enough courage to ask them to dance. Finally one young man got up his nerve sufficiently to walk across the hall, and he asked her for a dance. She looked him up-and-down very slowly, and said: "No. Thank you."

The public humiliation of that poor young man may have led him to commit suicide. (I do not know that: it is just a hypothesis.) Ladies, please be kind to us! We are so vulnerable!

Courtly love still exists, whether you like it or hate it. Men have to approach nervously to beg a lady to dance, and the woman graciously accepts (if she does). Sometimes you can insist a little, but not often. Thank goodness more and more women are happy to do the inviting, which evens out the risks. If you do want to dance, you must have the courage to insist. Sophie de Menton (one of the 100 powerful French women who signed the Open Letter on 9 Jan 2018 complaining that American prudery was pushing the #MeToo movement too far) said: "If my husband had not hassled me, I would not have married him." That is also a lesson in "leading."

When they described their Scottish holiday, my Virginian friends Trish and Julie told me how delighted they were to have been the beneficiaries of wolf whistles in Glasgow. "In America, after the age of 40 you become invisible," Trish told me. In the "battle of the sexes"and so long as there is no abuse of power (Harvey Weinstein) or physical abuse (Bill Cosby, Kevin Stacey), women know they are queens and on the dance floor we are merely courtiers. When it comes to economics and political power women are too often sidelined, as the film *Battle of the Sexes* illustrates for the world of professional tennis—and that is despite the battles of Billie-Jean King and the triumphs of the wonderful Williams sisters Serena and Venus. Only in Scandinavia have women broken the male stranglehold on money. Despite official government policy, in Britain and in America women still earn at least 25% less than men in business; while on the boards of companies —as in most governments—still only 5% or 7% are women. On the dance floor, however, we are equal.

Men and women can both lead dancing. I lead a waltz and when two women waltz together, one is the leader. On the Scottish dance floor however, Moira is the leader of the whole class as an RSCDS qualified teacher, and a very good one. To celebrate the twenty-fifth anniversary of the Richmond dance group, we organized our first Silver Thistle Ball in 2003. Our teachers Moira Turner and Stella Fogg composed a wonderful dance to celebrate the occasion, called *The Silver Thistle Ball*. Since I was one of Moira's demo dancers, I was lucky to be a member of the team that created this dance on the dance floor, and I have since taught it in France where dancers love it. *The Silver Thistle Ball* is popular in America and is one of the most beautiful of all strathspeys. You can see a presentation by the Richmond Silver Thistle Dancers on Youtube, where Moira (the blonde one) dances with Bern Runk, Allison her daughter partners Jeff Corrigan, and Valerie Brookeman (a St Andrews science graduate) is my partner.

You will hear music from the wonderful fiddle of Dr John Turner who plays the tune *Beneath the Willow,* from the CD *Many Happy Returns* where Dave Wiesler interprets his own tune on the piano with the gifted young fiddler Hanneke Cassel. I had thought *Beneath the Willow* especially composed by Wiesler for this dance, but Moira corrected me: "The dance was written for the tune, which haunted me after Dave and Hanneke released *Many Happy Returns.* We could not find a dance to fit the tune, so Stella and I devised one. We used (and modified) the recording to create a 3x for STB—*Beneath the Willow / In Memoriam Mary Kay / Beneath the Willow.* Both tunes are Dave's."

Every great Scottish dance has memorable music and a special "moment of perfection" that marks its composition. *The Silver Thistle Ball* contains a left-hand corner-pass-and-turn figure—known as "Heart to Heart" because this is the shape it forms on the dance floor—which demands exciting precision on the one-bar left-hand turns in the middle of the set, both for the corners and for the dancing couple. These turns in the Heart-to-Heart are where *The Silver Thistle Ball* sets itself apart ... together with the precision of the mirror reels, which require all dancers to be lined up on the sides on the even bars, and crossing or weaving on the odd-numbered bars. As Stella loves to put it, "You must all be in a straight line for one nano-second..."

THE SILVER THISTLE BALL

Strathspey 3 x 32 bars for 3 couples in a 3-couple set. Devisors: Stella Fogg and Moira Turner 2003.

Music: *Beneath the Willow* by David Wiesler on the CD *Many Happy Returns.*

This dance was written to celebrate 25 years of RSCDS dancing in Richmond, Virginia.

Bars 1- 8 : 1s turn RH, cast 1 place, ¾ turn LH and cast to left out the end to 2nd place own side;

Bars 9-16 : 1s dance LSh Pass &Turn with 1st corners (corners also turn LH), turn LH and dance LSh Pass & Turn with 2nd corners and pass LSh to 2nd places;

Bars 17-20 : 1s+3s Set&Link,

Bars 21-24 : 3M+2s (at top) also 3L+1s circle 3H round to left, crossing to 2nd place on own side;

Bars 25-32 : 2s+3s+1s dance reflection reels of 3 on own sides (3s out and up to start).

At the end of the first round and with perfect timing, second couple arrives in first place to begin the dance again with that strong right-hand turn, the cast, and then a three-quarter turn that propels the man out of the top as the lady dances out at the bottom, the two dancers bidding farewell to each other with a long, languorous gaze .... perfect for phrasing and for eye contact! Then follows the Heart-to-Heart with those strong one-bar left-hand turns, allowing the dancing couple to follow their corners into the set-and-link position. Out of this move, a new dancing couple takes over to circle top (the man) and bottom (the lady) before easing out and crossing into second place for the reels. Such an elegant set of flowing moves! Some of Moira's dances are impossibly demanding, but not this one. *The Silver Thistle Ball* flows with the grace of a waltz, and it should find a place on every dance program.

9

VELETA WALTZING TO ST LOUIS WITH
CHRISSIE AND LESLEY OF PAISLEY

H aving told you about wonderful complicated waltzes, kids, I should describe some of the simple family dances and waltzes I enjoy. These days a birthday party seems to require a hired hall and costly professional entertainers. We used to party at home, playing games—team quizzes, traditional party games, hide-and-seek or sardines, dressing-up for charades—and dancing. Vinyl records on a turntable provided music for dancing in the sitting room, with the furniture and carpets pushed to the side.

I remember dancing *The Veleta Waltz* with my maternal grandmother 'Mumsmum' and with her friend Aunt Rebie (an entertaining spiritualist and medium), with my mother's lovely best friend Paulette who taught us all how to appreciate France, and with my mother who was a much better dancer than any of them. The internet shows swishy *Veleta* moves with partners turning back to back, then swinging round perfectly to face each other—slick and elegant. Family parties and ceilidhs (pronounced KAY-ly) are simpler. You hold inside hands, and waltz forward (or six running steps if you are energetic), then face, take hands and chassé sideways. Then you repeat all that in the clockwise direction. On bar 9 you waltz once round with your partner, chassé two more steps and then waltz again for four bars.

THE VELETA WALTZ

Waltz n x16 bars for any number of couples dancing aound the room. Devisor: Arthur Morris.

Created in 1899 for an annual competition run by the British Association of Teachers of Dancing.

Start facing anticlockwise around the room with nearer hands (M right, L left) joined, L on Man's right.

Bars 1-2 : Starting with the outside foot, dance six running steps forward, finishing facing partner and taking both hands (as in a strathspey poussette);

Bars 3-4 : Chassé anticlockwise two steps, finishing by releasing hands (M right, L left) and facing clockwise with nearer hands joined;

Bars 5-8 : Repeat bars 1-4 in the opposite direction (and with right and left interchanged), finishing by taking waltz hold;

Bars 9-10 : Waltz once round in the anticlockwise direction around the room;

Bars 11-12 : Retaining waltz hold, chassé anticlockwise two steps;

Bars 13-16 : Waltz round twice, making some progression anticlockwise around the room, and release waltz hold to finish facing anticlockwise with nearer hands joined.

Dance Notes : To make the format simpler for family or ceilidh dancing, Bars 9-12 can be used simply for two steps outwards (woman going backwards) and then two steps inwards (man moving backwards) before moving into the waltzing on bars 13-16. Professional dancers produce a more flamboyant choreography, notably in their turning waltz-style on bars 9-10. Experienced waltzers can introduce their own variations.

There is also a progressive version with the following modification:

Bars 13-14 : Waltz once round, making some progression anticlockwise around the room, finishing by removing hands (M right, L left) but retaining joined hands;

Bars 15-16 : M raise joined hands so that L can dance under the joined arms to finish beside the next M anticlockwise, both facing anticlockwise with nearer hands joined.

Celts were said to have danced clockwise (or sunwise) in circles on happy occasions. Anti-clockwise was the direction for death mourning dances. *Widdershins* is the Lowland Scots expression for counter-clockwise or 'lefthandwise' = walking around something while keeping it on your left, and *widdershins* (a German or Saxon word) was traditionally associated with the Devil. I do not believe that has much influence on the dancing we do today, although the roots of witchcraft are embedded in our dances and in our belief systems.

The opposite of *widdershins* is *deosil*—a lucky word that comes from Gaelic and means "right" = the direction one turns when going clockwise, following the direction of the movement of the sun as seen from Scotland, of course. In the Southern Hemisphere—Dunedin in New Zealand for example—the movement of the sun appears opposite to what we see in Edinburgh, even though the sun has not changed. Dunedin is Edinburgh the other way around. *Dun* in the Gaelic means a rock, a fortified place or burgh (German *Burg*).

One fun dance rooted in magic is *Nine Pins*. Three is a magical number, and nine (3x3) was an ancient sacred number of fulfillment, a symbol of wisdom and leadership. In the Middle Ages, nine-pin bowling was a popular game. In America nine-pins became ten-pin bowling; in Canada there is a five-pin variant. As a small boy in 1950, I had a game of nine wooden skittles or *quilles* and a wooden ball with which to knock them over. I still have them, and you grandchildren played with them when you were very small.

The game of five-pin billiards is said to have evolved in the Late Middle Ages from lawn croquet: when it rained, an indoor miniature version was created on a green wooden table imitating grass. I used to play this game as a boy in St Helens on the floor of my Maclean grandmother's sitting room, spending happy hours with my billiard queue and the ivory balls I was striking to hit the pins and score points. The board folded to become an elegant polished wooden box stored beside the window seat that looked out across Bembridge Harbour.

The dance-game of *Nine Pins* is an amusing combination of musical chairs and pig-in-the-middle, danced in a square set with one person in the center. Two couples pass across and back; the others do the same; and now the men circle around the dancing ninth pin. When the women come in for hands across, the ninth dancer joins the wheel which continues turning until the music stops. Each dancer now leaps into an empty space, leaving one person as ninth pin. Second time around, the women circle and the men make the wheel so that the genders even out: the identity of the ninth pin has no importance. When we danced this around midnight in St Andrews under Rachel's skilled direction, our Italian teacher Samuele suddenly jumped in as a tenth person. He was the quickest to spring out again when the music stopped .... leaving two pigs (or pins) in the middle amid much laughter.

NINE PINS DANCE

Reel unlimited for 9 people in a square set: a fun fusion of Pig-in-the-Middle and Musical Chairs.

This dance, also known as *The Prisoner*, was published in 1869 as *Quadrille Nine-Pin* (Spencer)

Bars 1-4 : 1s and 3s dance across the set, and back again, the 9th person sets in the middle;

Bars 5-8 : 2s and 4s repeat;

Bars 9-12 : 4 men dance a circle round the 9th person, and back again;

Bars 13-? : 4 women dance five hands across with the 9th person, and back again for as long as the music lasts.

AS SOON AS THE MUSIC STOPS, each dancer tries to jump back into one of the four square spots. One person left in the middle becomes the new ninth pin.

REPEAT with the women dancing first, and the men dancing five hands across with the 9th person, and back again for as long as the music lasts. This means that one of them will be left out, and the 9th pin may be alternately a man or a woman. Or not.

If someone else joins the dance, there will be two people in the middle.

More than two in the middle becomes too many: two is company but three is a crowd.

The most crazy place I ever danced *The Valeta Waltz* and *Nine Pins* was in St Louis du Sénégal, the decaying former capital of France's West African empire. We went there to dance. Small African kingdoms with no firearms provided an easy target for brutal conquest by a French Army desperate to recover its honor after defeat in the Franco-Prussian war of 1870-71 that resulted in the unification of Germany. That is how West Africa came to be French.

Meanwhile other European powers carved up the rest of Africa, establishing trading stations on every African river estuary. The Congo was brutalized by the Belgians. The Portuguese traded out of Guinea, Mozambique, and Angola from where they launched the slave trade. The Gambia became a British colony. In the 1980s your grandmother and I ran rural development programs in The Gambia. One year on November 30th, a couple of Liverpudlians joined us at the St Andrews Ball. Linda and Paul (not their real names) were Scottish dancers living in St Louis where Paul was an agronomist. Linda taught Scottish dancing to.... Yes, you may well ask: "to whom ?" That was a question we asked ourselves. We decided to find out. Our friends Phil and Lesley Hanlon were receiving her parents for Christmas: Laurie and Chrissie Morton were both doctors and delightful. St Louis seemed like a great place to visit, so we organised a migration of Scottish country dancers from Banjul to St Louis to dance with Linda and Paul. What could be more exciting—or more incongruous—than dancing in the New Year in St Louis du Sénégal?

We were nine travelling in a minibus, plus our driver: our two children were with us as well as the Hanlons, the Mortons and our RSCDS teacher Margaret Fell. Two other cars joined us: a total of 17 dancers from Banjul descended on St Louis to celebrate Hogmanay. Linda knew we were coming, so the look of horror on her face when we rang her doorbell caused us as much astonishment as amusement. In response, I found a small hotel with rooms for the Poultons, Hanlons and Mortons, which had a bar and patisserie. There we spent happy hours in laughter, while Margaret—our children's best friend—and our kids shared a room in Paul and Linda's house. We danced there with the six beginners in Linda's class: a couple of Dutch development workers and four confused Senegalese adolescents who were practising their English more than their dancing.

Since we were seventeen dancers from Banjul, mostly we danced with each other. In addition to some simple Scottish country dances, we had ceilidh dances suitable for beginners and for a Hogmanay dance. *The Valeta* was one I danced with Lesley—together with *Nine Pins, The Dashing White Sergeant* and the *Circassian Circle*. The most amusing was *The Flying Scotsman* named for Scotland's most famous railway engine. I danced it with Lesley's giggling mother Chrissie who could hardly believe she had come fall the way from Paisley to dance *The Flying Scotsman* in northern Senegal. What a laugh! After the tame version which has people dancing around behind the lines, we began the alternative version which involves the women holding hands and zigzagging around each of the men standing in line. When the men started dancing in between the women and the music began to get ahead of the dancers, the Senegalese began to understand how much fun ceilidh dancing can be. They enjoyed *Nine Pins* as well.

THE FLYING SCOTSMAN (4-couple version)

Jig 4 x 32 bars for 4 couples in a 4-couple longwise set. Devisor: Hugh Thurston

RSCDS Medal Tests for Young Dancers. by Hugh Thurston: Sixteen New Scottish Country Dances 1946–57.

The *Flying Scotsman* railway service has been operating between Edinburgh and London since 1862.

Bars 1-8 : 1L followed by 2L3L4L cross, cast behind 1M, cross below 4M and dance up to places;

Bars 9-16 : 1M2M3M4M repeat bars 1-8 around Ls, all finishing in places;

Bars 17-20 : 1s take both hands and slip down the middle;

Bars 21-24 : 1s slip up to finish in 4th place while 2s3s4s step up;

Bars 25-32 : 2s 3s 4s 1s take both hands with partners and slip down the middle and back.

Dance notes: It can be danced in five or six-couple sets.

In any ceilidh or Hogmanay dance, the first sixteen bars suffer a variation: instead of dancing round behind the opposite lines, the women (and later the men) will join hands and dance as a unit in-and-out around the people in the opposite line until they get back to place. This is more fun and of course requires a very quick movement. Often the men have to set off before the women have finally reached their places. If there are five couples (or even six) then the music available makes it impossible to complete the movement correctly, with attendant laughter and fun.

Bars 25-32 are often done in lines holding hands, instead of with partners, representing the railway tracks.

The journey was as important as the destination. Driving north to St Louis we passed through Tivouane, center of the Tijiania Sufi Brotherhood with a mosque that has one of the largest domes in the world, funded by Saudi Arabia as part of their "checkbook imperialism" foreign policy spreading the intolerant creed of Wahabbism. On the way back south, we visited Touba, home of the Mourid Sufi Brotherhood where the beautiful mosque was built by Senegalese disciples of the late Cheikh Ahmadou Bamba. Mouridism is an African anti-colonial Sufi movement that began in protest against French occupation and which is now—as our Mourid guide explained unambiguously—against Arab imperialism. Islam is no longer an Arab religion: it has become a world religion, a fact that Arabs find hard to digest. The largest Arab nation, Egypt, is only the eighth-largest Muslim nation after Indonesia, India, Pakistan, Bangladesh, Nigeria, Iran and Turkey. The last three—like Egypt—all have a Muslim population above 70 million. We stopped in nomad camps, watered sheep, met camel herders and rode dromedaries. In addition we enjoyed the travel and the conviviality of community singing in the minibus. After they returned to Scotland, Lesley's parents never stopped talking about their Scottish dancing pilgrimage through West Africa.

10

PAULINE AND THE HEALING POWERS OF
THE DANCE COMMUNITY

F riendships are the basis for human life, and they come in many forms. Keep up with your friends, children, and make sure that they know how much you love them. Dance friendships are of a special nature. I have danced with people for twenty years and in different countries whom I count as friends although I know next-to-nothing about their lives. What we love about each other is the dancing. After several years, I saw Jo again in the Younger Hall at St Andrews and I knew her at once from her smile and her beautiful dancing. She is the doctor who told me that some women in Edinburgh are so physically unfit that even lifting their arms to hang out the washing on the line (instead of throwing clothes into the dryer) provides them with a measurable difference in terms health and heart exercise. We seldom meet, yet Jo and I are dear dancing friends. Friendships are precious. I know that some of the ladies in my dance groups look forward to my weekly hug at Scottish dancing: my weekly hug may be the only physical human contact they feel in a week (or in six months if I am traveling overseas). They love it! I know they love it because they tell me so. When I walk into the class, the ladies almost queue up for their weekly hug: a simple way to promote the greatest happiness of the greatest number.

Not everyone wants to be hugged, of course; but in America especially, the lack of human physical contact is painful. Sometimes in the street I see young men and women—often young evangelicals—with posters offering "free hugs" who are hoping to break down the barriers of white Americans who are so suspicious of, so afraid of other people. Dancing offsets some of the chill of this white, northern, social (anti-social) culture: dancing is fun, spontaneous, and compensates for the lack of human contact and spontaneity in many lives. The more hugs the better, I say! Groups who offer "free hugs" provide a valuable service to their city. Princess Diana once made a memorable and important speech about love and community in which she stated something along the lines of: "Hugging is good for you. More hugging is better for you. An overdose of hugging brings only benefits."

So I hug my dancing friends, except for the one or two whose body language makes it clear that physical human contact makes them uncomfortable. Or perhaps they do not like my smell. There is nothing sexual about the hugging. Americans tend to confuse physical contact with all sorts of issues that exist only in American culture. Touching is not a part of white American culture, and I know plenty of Scots who do not care for physical contact. Sometimes I wonder how Scottish couples manage to make so many babies. Thank goodness for whisky.

Dancers have to touch, otherwise they cannot dance together. So probably dancers in the USA have a higher tolerance for hugging than other white Americans: this is an important distinction because Black American culture and Latino American culture are more human and friendly and huggy. Cultures are different. A homogenous American culture does not exist.

Dance friendships revolve around a common love of music, a joint sharing of the music through dance. Music is the magic that creates dance. When people arrive from all over the Eastern Seaboard to the Richmond Scottish Christmas Dance, or to the St Patrick's Dance in March, I greet old friends like Ellen, Eva, Holly, Pam and Pat with a hug of genuine affection, although I may not even remember their surnames. I have no idea where they live or what they do for a living, yet they are dance friends of 20 years and we love each other through dance. There are other communities of course, where friendships develop through shared interests: church memberships, knitting groups, sports teams, pubs and coffee houses, lunch clubs like Rotary, Jack & Jill, or Kiwanis, but most of these activities involve opportunities for talk: people get to know one another as people, and they may like each other or not. When we are dancing, we do not waste much time on talk. We do not know whether we like each other as people, but we love each other as dancers. The dance community resembles rather the lives of soccer or basketball or hockey teams, where the physical sharing of the sport is what brings people together.

While the friendships are genuine, one of their advantages is that they do not need to become deep. In any dance group there may be real buddies, of course, and family members too. With some dancers I have built deep friendships; but there is a common—and different—general level of friendship that requires little personal commitment, and yet brings real value. Peg Shealey and her family in Virginia (Malcolm, Becky, Anna, Jacob) are a great example of dancers whose arrival adds value to an evening. They lift the spirit of the whole dancing group because their happiness communicates love to everyone else in the room. By dancing with obvious joy, they bring spiritual healing to tired friends. It is a precious gift. How they run their daily lives I have no idea, but they are lovely to dance with. So, my sweet grandchildren, try to look happy. If you look happy, you will feel happy and you will make others happy.

A powerful example of dance friendship and healing occurred on Sunday 15th April 2018: as the Richmond Springforth Contra Dance Weekend drew to a close, I thanked one of our visitors for dancing the last contra with me. Pauline (I have changed her name) had come down from Maine to visit her daughter in Roanoke and had timed her visit to take in Springforth, which is one of the best parties of the year. Smart lady! I had found her a delightful dancer and person as we danced and flirted gently over the three days. Pauline was probably around 60 years old, with a cheery face and sparkle in her eyes. The sparkle came from the music and from her interior beauty. I think Pauline from Maine has deep internal calm. I guess she is a loving mother and grandmother, and she might be a teacher; if she is in business, then it is probably an environmentally oriented business where she derives as much pleasure from her activity as from the money she makes. But I really have no idea. All I know about Pauline is that she came down from Maine and she was born in Roanoke. Little enough, and yet we became real friends through dance.

As I hugged Pauline at the end of our dance weekend and wished her a safe journey to Roanoke, she said something of great importance that I could not imagine happening in any other context than dancing. Except, perhaps, in the theater. "I want to tell you that you have made this weekend really special," she told me as we hugged. "My husband died two years ago. He was a wonderful dancer. Somehow, you have touched somewhere inside of me and made this a wonderful weekend."

I said I was glad, and I held her tight. "That is a tough place to be," I said. "Losing a loved one is very hard, and I can tell that you are a very strong person who has dug deep to get though it. I hope this weekend has helped you come through some of the pain. Take care of yourself." We kissed with tears in our eyes, and as she left, I went off to sweep the floors of the beautiful Ginter Community Center where we hold our contra dances. Then I came home and wrote this memory of a sweet dance encounter.

11

YOUR GREAT GRANDFATHER HEALED DOLLY WITH SCOTTISH DANCING

My father—your great-grandfather dearest Liam and Isa—was a generous and loving man, a popular medical doctor devoted to family and to people. Every Wednesday evening, a group of Scottish dancers met to dance in my parents' home in Sussex. One Wednesday evening over tea and biscuits at half-time, a lady I shall call Dolly told me that my father's dancing had changed her life. One of the nice things about dancing is that is it usually inexpensive (just three or four dollars per evening, or a packet of cookies, or nothing at all) and there is no alcohol. You have to be a sad person to believe that alcohol is a necessary part of having fun. On the contrary, alcohol is a mood-enhancer: if you are happy, a couple of glasses will make you happier, and the same couple of glasses—if you are feeling morose—can push you into depression. Raised by his Scots Presbyterian mother, my father never allowed alcohol in our house. Country dancers usually drink water and eat a cookie at half-time. British ladies always brew a pot of tea: one of them slips out before the half-time interval to put the kettle on.

Alcohol consumption is a problem in all the Celtic nations and in much of northern Europe. In 2018 the Scottish government sharply raised the cost of drinking alcohol in order to reduce health problems and their cost to hospital emergency services. Here is a story about too much drinking, and how it can make you foolish.

Once upon a time, an elderly man was sitting in the Blue Bonnet pub, finishing his drink. He called out to the barman to bring him another. "No more, Joe, said the barman: you've had more than enough for one night."

Grumbling to himself, the customer gathered up the dominoes into a pile, pushed himself up from the table, turned towards the door, and fell over. Cursing to himself, he crawled to the door and used the handle to haul himself upwards. But as soon as he let go of the door, he overbalanced. Hoping that the cold night air would sober him up enough to stand, our hero crawled out of the pub, took hold of a lamp post and pulled himself into a standing position. He could see the front door of his house from where he stood. "Only a few steps to make it home," he thought, pushing off from the lamp post and launching himself in the right direction ... but he fell flat on his face.

So Joe dragged himself along the pavement to his front door, fished out his key, and unlocked the door, making as little noise as possible in order not to wake his wife. He pushed open the door, and was dismayed to see his wife standing there with her hands on her hips and a glare on her face.

"I tried not to wake you, Dearie," said Joe nervously, looking up at her from the front step.

"Not wake me, you Ijiot?" cried his wife. "I was woken by a phone call from the Blue Bonnet, to tell me you've forgotten your wheelchair again."

Sitting in the Island Cottage during a pause in the dancing, Dolly explained how helpful Scottish dancing had been for her. "I was very depressed after my divorce," Dolly told me as we sipped our tea. "For two years I barely left the house. I had forgotten how to socialize and I lived in a depression that I know now was largely of my own making. Then I met your father, who replaced my family doctor during his holidays. After he had renewed my prescription for pills, he invited me to come to his Scottish dance group. He gave me the phone number of someone who lived not far from where I live and suggested that I call them to car-share. I decided to try it. I called the number, and the friendly person on the other end of the line said they would collect me at 7pm so as to arrive by 7.30 for the dancing. Everyone was so welcoming in the dance group that I felt better than I had felt for the past three or four years. The next week I came back again, and that was three years ago. Now I rely on this dance group to keep me sane. My Wednesday evening dancing is the focal point of my social life each week. And I no longer take any pills."

I told my mother about this conversation, and how wonderful Father's dance group had been for Dolly. As a doctor, it seemed that he had performed an act of healing through dance.

"Yes," said my mother. "Dolly had a terrible time. After fifteen years of marriage, she came home one day to find her husband wearing her clothes. She thought it rather odd, but it became more than that: at first he wore her clothes every night; then he went off to buy more women's clothes that fitted him better, and very soon Dolly no longer knew whether her husband was a man or a woman. She dreaded visitors coming to the house. She dreaded seeing people. She no longer dared to go out with her husband, and she was terrified if anyone came to the door. It took her five years before she summoned up the strength to demand a divorce, by which time she was so stuck in her house and her defensive mental walls that she no longer went outside or met anyone. Luckily she found Scottish Country Dancing, and she has rebuilt her confidence. It shows that doctors who dance have a broader range of options to offer their patients than doctors who do not dance."

I know a number of women who have joined dance group on the recommendation of friends or doctors to help them recover from a divorce. Going out and developing non-demanding relationships with other people, in a non-sexual environment, appears to be beneficial for emotional and mental stability. Research also shows that dancing is the best antidote for senile dementia and for delaying Alzheimer's syndrome: the reason being that it combines physical and mental activity. Dance requires a focus on balance and coordinated movement, together with healthy exercise and the memorizing of formations and directions, while harmonizing this whole sequence of functions to music. Dancing is good for the back and good for the brain. But you do need to take care of your feet, ankles, knees and hips.

My friend Dr Greg Toler had both his knees replaced: they were worn out, they were hurting, and they stopped him dancing. Once he had his new titanium knees in place, Greg was able to come back to Scottish dancing and of course his lovely wife Mabel Macdonald (from Prince Edward Island in Canada) came with him to make sure he behaved. I am certain that the love and support of the dancers in our Richmond group were part of his healing process and a strong part of his motivation to "get back" to his old ways. Dancing is healing! At a recent conference, a medical researcher was presenting findings showing the benefits of dance for older people. In the Q&A session someone said that they were keeping their mind very active with crosswords and sudokus, and they thought this should protect them from senility.

"I am sure that crosswords and sudokus are beneficial, replied the speaker: but the research shows that if you want to delay Alzheimer's or avoid senile dementia, you should dance."

A Canadian study for a university thesis in 1988 concluded that dance is good for reducing both stress and weight. *"A Little Bit of Weight is Taken Off,"* said one of the respondents, explaining her lessened stress levels and providing a title for the M.Ed. thesis. Balancing and managing stress was associated with new "Leadership" skills. For both mental and physical well-being, therefore, an activity program based on Celtic dances (Scottish and Irish) is beneficial.

Ideally at my age, you should keep fit to dance. Many people put it the other way around: "I dance to keep fit" they say .... But that can also lead to injury. What you need is a general fitness regime of which dancing is a part. I do stretching before and after dances to avoid pulling muscles while dancing and to keep away very painful leg cramps while I am asleep. After strenuous dancing your feet and tendons should be relaxed in cold water, while your muscles need to relax in hot water. At St Andrews when I am dancing intensively, I wash my feet after a dance in cold water in the hand basin before stretching my legs and back and neck under a hot shower. Then in my bedroom I roll out a yoga mat and do some more rolling and stretching before bed using Pilates movements developed specifically for dancers.

Because of my work in peace and anthropology, I need to keep supple. I want to be supple. I still know how to fall safely from youthful days of judo and rugby. I can cross my legs and sit on the floor for hours—a necessary skill for sitting to discuss disarmament prospects with Afghan insurgents, Sahelian rebels or Cambodian monks. While cross legged, I can still bend forward and put my forehead on either knee—not a skill that is needed for village life, but valuable for keeping a dancer supple. One of my dance friends showed me his new step counter, called a FitBit. "The rest of me," he joked, "is the unfit bit." Personally I do not use a step counter, but in hotels I always walk upstairs (I usually reach my destination before other people have even found a free elevator) and I often walk 2 miles to the market: keeping fit so that I can dance, dancing so I keep fit.

Dancing brings health benefits to young people as well. Many girls in America and Europe develop terrible posture with rounded shoulders and bent spines (heavy bags of school books with badly-adjusted shoulder straps do not help). Beautiful women have good posture. Good posture means taut back and stomach muscles that protect the body against future aches and pains. Pilates teachers describe the muscles of your stomach and diaphragm as "your second backbone" because they support the spine. Women from West Africa are so striking partly because of their wonderful posture. They carry loads on their heads—in order to keep their hands free—which means that their back and spine are used with maximum efficiency. Most girls and women in Europe and America with good posture and straight backs have been taught dance. You can tell a woman who dances by her elegant walk and the way in which she holds and knows her body. The same is true for men: dancers, and for soldiers who march hold themselves erect. Marching is a simple form of dancing, often done in time to the music of a regimental band. I sometimes reply to people who say they cannot dance: "If you can walk, you can march; and if you can march, you can dance."

Armies always have regimental bands and regimental marches. Scottish regiments have regimental pipe bands for a reason. Music is good for the soul, good for reinforcing camaraderie, and good for keeping time with the other members of the regiment: the basis of military discipline. The hours and hours that soldiers spend marching around the parade ground are not simply a way of killing time: they are a way of building camaraderie, team spirit and discipline. Marching to music is more enjoyable than marching to the sound of your own footsteps. When the regiment marches with its band playing, its members feel invigorated and there is a lift in the morale of the troops. When the pipes are playing, the soldiers' blood begins to race and their marching feet barely touch the ground.

Happiness can be created by music, and by the way in which a person's body and mind fuse with music. Dancing works better than marching to develop an intense relationship with music. When I hear Scottish dance music, my walk quickens. When I hear the bagpipes, my blood races and I cannot remain seated. If the pipes are playing, I have to stand to see the pipers. Sometimes I cannot simply stand still: I have to dance. Africans have a similar relationship with music to the Scots. I have lived my life in the two cultures: African and Celtic music and rhythms move me both spiritually and physically. I sometimes explain to people, "The music enters my ears and flows out through my feet as I dance."

12

DANCING FOR SCOTLAND'S NATIONAL POET WITH BESS, TIKKI, JEAN AND MARY

B irthdays. How we grandparents do love coming over to your home to celebrate our grandchildren's birthdays! Your French-influenced Mamie buys beautiful garments and other presents while your Scots-influenced Papy frowns at the extravagance and over-expenditure on 'objects' and tries to offer love, postcards, soccer practice and colored balloons instead of yet more and more toys. But I do buy you books—usually humorous books (in French).

The Scots love birthdays and birthday cakes (the national sweet tooth). One of Scotland's great cultural events, dearest grandchildren, is the annual birthday of our national poet Rabbie Burns, the poet of Ayrshire and cultural beacon of the 19th century Scottish Enlightenment that included philosophers (Francis Hutcheson and David Hume), sociologists (Adam Ferguson), economists (Adam Smith), agronomists (James Robertson) and engineers too numerous to mention. In the cultural arena, the unchallenged star of the Scottish Enlightenment was Robert Burns, who collected music and legends and beautiful women from the countryside while composing some of Scotland's finest poetry. Medieval Gaelic literature was oral and has mostly not survived, although there were important poets in the Gaelic such as the blind harpist Turlough O'Carolan (1670-1738) in Ireland. Burns was no Gaelic-speaking Highlander: Robert Burns was from the La'land-speaking Sassanach (Saxon descendants) culture of the Lowlands. To earn a living, Burns became a tax collector for the same Hanovarian kings who were destroying Highland culture. The Anglicizing of Scotland included the salary of Robert Burns.

Winter can be a dreary time in the British Isles. Grey skies leak permanent cold drizzling rain that drips into your collar, running down your neck into the very marrow of your bones. Scotland has more honest weather, especially in St

Andrews on the East Coast, where the North Sea winds either blow away the drizzle or turn it into an honest gale of rain driving into your face at 45 degrees—a truly bracing, thrilling experience. For those who fear such honest saucy weather, my friend Lesley Hanlon has written a haiku that explains how dancing cures your woes:

> *Cold winter months*
> *Listening to the silence within*
> *Discordant notes transform to melody*

The melody that transforms discordant winter into joy and music will be a reel or a jig, or one of the many Scottish songs collected or composed by Rabbie Burns. But first or all, before the music, comes the ritual of Burns Night that must follow tradition. It starts with the Selkirk Grace he composed:

> *Some hae meat and canna eat,*
> *And some wad eat that want it;*
> *But we hae meat, and we can eat,*
> *And sae the Lord be thankit.*

We do not celebrate Burns' birthday with cake, but with haggis, the Chieftain o' the Puddin' Race. Every Burns Supper includes a haggis, normally served with neeps and tatties (mashed yellow turnips *rutabaga* and smashed potatoes). Haggis is a great delicacy and every grandmother has her own recipe. Basically haggis is a sausage (in your local fish and chip shop), or a giant sausage pudding composed of oats and offal—add onions, salt and pepper and a bit of mashed turnip to taste. Yummy.

In Virginia I told my friend Harold Deaver about Burns Night and haggis. Harold is an English country dancer from North Carolina who doesn't know Scotland. I explained that the haggis is a Scottish bird with one leg shorter than the other, which is hunted and trapped by chasing it round and round as it moves up to the top of the hill. Plenty of Americans believe this story. "I think your Haggis Bird is a bit like the Carolina Ono Bird," said Harold. "The Ono bird has balls that hang below his landing gear, and every time he comes in to land you can hear him cry 'Oh! No! Oh! No!'"

At a formal Burns Night, haggis is the central attraction. The pipes strike up in the kitchen, or in the yard outside, and their magical strains grow stronger as a piper marches into the dining hall followed by two important personages: the bearer of the haggis and the bearer of the whisky. The piper having stopped, he receives a wee dram, with which he toasts the haggis and the assembled worthies. And now, some poet steps forward to salute this gleaming, steaming, delicious

Scottish delicacy immortalised in Burn's poem: of which here are just the first two stanzas, with a translation supplied by the Alexandria Burns Club in Virginia.

ADDRESS TO A HAGGIS
Fair fa' your honest, sonsie face,
Great chieftain o' the pudding-race!
Aboon them a' yer tak your place,
Painch, tripe, or thairm:
Weel are ye wordy o'a grace
As lang's my arm.
The groaning trencher there ye fill,
Your hurdies like a distant hill,
Your pin was help to mend a mill
In time o'need,
While thro' your pores the dews distil
Like amber bead.

ADDRESS TO A HAGGIS—TRANSLATION
Good luck to you and your honest, plump face,
Great chieftain of the sausage race!
Above them all you take your place,
Stomach, tripe, or intestines:
Well are you worthy of a grace
As long as my arm.
The groaning trencher there you fill,
Your buttocks like a distant hill,
Your pin would help to mend a mill
In time of need,
While through your pores the dews distill
Like amber bead.

Then our poet kills the haggis. I once heard the Address to the Haggis given by a soldier from the Black Watch Regiment, a specialist in unarmed combat. When he reached the words ...

His knife see rustic Labour dight,
An cut you up wi ready slight,
Trenching your gushing entrails bright,
Like onie ditch;
And then, O what a glorious sight,
Warm-reekin, rich!

... instead of picking up a knife from the table and slicing the haggis open, the soldier stretched out his arm over the dish and we heard a sharp click. His hand flashed downwards and slit open the haggis with one stab of his flick-bladed knife. I felt quite queasy.

After the Selkirk Grace and the Address, Burns Suppers can take various forms, but I expect some dancing, together with more Burns songs and poems. Drinking whisky and hearing long speeches (*A Toast to the Immortal Memory of Robert Burns*) are not sufficient for me even when they include the amazing love poems (and songs) and saucy stories about Burns' marriage to Jean Armour, or his illicit-but-passionate love affairs with Bess Paton and Mary Campbell (not forgetting Nelly Kilpatrick or Peggy Thompson who were his earliest short loves). I am not condemning Burns: passion is something I understand. It is only thanks to his passions that we are able to enjoy Burns' finest poetry: "My Love is like a Red, Red Rose"; "The Highland Lassie O", "Highland Mary"; "To Mary in Heaven"; or the sad song "Ye banks and braes o' bonnie Doon" which I have sung as a duet in concerts with my dear friend Marjorie Falconer. I might sing it to you some day, children. The song ends sadly but beautifully:

> Wi' lightsome heart I pu'd a rose
> Frae aff its thorny tree;
> And my fause lover stole the rose,
> But left the thorn wi' me.

When we moved to Virginia in 1999, I started travelling to Charlottesville every January 25th (or on the nearest Saturday to Burns' actual birthday) where the RSCDS dancers celebrated Burns at the historic 18th century Mitchie Tavern: a hostelry frequented by Thomas Jefferson and other Virginian luminaries who were contempories of Robert Burns (1759-96). After a good dinner, we enjoyed short and witty speeches (a toast to the Lassies, with a reply from a Lassie); stories about Burns, a noted philanderer ("Burns was active in many fields, especially in the field behind Alloway Church, in Ayrshire"); amusing sketches and stories in the ceilidh tradition. Soon I suspect the tradition will include a reading of Murray Lachlan Young's hilarious Burns spoof *Ode to a Scrotum* that everyone can hear on YouTube. Our Virginia Burns evening always included a dance demo in the Mitchie Tavern fireplace (space being limited) by the Charlottesville dancers including the Beltons (Bob and Celia), the Markhams (Howard and Pat) and the Murrays (Jim, Bess and Tikki).

I had a special link with the Murrays: when we first met, Jim Murray asked me if I was a descendent of the great zoologist Sir Edward Bagnall Poulton—to which, of course, I said yes. The distinguished Emeritus Professor Murray said he was raised on my great grandfather's work on evolution and mimicry (the way in which especially butterflies imitate the colors and shapes of nastier species as a disguise).

This expertise made EBP the British Army's advisor on camouflage during WWI. EBP had Welsh-Irish ancestors, but his very Scottish obsession with economy led him to re-use every envelope. The British government mimicked him, designing reuseable envelope stickers that were used by every government department at least until the 1970s. I should add that EBP married a beautiful and distinguished lady, Emily Palmer, a geologist and an heiress who was daughter and brother of Quaker biscuit-makers in Reading, England. The Palmers and Poultons were patrons of women's education (Reading University, Somerville College, Oxford, Malvern girls' school). Metal tins of Huntley and Palmers biscuits fed the British Empire. When the engagement was announced, a student wrote on the blackboard: "Dr Poulton has taken the biscuit." Seeing this, my great grandfather picked up the chalk and added: "and the tin as well." Portraits suggest that our handsome "Poulton features" come from Emily, Lady Poulton who was also the source of our love of music.

One January I was visiting Chichester, where your great-uncle Rory was organising the dancing for Burns Night. "Great, he said: if you are here we can dance *The Shepherd's Crook*." You can admire this dance for three people (normally a man and two ladies) on YouTube. *The Shepherd's Crook* is a traditional highland dance, recomposed as a demo dance with exciting choreography by Mary Isdale McNab of Vancouver, Canada (one of the McNabberies, as they call them over there): it not to be confused with an RSCDS strathspey of the same name from Book 10, although they may have common roots. Rory was sure we would find a lady as third person, and we did. "What shall I do, she asked, while you men are dancing the highland steps?"

With characteristic Poulton bluntness Rory replied: "It really doesn't matter what you do, so long as you keep out of our way. No one will be watching you: they will all be watching the two men in kilts! When we have finished, we will come and collect you." This, of course, is exactly what happened. Everyone loved our dance, even the lady we were abusing. I hope that you grandchildren will dance *The Shepherd's Crook* one day. You will need to know by heart the order of the McNab dance steps so that you can repeat them to yourself during the dance.

THE SHEPHERD'S CROOK SUMMARY

Highland dance for 3 people arranged by McNab

Down and back; Rocking step; The Crook; Schottische x2; Reel; Huntly crossover step; Circle; Highland Fling.

The most astonishing Burns Night I ever attended was in Brittany, France. Claudine Auriacombe called me from Vannes and asked if I would attend the 2006 Burns evening being organised by her English language teacher. Your grandmother and I drove south to the Morbihan region of Brittany and stayed the night in Eric and Claudine's beautiful house, which was once a grain mill driven by tidal flow: there is a harbor on one side of the house and a tidal mill-pond on the other. Exquisite!

200 Bretons were awaiting us in a hall with their teacher: a retired engineer from England who had lived for ten years in Scotland and who had decided that Burns would serve as an excellent English-language subject for his students. Fortunately, the whole evening was French-speaking—no French person learning English should expect to understand a single word of Robert Burns' Scots dialect. Very few of the guests were actually studying English, and not one of them had any idea who Burns was. I was the only person present with any claim to a Scots heritage, and I was the only man wearing the kilt apart from an amazing piper called Armel Denis, a charming Breton musician who learned the pipes in Glasgow where he won several piping competitions. Each time Armel piped a reel, I entertained the 200 Bretons with some highland dancing.

Haggis was served in thimbles with miniature spoons, rather like a caviar delicacy. We did some ceilidh dances, including *The Gay Gordons* and *The Dashing White Sergeant* which had been taught to a few of the English language students. Claudine was very excited by the success of the evening—and I was amazed to have celebrated the biggest Burns Supper in my life with a mass of people who had never even heard of Robert Burns. Your grandparents taught *The Gay Gordons* by demonstrating the steps. Here is what you do:

THE GAY GORDONS :

Ceilidh reel-march for any number of couples dancing counter-clockwise around the hall.

The famous Band Master Victor Silvester says in " Old Time Dancing" (1949) that *The Gay Gordons* was created between WW1 and WW2 in response to a craze for march-style dances: named for the Gordon Highlanders.

Bars 1-4 : Taking two steps forwards with your arm over your lady's shoulder in allemande hold, you both then swivel and continue two steps backwards in the same direction: walk or dance as you like;

Bars 5-8 : Repeat, so that you finish back where you began: and since everyone should be going around the room in a circular pattern, no couple should bump into any other couple;

Bars 9-16 : The lady turns under the arm of her partner, who provides a middle finger pointing downwards so that she can turn around it as many or as few times as she cares to do (probably once, and not more than three times) while the man sets, or lilts or walks with small steps as he admires his partner;

Bars 17-24 : Polka with your partner using the step: 1,2,3,hop; 1,2,3,hop; finishing facing around the hall with your partner in the original allemande position, ready to walk forward once more.

No one really needs to teach *The Dashing White Sergeant*, which can simply be marched in time to the music. Circle, set and turn, reel or swing, and then forward and back: so simple. Bars 17-24 should be danced as a reel of three, but for non-dancers it is safer to replace the reel with arm swings—which is how I led it at Claudine's ceilidh.

THE DASHING WHITE SERGEANT

Reel n x 32 bars danced by one set of 3 people facing another set of 3 people, progressing in opposite directions around the hall. Traditional 19th century popular dance: RSCDS Book 3

Words to the song were by 18th century General John Burgoyne. The 1826 music by English composer Sir Henry Rowley Bishop created a dance inspired from Swedish circle dancing that was fashionable in Victorian Britain.

Bars 1-8 : All circle right and back = 6 hands round and back;

Bars 9-12 : Center dancer sets and turns 2 hands person on right;

Bars 13-16 : Center dancer sets and turns 2 hands person on left (popular variation—turn person on right RH, turn person on left LH);

Bars 17-24 : All dance reels of 3 with center dancer passing LSh with person on right (popular variation—RSh to person on right): but in a ceilidh it is often better to swing the side people with locked elbows, alternately right and left, to avoid confusion for people who do not know the reel;

Bars 25-32 : Both sets of 3 advance and retire twice, passing through (or under arches) to meet the next set of 3 coming at you around the hall.

13

CONTRA DANCE WITH LAURA IS IRISH-AMERICAN FUN ON SPEED

When the Irish dance, they dance fast; precision is not usually a part of the equation. *River Dance* has changed the way in which the world perceives Irish dancing. It is marvelous fun but *River Dance* is Irish tap dancing, a spectacular show-dance very different from my sort of community dancing. I always told my children: "The Scots have the best dances and the Irish have the best parties." Like their Scottish cousins, Irish communities and families dance a lot. When they dance, it can be exhausting: their dances seem to last for ever. Sometimes I have the impression that quantity pleases the Irish more than the quality of their dancing.

Waves of Tory—named for a rocky outcrop (the Irish call it an Island) off the coast of Donegal is a great example of the difference between Scottish and Irish ceilidh dancing. The Scottish Dance Directory gives instructions for a five couple set (an Irish family). In Irish parties, a 30-couple set is more likely and they drop the boring part that involves walking in pairs and dividing as in a Grand March: the RSCDS dance video from Liverpool shows a set of fifteen couples walking this Grand March part. Excitement only comes with the waves!

At an Irish ceilidh no one bothers with instructions: the announcer tells partners to face each other for *Waves of Tory*, and the jig music immediately launches the over-and-under movement of waves. Couples going up the hall raise their arms and those coming down duck under the arch, and IMMEDIATELY the downers raise their arms as the uppers duck under their arch, and the waves go on and on, up and down. When you reach the end, you turn inwards, take hands again and go all the way back, over-and-under until the music breaks down, or one of the dancers dies of exhaustion. The

Irish use no steps, they go as fast as their beer consumption allows, and usually they do not listen to the music—yet the music has the effect of moving the waves and so a semblance of harmony is achieved. It is great fun for a ceilidh or a wedding.

WAVES OF TORY

Jig n x 48 bars for 5 couples in a 5C set (RSCDS version) or for unlimited couples (Ireland).

There are many versions of this dance in the villages of Ireland and Donegal, where Tory Island lies.

Bars 1- 8 : All Adv&Ret, all advance and cross over with Ladies dancing under Men's arches;

Bars 9-16 : Repeat back to places but Men dance under Ladies' arches;

Bars 17-24 : 1s Slip-Step down to bottom and back again;

Bars 25-32 : 1s followed by 2s+3s+4s+5s cast and 1s make an arch at bottom as 2s+3s+4s+5s dance up under arch. 23451;

Bars 33-48 : 2s+3s+4s+5s face and dance down as 1s dance up under 5s arch as 5s dance down over them and 1s dance over 4s and 'under and over' to top etc. and as all reach bottom/top they turn about and dance up/down 'under and over' back to places 23451.

Dance notes: At a ceilidh, I recommend starting with the waves bars 33-48 and don't worry about the rest.

The Waves of Tory dance illustrates the history of the Conservative (Tory) Party's relationship to Europe: up-and-down, Yes and No. In support of peace Winston Churchill supported Adenauer, Schumann and Monet's European movement, but without Britain. In 1961 Harold Macmillan wanted Britain in, but de Gaulle said '*Non*': only in 1973 did Edward Heath take the UK into the European Economic Community. Margaret Thatcher signed the Maastricht Treaty in 1986, but later changed her mind, giving momentum to what became David Cameron's ill-conceived and mis-managed Brexit referendum. All of these people were Tory prime ministers. What a mess! At least the dance *Waves of Tory* obtains continuity and coherence from the music.

Contra Dance seems to have evolved in New England from English country dancing as a reaction against the staid (and sometimes boring) square dance tradition. I think it was the Irish jig influence in Irish cities like Boston that made Contra much faster than English, and more fun than square dancing. Contra's particularity is based on a 4-count balance and a 12-count swing, usually swinging both your partner and your "opposite" or "neighbor" before the two couples separate to progress up or down the set. Mainly danced to jigs (6-8 time) and reels (3-4 time), contra dance is done in lines with men facing women which is how many French and Celtic dances are presented. A band produces music and a caller tells people what to do. In contra dance the calling stops after a while, when dancers have the formations in their heads. Unlike its cousin American Square Dance, the calling is not an integral part of the dance itself. I do not care for square dances for that reason: the voice is more important that the music, and I love dancing to music.

In Richmond, Virginia contra dance is organized by TADAMS, the Traditional American Dance and Music Society of which I have been an enthusiastic member since 1999. Even though I seldom dance now in Richmond, I pay my membership each year in order to support TADAMS and the wonderful world of dance in Richmond's Ginter Park Community Center, which is a great contra venue with an excellent wooden dance floor. One of the lovely aspects of this TADAMS contra community is the frequent presence of children. Wendy and Robert in Richmond, for example, brought their kids Alex and Rachel when they were small enough to curl up in a blanket and sleep on stage behind the band—great immersion in live music. I danced with Rachel when she was five, and again when she was fifteen. She refused to dance between the ages of 8-12, sitting in the corner playing with a telephone; dancing would have served her better, but anyway she and Alex have dance music in their bones. Great educational experience. I also took my kids to see and hear and feel live music whenever I could.

A great band produces a great dance, and the caller provides the interaction between dancers and musicians. Often the best musicians and callers are also great dancers: they understand how the parts of a ball fit together. Famous bands like Atlantic Crossing, Nightingale, Swallowtail, the Elftones, the Groovemongers, Toss the Possum, Wild Asparagus, famous musicians like Rodney Miller, Elke Baker, David Knight, Dave Wiesler and others know how to vary the contra music, starting slow and building excitement. They feel the dance, just as the dancers feel the music. Often a band will add an instrument that builds excitement: clogging rhythms, a bombarde, a mouth or jaw harp, or a variation of the pipes ... one New England band called Pig's Eye Landing produced fiddle-sticks, sticks like chopsticks with which one musician beats out a rhythm on the strings of a fiddle even as the fiddler is still playing his reel. So exciting! In contra dance, you hear the rhythms. For each couple, the leader's interpretation of the music can heighten excitement in the dance. If you want to see what contra looks like, the YouTube video of a dance called *Rockin' Robin* (by Rick Mohr) includes some people I dance with.

Women and men alike introduce extra turns and spins into their dancing, and men (or women who are leading) are expected to provide a strong lead and to catch their partner when she spins. I enjoy teaching beginners how to spin safely, but the real excitement comes when I am dancing with an excellent and experienced lightweight dancer who spins fast and who loves to spin. I use various ways to spin ladies, and the variations left, or right, or first-left-and-then-right, sometimes slower and sometimes faster, are what makes it exciting for the skilled ladies who get to dance with a different man at every turn of the music. In most dances the lady spins with her partner every 12 bars or 18 bars, giving the leader the chance to experiment with the styles his partner prefers. At the end of one Springforth Ball, the band played a wonderful set that lasted 15 minutes. I had invited a lady I did not know called Laura Duncan. As we danced we moved faster and faster, knowing each other better and better, becoming more and more excited as the music kept us moving on and on and on. At last the set ended and we hugged, sweaty and happy. Laura said: "Great lead!" The perfect compliment.

I should explain, dearest children, that the expression "lightweight" in the context of contra dance has nothing to do with the size or shape of a woman: it has everything to do with the way she handles her own weight. I know quite small women who are heavy, for their whole weight hangs off my backbone when they dance—tiring on the body and bad for my back. And I know some big women who dance like angels on the head of a pin because they hold their weight above their own center of gravity. Big or small, tall or short, those are the "lightweight" women with whom we men love to dance.

Contra dance is not for everyone, especially not for women who dislike sweaty men. I change my shirt at half time, and so does my friend Jeff; but many of the men (and some of the women) get wetter and wetter. One of my lady friends told me that she danced at the Summer Soirée event with a man who brought 34 shirts and changed his shirt every 15 minutes. She added that she went through 10 dresses during the weekend: but a lady requires longer to change, and more privacy. The Summer Soirée in Asheville, North Carolina advertises itself as "the Hottest Event on the Calendar"—both the temperature and the dancing.

I obey one rule: I always wear a white shirt, with an A-shirt or singlet beneath it to absorb perspiration. I remember one occasion when a student attended a Richmond contra dance in May wearing a light gray T-shirt. At half time it had become a dark gray top that was dripping wet, and her long hair was dripping traces of sweat across the dance floor. It so happened that I had a spare white T-shirt in my bag, so I went across to chat to her. I did not feel able to raise the subject myself, but fortunately she told me, "I feel terrible, I am soaked and I didn't bring anything to change into." Feeling virtuous, I offered my clean T-shirt, and passed her a towel as well. Her gratitude turned into friendship and I went to see her graduation exhibit at the VCU School of Arts, where she had filled a room with some sort of stretched resin stuff that hung and floated across the space. Visitors were invited to lie on the floor, and look up at the ceiling through this web of resin cobwebs. I duly lay on the floor and wriggled around the room on my back, looking at the shapes and strands. Very creative.

At the start of a contra dance, I usually invite beginners and I hope to give them a great dance experience. I know the rhythm of jigs and reels and I try to share this with new partners. If the beginner is a natural dancer, I will push her as far and as fast as I feel appropriate so that she can begin to feel what top-flight contra is like, with its exciting spins and whirls. The ultimate target is the "buzz-swing" which is thrilling .... but not as exhilarating (or dangerous) as the Scottish Reel of Tulloch swing, where the two dancers place left hands behind their backs, holding the right hand of their partner. In Virginia, the only person I dare do a Tulloch swing with is Moira Turner: one nod and we are in it and spinning at 90 miles per hour like we did when we were twenty years old in Scotland. You need to know your partner and to have full control of your own body, balance, weight and handgrip in order to come out of your spin at the exact split-second to end on the precise spot where you both need to be on bar 8 of your set.

In contra, I advise beginners to walk around in time to the music. "As long as you walk, you have control and a strong or clumsy man cannot do you any damage. If you know the man you are dancing with—and if you trust him—then you can be more adventurous and let him spin you." Then I show my beginner some of the spinning techniques. First: the outside of your right foot is placed against the outside of your partner's right foot (never inside or you will both fall on your faces). Then you begin to pivot slowly, pushing off with your left foot as though on a scooter, and lifting the ball of your right foot very slightly to allow the turn. As you gain confidence together, the spin can get faster. Each partner is holding the other upright through the other's back or shoulder. If the lady is the right height and weight for me, I find the ideal spin position is to fill the palm of my right hand with the lady's left shoulder-blade: if she leans into my hand, the straight line running from her left shoulder to her right foot provides the perfect pivot for a good spin. It is a question of physics.

If my partner is light and confident, we sometimes use other techniques. Holding left hands above your head, and with right hands on the other's left hip, allows for a wonderful spin with the eyes locked, and the lady can turn out at the end of the spin straight into a circle flowing leftwards with the oncoming couple. Occasionally I will spin a very skilled lady with a single hand behind her shoulder, raising my left hand in the air as for Highland dance. One of the skills of being a good "leader" is to offer new ideas to your partner: but the key thing is to know what you are doing and to respect the phrasing of the music. If in doubt, keep it simple and repeat what works. Never try something complicated with a lady who is not fully confident of what she is doing and where she is going. The biggest contra crime is spinning a lady who does not want to be spun, using brute force. A man can dislocate someone's shoulder if he is strong and clumsy. Simple is safe. When I meet an unknown lady coming down the line (for example in Glen Echo, Maryland where there may be 300 dancers and I only know six of them), I find the best thing is to ask the lady, " Do you want to spin?" She will tell me if she does, and then I can raise my arm and give her the thrill of a great spin into the arms of her next partner.

In which case I must turn around quickly myself for here is another beautiful dancer headed into my arms, and I have to be ready to catch her! Ah! Bliss!

14

A CONVERSATION ABOUT DANCE ETIQUETTE WITH TOM HINDS, LIZ AND ELKE

T om Hinds is one of the best callers and dance composers on the US East Coast contra circuit. He lives in Virginia. My relationship with Tom is a perfect example of dance friendship since the only thing we know about the other guy is what we have seen on the dance floor. I only know that Tom is a great dancer and a great caller. So I was surprised to receive an email from Tom one day back in 2017, asking for my advice—not so much about dancing as such, but about social etiquette on the dance floor. Like many dancers, Tom enjoys various styles of dance and it turns out that he had seen me when I attended an English dance session near Charlottesville.

> *Robin,*
> *Tom Hinds here. Linda Salter gave me your email address but I'm not 100 percent I have the right person. Are you Scottish and did you attend our English dance in Ivy a year ago? If I've got the right person I'd like to ask you a question or two about your experience at that dance. Thanks.*

I confirmed to Tom that he had found the right man. He saw my face at the English dance session and he thought I was the guy whom he had seen wearing the kilt on the contra dance floor. I wear the kilt for both Scottish and contra dancing because it feels good. The kilt is so comfortable for spinning and turning. Also, Liam, women LOVE a man wearing the kilt, and for two reasons. Firstly, many women love to see a man's strong and muscular legs. Secondly, the kilt divides the man vertically into three equal parts, which is more elegant than shirt-and-pants. Above the kilt is my clean white shirt with a scarf or a tie; below the kilt are my clean white stockings with flashes; and in the middle of the kilt sits my sporran that—especially if it is made of sealskin—every woman would love to stroke. I often tell adolescent boys who feel awkward: "If you wear the kilt and dance, girls will love you. They love the kilt, and they love a man who can dance. Even if they do not tell you so, trust me that it is true: a boy in a kilt is a WOW with the girls."

By the way, kids, the expression "Wow!" was originally a 16th century Scots expression for astonishment, admiration, shock or whatever. It was first used in print in 1513 in Scotland, and is now frequent throughout the English-speaking world. You may say "Wow!" It is your heritage.

Tom Hinds told me that he had heard complaints about his English dancing when he introduced a few contra-style extra turns into the dancing. Some of the English country dancers are very staid. He had heard me in Charlottesville giving the occasional whoop, occasionally clapping to the music and generally trying to make the dancing more lively. Had I had any negative feedback, he wondered, about my antics?

I chuckled when I read Tom's message. While most dancers envy me my courage and my good humor, I do know a few people—very few: I can think of just one musician, and maybe three dancers—who hate it when I clap and whoop on the dance floor. An excellent musician called Liz does not like it when I clap because she says that I usurp her right to determine the beat. So when Liz is playing, I am restrained. Most other musicians thank me for responding to their playing, saying that my clapping and whooping gives them energy and pushes them to play harder in response to the enthusiasm of the dancers.

On one occasion at the Richmond Highland Games, Liz was playing a concert of dance music with the wonderful fiddler Elke Baker: they call their duet *Terpsichore*, the Ancient Greek Muse of dancing and choral singing, and we are lucky that they often play for our Richmond dances. Someone told me that Liz would take exception to my entertaining the crowd with some Highland steps while they played. I laughed and replied that my experience of entertaining people was as great as hers. I know how to whip up a crowd! At the Richmond Folk Festival I regularly produce an impromptu two minutes of dancing on stage when a good reel is being played, and I instantly have 3000 people clapping in time to the reel. When I have attended concerts of the world-famous Battlefield Band—one of Scotland's most famous folk music groups to play in Virginia—I have always worn the kilt. Each time the bagpipes began to play, I would go up on stage and dance for a couple of minutes. The musicians were delighted: they could literally feel the audience lift and the noise level rise. A dancer bridges the space between the musicians and the spectators. At my time of life I know what I can do, and what I want to do. I had no hesitation in reassuring Tom Hinds.

THANKS, TOM

I am old enough now, Tom, not to care whether people like my antics on the dance floor or not, but in general terms I know that I do bring extra energy and enjoyment to the others' dancing. I know that 90% of bands are grateful for enthusiastic response from the floor, which explains some of my "hooching" (the rest is pure joy and enthusiasm). If the dancers return the energy to the band, the band gets stronger and the musicians feel better. This two-way street is what makes a dance really successful.

ALSO I know now that I am a good folk dancer, and one whom women enjoy dancing with (it took me 50 years to realize this—but I am sure of it now!). When a dancer in a kilt enters a room, people perk up. I have been invited to weddings simply because the hosts hoped I would turn up wearing the kilt.

One time when I was leaving at half-time through a contra dance in Richmond (I was tired after dancing Scottish all afternoon), a fellow-dancer called Greg told me, "When you leave, there goes half the energy of this whole dance hall." So the antics of a few individuals can really "lift" a dance floor, especially if there are not a lot of dancers. When I dance in the Younger Hall in St Andrews during RSCDS Summer School (the "Olympic Games" of folk dancing)—with 250 dancers on the world's best dance floor, of whom 100 are wearing the kilt—then nothing I can do will "lift" the dance. St Andrews dances are lifted by their own momentum and by the brilliance of the band and the dances. But in a smaller hall like Richmond or Norge, with 50 or 60 dancers on the floor, then one or two people can sometimes "carry" the dance and push the music to a higher level: "kick it up a notch" as Emeril, the Portuguese cook and TV presenter, likes to say.

So you have heard complaints? I say: "Ignore them!" Your national reputation as a caller and dance creator gives you the latitude to do whatever you want. IT IS ALSO TRUE that one person complaining does not represent the whole community: it is often the negative elements who make themselves heard loudest. So if you wanna add in a spin, just do so because 70% of the dancers probably enjoy the extra twist.

Hope to see you on the dance floor one of these days, and soon!

very best wishes

Robin

15

ST ANDREWS HAS THE WORLD'S GREATEST DANCE FLOOR AND UGLIEST NUN

I have told you about St Andrews, kids, one of the world's most beautiful small cities with its fabulous West Sands beach stretching for two miles; its East Sands and picturesque fishing port. This is where the 4th century monk Regulus came from Patras in Greece to bring to Scotland the bones of St Andrew, one of Christ's twelve apostles. St Andrews has a long religious history and the city is filled with ghost stories and places where the Reformation burned its martyrs. If you were to spend just one chilly night in the Bottle Dungeon, dug out of the rock under the dramatic-but-ruined castle of St Andrews, you would hear the waves of the North Sea beating against the castle foundations, mingled with the groans of those prisoners who, once dropped into this dungeon centuries ago, knew they would never come out again. By the time anyone gave them a ladder to climb out of the pit, they were too weak to climb. Dropping a prisoner fifteen feet down into that dungeon would break his leg and leave him in agony. The Middle Ages were filled with cruelty.

Walking uphill from the Royal & Ancient Golf Club, along The Scores roadway you reach a Martyr's Monument perched on the cliff edge and overlooking The Butts where medieval citizens were ordered to practice archery instead of playing football. Below is a pool of water visible in the rocks at low tide. This is the Witches' Pool, where people suspected of witchcraft are said to have been thrown during the 16th and 17th centuries around the same time that the Salem witches were being burned in Massachusetts. If the old women suspected of witchcraft sank and drowned, then they were deemed innocent and could be buried in the churchyard. If they floated, the women were judged guilty and burned at the stake. You can hear their spirits moaning around the Witches' Pool when the wind is whistling on dark rainy nights. The Martyr's Monument records other nasty burnings from the time of the Reformation.

Outside the university chapel the letters PH are written in the medieval paving stones: university professor Patrick Hamilton was burned here in 1528 for his Protestant reforming beliefs, becoming the first martyr of the Scottish Reformation. The wood was wet, and PH took six hours to burn; his ghost wanders the university cloisters on windy nights, howling with pain from the flames that are devouring his flesh. His face is said to have burned into the stonework of St Salvator's College where he died: you can see him in the 5th stone above the arch, watching you. We always avoid stepping on the PH and any other martyr's marker. In the ruins of Blackfriars you may meet the unhappy Alexander Campbell, one of those who burned Hamilton and who was struck down the following day—the revenge of God, according to popular belief. If you venture into St Rule's Tower, beside the cathedral ruins, you may meet Prior Robert de Montrose, who was stabbed here in 1393: he is a friendly monk, far more friendly than the ghastly disfigured woman of Nun's Walk, down by St Leonard's Church near the beautiful gardens of St Leonards School: this young woman in a grey cloak is said to have cut off her own nose, ears and lips to avoid an unwanted marriage, before becoming a nun. Nearby a ghostly little three-legged black dog runs around above the ground: he died in a snowfall when the snow lay one foot thick but no one knows how the dog is related to the disfigured Nun of the Walk.

Cardinal David Beaton may haunt the castle. After he had watched the reformist preacher George Wishart burning at the stake in front of St Andrews Castle, the Cardinal—the last Scottish Cardinal before the Reformation, who was also Chancellor of Scotland, Archbishop of St Andrews and Papal Legate—was murdered by vengeful Protestants who broke into the castle on 29th May 1546. One of them was John Knox, who had been Wishart's bodyguard. Beaton's body was hung upside down from the battlements. Although Ethie Castle near Arbroath claims his ghost, Cardinal Beaton is more likely to haunt the castle where he was killed. Dundee claims the ghost of Beaton's mistress, Marion Ogilvy (erudite daughter of the first Lord Ogilvy) who waves a white handkerchief across the water to her erstwhile lover Cardinal Beaton in St Andrews. Well she might wave to him: Marion and her lover, the theoretically unmarried Cardinal, produced and raised eight children together.

The medieval castle and medieval cathedral are largely ruined: the cathedral was destroyed at the behest of vicious John Knox, who had previously been an ordained Catholic priest. Engineers love visiting the mine and counter-mine dug during the Reformation in battles to control St Andrews and capture its castle. The medieval university where I studied is in great form: founded in 1410 (it received a formal Papal Bull in 1413) it is the oldest university in Scotland and the third oldest in Britain after Oxford and Cambridge, regularly being cited among the top universities in Europe. Here students for 600 years have worn the famous red academic gown. I gave mine in 2017 to a nephew, Jack Symonds who is studying astrophysics at St Andrews and is now dancing in my scarlet gown. St Andrews is home to seven 18-hole golf courses and the historic Royal & Ancient Golf Club, "Home of Golf" with the famous pub called "The 19th Hole" sitting beside the 18th green of the Old Course. Having told you about all these beauties, lovely grandchildren, I must tell you that St Andrews in summer is also the world center for dancing in a town where the summer daylight lasts until nearly midnight. The best place in the world for a holiday and I try to come to St Andrews at least every second year.

For four weeks every summer, the Royal Scottish Country Dance Society holds its Summer School in St Andrews. We stay in the student bedrooms of University Hall and a neighboring building named after Agnes Blackadder, the university's first female graduate who received her M.A. on 29th March 1895 and went on to achieve eminence as a consultant dermatologist in London. The food is great, the sun always shines and the dancing is amazing. You wake at 7am to the wonderful sound of a piper marching in the gardens below your bedroom window. One year, I looked out of my sunlit window and noticed that this week's kilted early morning piper was ... a Japanese woman! They offer a huge breakfast offering Scottish specialties like porridge, kippers and black pudding as well as the "Full English" and as much fruit and "Continental Breakfast" as you could wish for. After breakfast two hundred dancers set off on foot through the gardens for their classes. Teaching takes place in church halls across town, each one with a wooden floor and a pianist: levels go from "beginners" and "children who have never danced before" to "very advanced high impact" and "qualified teachers only."

One note of caution: even if you adore smoked kippers, I do not recommend eating them before dancing—it is the breakfast dish that keeps on giving. The internal belch of kipper fumes is not what you want to taste when you are trying to perfect your pas de basque.

We have two classes every morning during the week, with two different teachers and two live musicians (well, they would not be much good if they were dead musicians). Each traditionally receives a gift and a "thank you" card from the class because all teachers and musicians provide their services free. Scottish country dancing thrives thanks to people who are generous with their skills and passionate about Scottish culture, music and dance. In the afternoon these days I tend to rest, or talk through dances for some of the foreigners who are preparing a Younger Hall dance. Some afternoons I give guided tours of St Andrews and its ghost stories to dancers from other countries. Other people go off to swim, play golf, go putting, visit the cute fishing ports along the coastline of the East Neuk of Fife—where artists love to paint—or tour the jewel of Fife: fortified Falkland Palace and its gardens, its Rennaissance Royal Chapel and real royal tennis court—the oldest in Britain where Mary, Queen of Scots played. The tennis court was built by her father, James V, and this was Mary's favorite palace. Falkland Palace reminded Mary of her childhood in the French court.

Every evening in St Andrews we have ceilidh and social dancing, with "big" dances on Thursday and Saturday: and "big" means that they take place in the Younger Hall, the university's graduation hall where the world's greatest dance floor was built by Scotland's Younger beer family. In 1884 Louis Pasteur visited the Younger brewery in Edinburgh to see how his 'pasteurization' technique had improved the keeping qualities of their beer. His visit coincided with the 300th anniversary of Edinburgh University (only 300 years: such a young institution). In response to Pasteur's horror at the appalling state of Edinburgh's public health, the Younger family funded in Edinburgh the first public health Chair at any university (named for Bruce and Usher, two of the generous brewers). To St Andrews University the Youngers donated this magnificent graduation hall, housing the music department and a sprung dance floor (nowadays called a spring floor) composed of wooden boards each of which is individually fitted with metal springs. Modern American sprung floors are based on a layer of foam, a pale imitation of the Younger Hall where the feel of the floor is so wonderful: it absorbs shocks and responds to dancers, giving extra bounce. When 200 people dance in the Younger Hall, the floor takes on a life and movement of its own. I hope you grandchildren will dance there one day.

These Thursday and Saturday evening dances are the Olympic Games of Scottish Dancing. Dancers come from all over Scotland for great dancing and fine music, even if they are not attending the daily classes. The dancing is of high quality and the dances are complex. Back in the 1960s, when we of the St Andrews University Celtic Society organised our annual Highland Ball, dancing was stressful. There were no pre-dance briefings then. The band would play four bars of music, the sets would form, and the dance would begin with a chord and a bow. No one even announced the name of the dance: you were expected to read your dance card and know your dances. I was a young, less confident dancer in those days. We studied and practiced beforehand and re-read the dance instructions before each dance. 50 years on, I have more knowledge, more experience, and we now have briefings before each dance—partly because the Society has so many great new dances.

There are easy dances as well. More than a dozen dances are named after St Andrew, of which the most popular is *St Andrews Fair*, written by the famous dance devisor Roy Goldring. It is a good dance with which to begin a program, for it is easy in conception, it flows nicely and it is not too demanding on the legs: the turn-and-chase figure, for example, and the circle in between are pleasant formations that help warm up the leg muscles as people dance around the set.

ST ANDREW'S FAIR

Jig 8 x 32 bars for 3 couples in a 4-couple longwise set. Devisor: Roy Goldring. 5 Scottish Country Dances.

During the 12th century St Andrews became a burgh with the right to hold a weekly market and an Annual Fair.

Bars 1-4 : 1st couple cross by the right and cast 2 places;

Bars 5-8 : 1s cross by the left and cast up to 2nd place on own sides;

Bars 9-12 : 2s 1s 3s turn partner by the right halfway, retain hands and set;

Bars 13-16 : All chase clockwise halfway to own sides;

Bars 17-24 : 3s1s2s 6 hands round and back;

Bars 25-28 : 3s 1s 2s turn partner halfway by the left, retain hands and set;

Bars 29-32 : All chase anticlockwise halfway to finish 2s1s3s on own sides.

16

CATRIONA AND OTHER MEMORIES IN THE YOUNGER HALL

My first sight of the Younger Hall was in 1965, for the September graduation of students who had not received their degrees in June. Presiding was Sir Malcolm Knox, Principal of St Andrews University 1953–1966 (Americans would call him the president) and a distinguished professor of philosophy. To my amused astonishment, the medical students in the balcony started singing their favorite graduation song: "Oh Sir Malcolm, do not touch me!" to the tune of Glory, Glory, Hallelujah! It continues: "Oh Sir Malcolm, do not touch!" "Oh Sir Malcolm, do not!" "Oh Sir Malcolm, do!" "Oh Sir Malcolm!" "Oh Sir!" "Oh!"

I could see Sir Malcolm and the university bigwigs lining up, and the University Principal did not look amused. Led by two great medieval maces, the graduation procession began to enter the Younger Hall down a middle passage between the seats. The singing changed: "The animals came in two-by-two, Hurrah! Hurrah! The animals came in two-by-two, Hurrah! The animals came in two-by-two, the chimpanzee and the kangaroo..." sang the medical students and we young first-year students laughed in disbelief. Sir Malcolm Knox was not laughing.

More was to come. To the amazement of us *bejants* (the name given to first year students: it comes from the French *bête jaune* or 'green horn' but literally it means 'yellow creature') the medical students were now throwing paper streamers and rolls of toilet paper from the balcony as the medieval maces solemnly preceded the Principal and Deans down the center of the Younger Hall between the seated grad-uands. Deans and professors in long red gowns were brushing aside the paper streamers from their faces and tripping over the rolls of toilet paper unravelling around their feet. The chaos from the balcony above contrasted absurdly with the solemnity of the procession below ... or what was left of the solemnity in this riot of ridicule. In 1966, the rules were changed and no St Andrews graduation ceremony was ever again so noisy. St Andrews has made other progress as well: the last two Principals have been distinguished women academics. Professor Louise Richardson (now Vice-Chancellor of Oxford University) handed over in 2016 to Professor Sally Mapstone, who came to St Andrews from .... Oxford.

I stand and laugh at memories of that first experience of the Younger Hall, where later I received my own graduation scroll in a decorous ceremony in June 1969. Honorary degrees were awarded that year to Lester Pearson, peacemaker and Prime Minister of Canada, and Sir Michael Swann FRS, Vice-Chancellor of Edinburgh University, a distinguished molecular biologist who later became Baron Swann and Chairman of Governors of the BBC. These two eminent men were my fellow-graduates. I had the good luck to be invited (with my girlfriend) to a drinks party before the ceremony where I met them both and spent 40 minutes listening in awe to the wisdom of Lester Pearson. At the same party was my friend Su Swann, daughter of Sir Michael: they both graduated on the same day as me. Two weeks later, to our mutual astonishment, I walked into Horstone Cottage on the Isle of Wight to meet the new fiancée of my cousin Christopher Garnett, and his fiancée was ... Su Swann!

I remember with terror those St Andrews Highland Balls. We loved Bobby Crowe and his band and the band of Billy Anderson, who lived in St Andrews and who became a good friend. But without briefings, the dance pressure exerted by the adults was terrible. If we did not know our dances perfectly, we were dismissed with a contempt that only Scottish matrons are able to convey in a single frown. Today in the Younger Hall I laugh with joy at just being here in this space. The sprung floor beneath our feet undulates with the reels, jigs and hornpipes, while the boards glide smoothly beneath the steps of our strathspeys. No contempt, just shared joy and friendship. Great and lovely RSCDS! Marvelous music! Wonderful Younger Hall!

After student dancing, there were the walks on the golf course in what I remember as balmy summer evenings when the light did not fade on the kissing bridge until 10.30 or 11.00 in the evening. Golf is a game for the rich in countries like France and the United States, but in Scotland golf is a popular game for ordinary people. Golf was played on the West Sands of St Andrews 900 years ago. Mary Queen of Scots enjoyed playing golf in the 1500s. In 1754 the R&A was founded and ten years later in 1764 the 18-hole golf course became standard. The game was recently celebrated in the film *Tommy's Honour*, about Young Tom Morris who won the Open Championship four times in a row. He was the professional golfer who forced the wealthy 19th century aristocrats who dominated golf to treat professional golfers with respect and to pay them professionally. The film has great shots of the St Andrews harbour and other pieces of the East Neuk of Fife (that corner of the attractive Fife coastline where St Andrews lies, and which has other beautiful fishing ports like Crail, Anstruther and Pittenweem). You can still buy golf clubs in the St Andrews shop of Old Tom Morris, Tommy's father.

Americans are a big part of the St Andrews golf economy. There are bars full of young clean-shaven men with American accents whose eyes are glued to the golf channel. That is not all they do, of course. During World War II there was a popular saying about the GIs who were too attractive to British girls: "GIs are over-sexed and over here." The following golf story from my friend Wilbur in Washington D.C. follows a similar line of thought.

Golf partners John and Shawn had hired a car to drive to St Andrews from Prestwick airport near Glasgow. Unusually for Scotland, they got caught in a thunderstorm with heavy rain. They pulled into a nearby farm for shelter, and the attractive lady who answered the door said they were welcome to spend the night. "It's terrible weather out there and I have this big house all to myself," she said. "Since I'm recently widowed and so that the neighbors don't start talking, I will put you to sleep in the annex."

In the morning, the weather had cleared; so after breakfast with their hostess the two friends hit the road, reached St Andrews and enjoyed a great weekend of golf. Then nine months later, John got an unexpected letter from a Scottish lawyer. After reading the letter three times, he called his friend Shawn and asked, "Shawn, do you remember that good looking widow on the farm we stayed at on our golf holiday in Scotland about 9 months ago?"

"Yes, I sure do remember her," Shawn replied.

"Did you happen to get up in the middle of the night and pay her a visit?"

"Well, um, yes," replied Shawn sounding a little embarrassed "I have to confess that I did."

"Did you give her my name and address instead of telling her your own name?"

"Yeah, look, I'm sorry, buddy but I'm afraid I did. I should never have played that trick. How did you find out?"

"Her attorney just wrote to tell me that she has died. She left me the farm and one million dollars."

During the 1960s, students of St Andrews and town citizens could buy an annual golf card for ten shillings (50 pence) that allowed us to play on any of the town's five municipal golf courses. My favorite was the Eden Course, whose broad fairways and light rough matched my modest playing level. On long, light summer evenings in June, after exams, we could play the Eden until 10.30 at night. I tried playing the Old Course a few times. There was no extra fee, but I lost so many balls in the gorse bushes that I could not afford the Old Course. These days, millionaires reserve and pay a fortune for their space on the Old Course at St Andrews 12 months in advance. St Andrews golf has changed in the past half-century from a sport to a business, as the large number of hotels in St Andrews proves. Yet you can still hire a bag of clubs and go around one of the lesser courses for around £10 or

$20. Away from the elite Royal & Ancient Golf Club, Scottish golf remains a sport of the people.

If you walk west down South Street, children, you will reach the West Port built in 1587, which is the only remaining city gate. It was modelled after the Porte Saint-Honoré in Paris. Turn right outside the gate and walk along the path: you will see that the second building is called The Wee House. Yes, it is small; but the name refers to the fact that it used to contain the public toilets, before being turned into an attractive cottage. Hee! Hee!

As students we used to go out in groups to enjoy the West Sands, to play the putting greens (especially the very hilly green nicknamed The Himalayas), or simply to walk on the beautiful golf links. Sometimes there were just two of us. I invited both Alison and Catriona to Highland Balls—two of my favorite Scottish dance partners with two of Scotland's most beautiful girls' names. Catriona was my partner at my very first Highland Ball, one that I did not have to organize because I was in my first year. I didn't know that she had a non-dancing boyfriend who was furious with me. He was in the wrong: he didn't dance and he should not have wanted to spoil Catriona's fun. He was a medical student who decided to put a laxative into my drink as revenge. Fortunately friends of his (who told me later) persuaded him that I was the innocent party and it was up to Catriona to decide with whom she wanted to dance. Remembering the beautiful and intelligent Catriona revives a favorite Scottish limerick that somebody else wrote, and which has nothing to do with my old girlfriend.

Catriona, a pretty young lass
Had a truly magnificent ass.
Not rounded and pink
As you possibly think:
It was grey, had long ears, and ate grass.

The Highland Ball took place, naturally, in the Younger Hall. The only ballroom I know that compares with the Younger Hall is the vast Spanish Ballroom at Glen Echo, Maryland, where I go sometimes to dance waltz, contra, and swing. That 100-year-old sprung floor near Washington D.C. is sufficiently fragile that contra dancers are allowed only to use the outside parts of the floor: four lines of dancers are allowed, two on either side of the floor. A fifth line that could otherwise occupy the middle would dance where the floor might not be able to withstand the pressure of the "balance and swing" move where forty dancers stamping in the New England style, with hard heels, could set off vibrations that split the boards asunder.

These days in the Younger Hall I seldom even bother to read the program before a dance. I know that I can pick up the instructions from the pre-dance briefing, and I have already danced 95% of dances they will put on the program. Very seldom do I come unstuck. One Thursday evening at the Younger Hall, I had invited a Japanese lady who was in my class, and when I lined up in my set I asked my neighbor what we were going to dance next. "Muirland Willie," he replied. I had not danced *Muirland Willie* in ten years.

"Will you remind me? I have a beginner as my partner."

"You'll have a tough time getting a beginner through *Muirland Willie*," my neighbor told me: "Each couple in the set does something different, and all of them at the same time."

I did then have a moment of doubt. But it was too late to pull out of the set, and I could neither disappoint nor humiliate my Japanese partner. I made clear with sign language that she should follow my every instruction, and I focused very hard on the briefing for this dance that I had known but had forgotten. And then we were off! We started at once as third couple: cross, cast to the top, all set, and cross to own sides. Easy. And now we are at the top: what should we be doing as 1s? Oh, Yes: lead down the middle to third place, and cast up into second place, and then all three couples set again, and cross. Then we can rest for 50 seconds. After the first sixteen bars of multiple changeovers from the top three positions, the rest of *Muirland Willie* is simple: the first couple (now in third place) leads up to the top, and sets. Then 1s and 2s set advancing, and dance the poussette to change places, so that 1s can dance it again with couples 3 & 4.

Now we are 2s: second couple set, cross down to third place, and set again. From third place, we cross, cast to the top, set and cross again .... Yes, we did manage the whole dance, thanks to a combination of my very firm finger pointing and the quick instincts of my Japanese lady partner in responding to my finger. Here I was practising another sort of "leading" and fortunately my lady was watching and following her partner carefully. If only all intermediate dancers would watch their partner so well! How can any worried dancer expect to receive directional help if she watches the floorboards ... the floor is the only part of a dance that is never going to move.

The final poussette is a lovely formation to progress, taking the two couples around each other and around the square all at the same time with the lively pas de basque step. Because the man begins on his left foot (instead of the normal right foot), the dancing feet of the man and the woman come out together in a point on every step, which is so elegant! It is also great fun to dance the poussette with a good partner using no hands. The best way to learn the poussette is to recite the ditty as you dance the eight bars: "Out to the side and quarter-turn; up or down with quarter-turn; into the middle and turn around; back; and back." In French it starts "*Hors du centre et quart de tour...*" The pas de basque poussette is very energetic and bouncy—not relaxing for the ankles when you are seventy years old. I used to love it as a student. In those ancient days, I could dance the poussette all night. Recently I attended a dance in France where the program composer had chosen three dances that included the poussette. Three? In one evening? On a floor made of plastic tiles laid over concrete? That is a lot of pas de basque! I was not the only person who felt that evening that my ankles had been abused.

MUIRLAND WILLIE

Jig 8 x 32 bars for 3 couples in a 4-couple longwise set. Anon. RSCDS Book 21.

John Playford in 1669 mentions the song describing Muirland Willie wooing Maggie with talk of his plough and three oxen, and a traditional tune *Lord Frog and Lady Mouse*—not a selling point for a modern bride.

Bars 1-4 : 1s cross down to third place and cast up to second place

WHILE 2s set and cross down to third place

WHILE 3s cast to the top and cross, all finishing on opposite sides;

Bars 5-8 : All set on the sides and cross with both hands to own sides;

Bars 9-16 : Repeat bars 1-8 from new positions;

Bars 17-20 : 1s lead to the top;

Bars 21-22 : 1s set;

Bars 23-24 : 1s & 2s set, advancing;

Bars 25-32 : 1s2s poussette.

Dance Notes: Don't dance this with a beginner! This is a complex dance for experienced dancers.

MARY STUART AND JEAN MILLIGAN SAVING SCOTTISH COUNTRY DANCING

I bet you never guessed, my lovely Franco-British grandchildren, that Scottish dancing came from France! *Oui! La Belle France nous a donné la danse écossaise!* Contra Dance and English Country Dancing also have French roots and I must tell to you how this came about. We have to thank that famous and mysterious lady called Mary, Queen of Scots. Amazingly, she was also Queen of France. Scotland and France have been allies forever, mainly because they were both bullied by the English. The English are often astonished to hear that they have exploited the rest of the world: amnesia and self-congratulation too often smother reflection about how the British Empire was created.

"An Englishman considers himself to be a self-made man, and he worships his Maker" is one explanation for England's poor understanding of history. Another, as Salman Rushdie recently observed, it that so much British history took place overseas. How many English schoolchildren learn about the repression of the Welsh, Scots and Irish by the English regularly invading the Celtic lands for 700 years from 1200 AD until the Easter Uprising of 1916? In 1922 formal independence came to most of Ireland, after centuries of slavery imposed by Anglo-Saxons. Few young people study the British Empire by analyzing the hundreds of thousands of deaths caused by the first three Anglo-Afghan wars .... the Sikh wars .... the so-called Indian Mutiny .... the conquest of Burma .... the Tasmanian genocide .... the Chinese opium wars .... the partition of India .... the creation of Israel, Lebanon, Iraq, Syria, Jordan, Kuwait, Saudi Arabia .... the colonisation (conquest and exploitation) of Africa .... the slave trade .... racism and slave exploitation in the plantations of Virginia and Georgia and the Caribbean islands .... the trade imbalances that still impoverish our ex-colonies .... South African and Rhodesian *apartheid*, and British support for racial separation? Not many schools in England emphasise these parts of history in their curriculum. Most British history teaching covers the follies of kings and the false glories of battles won, ignoring the women and children who have been the victims of all these wars. I want my grandchildren to be better informed than their comrades.

Although we live in a world divided into Nation States, this idea is quite new. The first Nation-State was the United States of America, which threw off the King of England in 1776 and had to invent something different. 150 years ago in the 19th century, the countries of Germany and Italy did not yet exist: their spaces were filled with small kingdoms, principalities and city-states. Seven hundred years ago, Europe was composed of lands that quite literally "belonged" to the feudal lord who ruled each estate. Even farmers "belonged" to the feudal lord: they were serfs (really slaves) tied to the land and not allowed to travel. The peasants of the manor of Hatfield Peverel in Essex were the slaves and subjects of the Norman lord Sir Ranulph Peverel (1030–1072), possibly one of William's bastards, who came to England with William the Conqueror in 1066. When the Black Death of 1348 killed off one third of Europe's population, agricultural labour became so scarce that lords were obliged to search for new workers, to pay wages to attract people to work for them, and only then did the slave status of peasants began to change. People did not think of The State. They thought only of their village, their lord, and Christendom, that wide community composed of ignorant people terrified of the Devil who worshipped the almost-as-frightening Christian God: "the rich man in his castle, the poor man at his gate" survived in servitude and in misery, hoping only for salvation (after the blessed relief of death) through the intercession of a kind and loving Jesus Christ. Scotland was not very different until the Reformation brought dramatic changes.

Mary Stuart, Queen of Scots, was born on 8th December 1542 in Linlithgow Palace to a Royal French mother named Marie de Guise, wife of James V of Scotland. Mary's father James died when she was six days old: she became Queen at the age of One Week. While Marie de Guise ruled Scotland as Regent, the young Queen Mary was betrothed at the age of six to the four-year-old son of the king of France. She went to live at the French court and the young couple were married in 1558, when Mary was 16. The following year her husband was crowned king and Mary became Queen of France. But François II died a year later in 1560, leaving Mary a widow aged 18. She returned to Scotland—where her mother had just died. The French-speaking Mary spelled her name in the French manner: *Stuart*. Her local Scottish cousins spelled it in the English way with a W: *Stewart*. In those days when most communication was oral, spelling was a matter of choice. Sometimes people used several different spellings, even in the same document, to show how clever they were in varying their spellings. If we now think of these two as separate names, it is because we spend years sitting on school benches where teachers obsess us with 'correct' spelling. Spelling Bees are an American national pastime, but your text-message generation will probably abandon spelling as an exercise.

Scotland was in the middle of the Reformation, torn between Roman Catholics like Mary and Protestants egged on by the radical preacher John Knox. My dancing story has no space for the fascinating plots and murders that dogged Mary Stuart's unhappy reign, her two Scottish husbands, the murder of her secretary or her execution by her English cousin Elizabeth I. Exciting though as they are, these events have nothing to do with dancing—except that everyone danced in those days. Queen Elizabeth always started her day with musicians, dancing a few energetic *galliards* to get her blood flowing. One day I will tell you children the story of Mary and Elizabeth, the cousins-who-never-met (despite a fake-news meeting described by the German writer Schiller in his play *Maria Stuart*), and teach you the *galliard*: it is a great Renaissance dance with plenty of acting and posturing.

Queen Elizabeth's cousin Mary was even more excited by dance, which was a big feature of the French court. When she went on her first tour of her Scottish kingdom, Mary discovered her Scottish subjects dancing in their barns and in their castles, and she loved it. She liked the music, she liked the dancing, and she told her French dancing masters to bring these Scottish Country Dances into her ballroom at Holyrood Palace, her home in Edinburgh. Note to myself: I must take my grandchildren one day to see Edinburgh and visit the palace.

The French court had many *contredanses*, which meant that—instead of round dances or line dances which also existed in the French countryside—the partners in the ballroom stood opposite one another in set lines *les hommes contre les dames*. In this sense, most Scottish and English ballroom dances are *contredanses*, and we dance them that way thanks to Mary Stuart.

The dances Mary found in the towns and villages of her kingdom descended from ancient Celtic reels—similar to the Danish and Norse word *ril*—danced for centuries in the barns and fields of Northern Europe, but evolving over time from dance styles still seen in the Baltics, the Balkans, in Syria and Greece: our inherited Indo-European dance traditions. Many of Mary's dances were probably what we would now consider ceilidh dances: easy social dances that anyone can join in and that everyone in the village knows like *Strip the Willow* which require minimum skill for maximum quick fun. Mary's French dance masters made them more structured.

By the way, kids, the best *Strip the Willow* is the one they dance in Orkney, where everyone dances all the time and it only stops when the dancers collapse or the musician drops dead. You saw all our cousins dance it at my 70th birthday party. In this *Orcadian Strip the Willow*, the first couple turns with the right arm, and then they both swing the second couple left arm, their partner right arm, the third couple left arm, and so on right down to the end of the line. As they turn the fourth couple, the second couple starts turning, and then they follow the first couple down the line. You need an organizer to make sure that there is enough space between the couples: if I see that one of the couples turning their way down the line has made a mistake, for example (which often happens in ceilidh dancing, where people cannot remember which is their left arm), then I hold on to the next couple for four or eight bars, to allow the congestion to clear down the line. It is great fun, but it is not great dancing. In fact I am not sure that most manifestations of *Strip the Willow* count as "dancing" at all.

The word *ceilidh* means different things to many people and derives from the Gaelic word meaning a 'visit' or a 'house party', or more usually an evening of "informal Scottish traditional dancing to informal music." Ceilidhs in the Lowlands tend to be dances, in the Highlands they tend to be concerts. The new RSCDS website states: "Today, the term Ceilidh dance refers to an informal way of dancing socially in Scotland."

Ceilidh dancing is a relaxed, non-competitive version of Scottish country dancing: Mary Stuart introduced formality to the ballroom and the more complex figures and steps that we love. We enjoy more complex dances than they used in past centuries and we have lots of new figures to master. Apart from old favorites, for experienced dancers it is the difficult dances that bring the greatest satisfaction: if you invest more, you get more enjoyment out of a dance.

For me, Scottish dancing has the following categories:

1. Ceilidh dancing is informal—its sole purpose is enjoyment. This is what Scots do at weddings, and it is a grand way to have a great party. Ceilidh dancing is the equivalent of barn dancing and is often done in barns. We did ceilidh dances in our sitting room at every family party since I was able to walk: I would list the *Boston Two-Step, Veleta Waltz, Circassian Circle, Gay Gordons, Strip the Willow, Dashing White Sergeant* and *Eightsome Reel* as my basic ceilidh dances.

2. Reeling = Scottish Country Dancing without much precision or variety, doing pretty easy dances. This form is found mainly in London and Edinburgh, or in aristocratic British homes where people cannot be bothered to learn proper dance steps.

3. Scottish Country Dancing is ballroom dance and is more structured with precise steps for reels, jigs and strathspeys. Not forgetting Scottish waltzes. This is Scottish ballroom dancing for joy and for elegance as introduced by Mary Stuart and as codified by the RSCDS: huge fun, sociable and extremely good exercise for both body and brain. It tends to attract people who like to think and who enjoy teamwork. To enjoyment—the primary purpose—we add artistry, style and precision. There are many new and interesting dances being written every year and the RSCDS publishes a new book of dances every year. There are 15,000 altogether. Several dances have been written to honor members of my family and friends. This beautiful dancing and its amazing music

is my passion—maybe my addiction—and these are the dances that we love to dance in St Andrews.

4. Demonstration or exhibition dancing is Scottish Country Dancing seeking perfection. It can be competitive, although I personally do not much care for competitions. This level is the most demanding. I love the discipline and precision of a demo team, the quality of the teaching and the quality of the dancers. This is the level where I find the absolute greatest satisfaction in dancing. This same quality can be achieved in a ballroom if your dance partners are demo level. Only with a partner who dances with good posture, perfect phrasing and precise step work can you achieve—for example—the full enjoyment and supreme satisfaction of the all-around diamond strathspey poussette. We had great fun for many years with the Silver Thistle Dancers in Richmond, producing excellent demonstrations that you can watch on YouTube.

5. Highland dance is a different animal, individualistic and militaristic. All soldiers in the Black Watch regiment, for example, learn highland dance which is used both for recruiting soldiers and for teaching army discipline. Highland dance is spectacular. Originally created by warriors and hunters with their arms raised like a stag's antlers, highland dance develops strong calf muscles and athletic skill. It is a dance art for young people. I used to dance the *Highland Fling, the Sword Dance, the Reel of Tulloch, The Shepherd's Crook* and I still do highland steps for French audiences because they have no idea that my steps are now imprecise. I don't mind dancing highland steps in old people's homes where the wheel-chair audience is amazed that I am still able to stand; or in front of people who cannot see well enough to know that I am staggering two inches off the ground instead of leaping twelve inches in the air. My ankles no longer have the elasticity needed for highland dancing.

6. Step dancing. Mostly done by ladies, step dancing—also known as "soft shoe national dancing"—is elegant and complicated. The Irish tap dancing style is related, and so is the clogging found in Virginia and the Appalachians, in the Netherlands and in Scandinavia. *Blue Bonnets* and *The Thistle* are two of the best-known Scots step dances. I learned *Blue Bonnets* at St Andrews Summer School under the kind but strict supervision of Ruby Wilkinson, but mostly her class was composed of ladies.

7. Hebridean dances are related to both Highland and Step forms of dancing, and probably derive from Scandanavian dances. I enjoy the *Hebridean Weaving Lilt*, a McNab composition danced with a running step. In Scandinavia and elsewhere, including in France and in Brittany, they have a dance they call the *Schottisch*, which varies in form but generally goes side-together, side-together, walk forward, walk forward,

and repeat. Sometimes it includes the *Highland Schottische* step. It is a
sort of hybrid dance, which seems to fit the Hebridean label.

8. *The Sailor's Hornpipe*. Originally an English naval dance, imitating the
   gestures of sailors on deck, this was one of the dances my mother taught
   me when I was five. I looked cute in my uncle Edmund's sailor suit,
   which was very fashionable for small boys between the wars. Hornpipes
   were used to distract and entertain sailors who danced to pipes in hard
   shoes. Now they are mostly danced in Scotland. Hornpipes (used for
   The Sailor, Pelorus Jack and other nautical dances) are synchopated reels
   accenting the first and third note: 1-2-3-4, 1-2-3-4. In 2017 the RSCDS
   decided to consider them henceforth as reels.

The co-founder of RSCDS, the late Miss Jean Milligan, used to tell us all
to "Dance with your Soul" (also the title of her biography written by Dr Alastair
MacFadyen and Miss Florence H. Adams). It is thanks to Miss Milligan—a
teacher at Jordanhill College who was very kind to her students provided they
danced well—and thanks to to her aristocratic partner Mrs Ysobel Stewart of
Fasnacloich who launched the movement by publishing a book of Scottish
dances, that the RSCDS became the force it has become. A group of 27 founder
members met at the Athenaeum in Glasgow to create the Society on 26th
November 1923, three days after Ysobel's 41st birthday. It was Michael Diack of
Paterson's, the Glasgow book publisher, who apparently introduced the two
women. The Scottish Country Dance Society's goal was to publish dances and to
support the revival of SCD. King George VI conferred the royal status to the
Society in 1951.

Ysobel was originally Miss Campbell of Inverneill House, who was born in
Autumn in Appin, Argyle. Many dances are named for Jean Milligan or for
elements of Ysobel Stewart's biography and that of her husband Major Stewart.
Ysobel was a Girl Guide Commissioner in Scotland, as well as bagpiper, wood-
carver, bookbinder, spinner, weaver, knitter of tartan hose, Gaelic speaker and
inveterate collector of dances. Without their diligence and dedication to creating
the RSCDS, none of us today—almost one hundred years later—would
be "dancing for the greatest happiness of the greatest number" in this worldwide
RSCDS sisterhood and brotherhood of Scottish international culture. After Ysobel
was widowed in 1948, she went to live with family in South Africa and Jean
Milligan carried the flame alone.

While we are thanking Mary, Queen of Scots for the creation of Scottish ballroom dancing, and the Milligan-Stewart partnership for codifying it, we should
also thank Queen Victoria for giving our dance format a serious 19th century
boosting. Reversing the repression of 1745, Queen Victoria adopted Scotland,
supported Highland dress and traditions and purchased Balmoral Castle as her
special home. Building on the favourable influence of Queen Victoria and Sir

Walter Scott's romanticizing of Scottish history, it is the RSCDS—under Royal patronage—that keeps the Scottish dance tradition alive.

The book title *Dance with your Soul* is also the name of a pleasant strathspey for four couples all dancing together.

DANCE WITH YOUR SOUL

Strathspey 4 x 32 bars for 4 couples in a 4-couple set (all couples dance). M Boekner Cameo Collection Vol 23.

Written for or in memory of Miss Jean Milligan and her biography *Dance with your Soul*.

Bars 1-8 : All set and 1s+4s turn with right hands moving down/up, 1Man followed by his partner dances out and down behind 3rd Lady to 4th place own side while 4th Lady followed by her partner dances out and up behind 2nd Man to 1st place own sides ;

Bars 9-16 : All dance right shoulder reels on sides ;

Bars 17-24 : 4s+2s dance the Rondel, while 3s+1s dance a reversed Rondel (1s dance up under an arch made by the 3s);

The Rondel involves three arches, one on the side and two on the main axis, with couples passing and crossing on each occasion. Women duck under the men's arms, and couples coming up dive under the arch of people coming down (unless it is reversed, naturally). Easy to understand if you know the jargon!

Bars 25-32 : 1s followed by 4s+3s lead up the middle between 2s and cast down own sides, all turn partners right hands, finishing in the order : 2341, ready to repeat the dance.

Angela Dreyer-Larsen, director of Scottish Traditions of Dance Trust, wrote about Scotland's youth and the 18,000 worldwide dancers of the RSCDS in *The Scotsman* newspaper on 11th November 2005: "There's been a little bit of a revival of young people dancing, as opposed to just 'shaking it all about' on the floor. Youth are responding to a lack of proper dancing in their culture. Ceilidhs are such a popular form of Scottish country dancing among the young because it's a relatively easy form to learn. No one gets upset if you take a wrong step. They're more likely to kill themselves laughing."

Scottish Dancing is no longer—sadly—a compulsory part of the primary school curriculum in Scotland. The Scottish government invests almost nothing in Scottish dance; nor do the authorities show any commitment to Scotland's Gaelic culture. My brother Rory likes to say: "If you pay peanuts, all you attract is monkeys." If the Scottish government does not promote the national culture, it will fade away into the monkey morass of Internet-Americana.

When Scotland was Guest of Honor at the Smithsonian Folklife Festival in Washington D.C. in 2003, the only person wearing the kilt apart from myself was Scotland's Minister for Tourism, who left after the first day. One kilt? The Scottish cultural display was pathetic despite the presence of Fiona Ritchie MBE, popular presenter of America's excellent National Public Radio program *Thistle and Shamrock*. The hundreds of Scottish Country Dancers and Highland Dancers living in the D.C. area were not invited to give even one display of dance. We should have been there every evening, showing off kilts and dances, and inviting people to join us for a daily ceilidh. I did see a lady trying to teach ceilidh dancing one afternoon. She was wearing pink shorts. Scotland's culture and music was eclipsed by the far more exciting Appalachian and African musicians on the National Mall. I spent the rest of the week with the Malians whose cultural offerings were so much richer. Did I say that the Scottish presentation was pathetic? Well, so it was! Edinburgh politicians focused on trade and fisheries, London finance and Anglo culture, do not sufficiently appreciate the value of Scottish culture and dancing. The Scottish National Party? Obsessed with the *National,* it is not Scottish enough for me.

Ceilidhs have become popular among the young because the dances are easy to learn and their parents all remember them fondly from their own youth. Everybody is welcome at a ceilidh. Edinburgh politicians might enjoy a ceilidh when they return from a cocktail reception in London. London? Aha! Here is one of my father's favorite Limericks from London.

> *There was a young lady of Twickenham*
> *Who bought some new boots to walk quick in 'em.*
> *She walked for a mile,*
> *Then sat down on a stile,*
> *Took off her new boots, and was sick in 'em.*

18

LIAM LEARNS STRATHSPEY IN 7 MINUTES WITH CATHERINE LEÏLA

For my 70th birthday, my dear Liam, when you were just seven years old, we organized an evening party for family and friends after an all-day Scottish dance for my dancing friends in Brittany. We hired a large tent with a dance floor, and we had a wonderful time. With your cousin Adam Brumder you kicked footballs. With Lucas Tillon you played African drums in support of my cousin Hugh and his wonderful accordionist Christine Taylor whose ceilidh band in London is named the *The Muckers of Geordie's Byre* and whose world music group is the *Walking Wounded*. I wonder how much of that day you and your sister Isabelle remember?

A lot of our family are dancers: parents, children, both brothers and Rory's wife Maureen ... while my sisters Alana and Lucie will dance if we insist. Lucie's gorgeous and talented daughters Tessa and Grace can be tempted onto the dance floor although they are—like the Garnett side of our family—reelers rather than dancers. I went Scottish dancing with lovely Chatty and Tor Garnett, who proved to be reelers. In 1969 I remember traveling down to the Isle of Wight from a holiday on Mull for my cousin Virginia's 21st birthday (she was born in Dunoon, Scotland), which we celebrated in Seaview with a ceilidh where Alana and I met her delightful future husband Peter Bottomley for the first time. At this typical family party we danced *The Eightsome Reel, The Gay Gordons, The Virginia Reel* (of course) with other barn dance classics. My 70th birthday dance program brought together all the Scottish dancers in Brittany under a marquee; there were no ceilidh dances until the evening. Some of my non-dancing cousins came in the afternoon. Oh dear! If you do not know your right from your left, instructions are useless. Having a PhD is no guarantee of "dance intelligence."

During the afternoon, Liam, you came along to see what was happening, and you danced *The Wind on Loch Fyne* with your aunt Catherine Leïla and me. I am very fond of this elegant strathspey for three couples in a triangle-shaped set. There are interlocking reels, stars and circles, and we danced them as a threesome with you between auntie and grandad. Bernard Gréau from Rennes—husband of dance teacher Françoise Harnard-Gréau)—filmed every dance. Their son Pierre-Samuel is a very good young dancer and computer genius, with a library of music on his well-organized Scottish dance computer. Bernard also filmed the reprise of the dance, allowing people who had missed out to join in for the second time through. I surrendered my place in the set and watched. What you now did—perfectly caught on camera—was to imitate the step by watching the dance. The video shows your concentration as you mastered the strathspey setting step in seven minutes. Two runs through of *The Wind on Loch Fyne* take seven minutes.

THE WIND ON LOCH FYNE

Strathspey 3 x 32 bars for 3 couples dancing in a 3-couple triangular set numbered clockwise, 1s facing down.

Loch Fyne is the longest of Scotland's sea lochs, stretching 65 Kms inland from the Firth of Clyde. There is always a pleasant breeze, sometimes a howling gale....

Devisor: John Bowie Dickson. Dunedin Book 1.

Bars 1-4 : 1s giving left hands cross down, pass 1L between 2s, 1M between 3s and meet;

Bars 5-8 : Taking nearer hands, 1s lead up between 2M3L, cast up (1L around 2L, 1M around 3M), meet and turn by the right halfway;

Bars 9-16 : All dance interlocking reels (pass partner right shoulder, pass next left shoulder, pass right around next, pass next left shoulder, finally back in original places turning partner ¾ by the right), finishing Men inside, Ladies outside;

Bars 17-18 : Men left hands across 2/3 WHILE Ls dance clockwise 1 place around the outside of the set;

Bars 19-20 : All turn by the right;

Bars 21-24 : Repeat bars 17-20 from new positions;

Bars 25-26 : 1s 2s 3s set;

Bars 27-28 : 6 hands round to the left (moving on 1 place);

Bars 29-30 : All turn partner both hands;

Bars 31-32 : 6 hands round to the left (1 place), finishing with 3s at the top.

Dance Notes:

If couples do not maintain the triangular shape of the set, especially at the end of each round, they will easily lose track of where they are: and the new first couple will not know where they are supposed to cross down.

At the St Andrews Summer School in 2016, there was a children's class for the first time, and they produced a demonstration at the Thursday evening dance. Why did it take the RSCDS 40 years to realise that we should be teaching children?

Why did Helen Russell, Marilyn Watson and Anne McArthur have to fight for 20 years to be allowed to teach children at St Andrews? Why were they blocked year-after-year by Old School fuddy-duddies who dislike or are afraid of children? The children's 'experiment' was a triumph! I was flabbergasted by the high quality of their demo on Thursday evening in the Younger Hall: in just four days, Anne and Marilyn produced a demonstration by kids from 8 to 10 years old who had never, ever danced before the Monday morning at 9am. These same kids come back and dance each summer in a new age group: we have made the breakthrough! When I saw you learning the Strathspey setting step in seven minutes, Liam, I realized that learning to dance is actually very easy when you have good teachers and good motivation from your parents. You could have been a member of that St Andrews demo. Perhaps, one day, you will be?

At Summer School 2018 I chatted during a dance break with Andrew and Alexandra, whose three children were enjoying the kids' classes as much as their parents were enjoying the advanced class. I told them how I had dreamed of bringing my whole family to Summer School in St Andrews where we could have explored the history, the beaches, the fishing ports, the Italian ice cream and the dancing. My kids would have come to love Scotland. We never came because children were not allowed at Summer School. My children dance beautifully and yet they feel no relationship with the RSCDS which deliberately excluded them, and several generations of other children like them. Was that stupid? Yes, it most certainly was.

If you ever do come to St Andrews to dance, your aunt Catherine might come with you and join the adult demo team. She danced very well during her teens. She used to say that dancing with adults in Cardiff (and before that in Geneva) offered blessed relief from spending all her time with other students. When we first turned up at the Geneva group, they loved our footwork but I sensed some unease. During the break, one lady was sent to talk to sixteen-year-old Catherine: "It is lovely to see you dancing. And who is your friend?"

"My FRIEND?" cried Catherine Leïla in horror: "That's my father." Relief flowed around the room that I was her real daddy and not a sugar-daddy. The physical similarity of our two profiles must have been obscured by my beard, or by someone's prejudice.

Dancing is a valuable social skill. Once upon a time, dearest grandchildren, when we were living in Brittany in the 1970s before your father was born, I received a panicked phone call from someone I knew in the reserve officers association of St Brieuc. He organized the annual ball of *La Rose et l'Épée*, and his ball cabaret act had just called off. Could I help? Since I was attending the ball and I did not want to disappoint the Roses or their Swordbearing Cavaliers, I promised to provide cabaret entertainment half-way through the dinner.

What a powerful social asset the kilt can be! Margaret Gilmore told me at her silver wedding reception, that the atmosphere changed when I arrived wearing the kilt: every guest perked up, paid attention and wanted to chat with me. In the case of *La Rose et l'Epée*, I called around and found a Breton piper who knew some reels. As he played the bagpipes on stage, I danced in from the other end of the ballroom weaving my way between the tables in reel time, clapping and hooching as I danced. By the time I reached the stage, my audience members were all clapping enthusiastically in time to the music, and they were well warmed up. On stage I performed two or three minutes of highland reel steps before I stopped to intro-duce myself and the piper.

Then we switched to strathspey: the piper played some more music (a bit too slowly) and I improvised some steps from the *Highland Fling* and *Barracks Johnny*. I then showed the assembled French officers and ladies how easy it was to dance the strathspey setting step as one-two-three-HOP! I made jokes about the beauty of Scottish knees and sporrans and had the 300 guests laughing. And then they all stood up in lines facing each other across the dance floor and I taught 150 French officers and 150 French roses how to dance the strathspey. SET: one-two-three-HOP! CROSS-two-three-HOP! SET-two-three-HOP! And CROSS BACK-two-three-HOP! Strathspey step teaching is improved if you say "One, Close, Three, HOP!" but that is not so easy to translate into French. Closing in third position was not relevant to my dancers. I fear that no RSCDS teacher would have approved the strathspey setting step and Alas! I did not tell the French that the strathspey trav-eling step starts by going DOWN with the back knee bent while the front knee remains straight. Pointed toes would have been pointless (Ha! Ha!) for my French cabaret turn. They may have danced badly, but my 300 French students loved their strathspey and my Breton piper didn't care one way or the other. One more triumph for Scottish culture? Possibly. Anyhow: *Vive l'Entente Cordiale between La France and L'Ecosse!*

> *Young Liam, on Papy's birthday,*
> *Danced* The Wind on Loch Fyne—*a strathspey.*
> *He mastered the step*
> *One, Close, Three, Hop! I bet*
> *He could still dance the strathspey today.*

19

HIGHLAND HAGGIS AND REELS FOR KIDS USING MARGARET'S RECIPE

Strathspey is pretty easy. Starting when he was eight years old your father Edward learned highland dance from world champions. His first teacher was the late and famous Billy Forsyth, whose smooth-design leather ghillies I wear for dancing. Billy always tied his laces around his instep, but I prefer to tie them around my ankle. Twice World Champion Highland Dancer and for 25 years Chairman and then President of the Scottish Official Board of Highland Dancing (SOBHD), Billy was also Director of the Edinburgh Tattoo dancers. You should ask your parents to take you to see the unforgettable Tattoo in Edinburgh Castle. Billy Forsyth was an ambassador for highland dancing around the world, and a good friend of ours.

One of his best stories concerned a Burns Night in Lima, Peru where he was asked to address the haggis before he danced. He walked out to the kitchen and found that the hotel had ordered a can of haggis from Scotland. Since they had no idea what it was, they had simply placed the unopened can on a silver platter. It is not easy to plunge your dagger into the heart of an unopened tin can! So Billy found a can opener, and moulded the cold haggis mixture as best he could with his hands to honor the Burns poem and make it appear something like a Great Chieftain o' the Puddin' Race. You, Liam, took less time to learn the strathspey setting step than it took Billy Forsyth to find a can opener, open the can, and create a Peruvian Haggis.

In those days, Banjul airport in The Gambia—like Lima, Peru—was served by the excellent and much regretted British Caledonian Airways. Part of their marketing was promoting Scottish = Caledonian culture. Every St Andrews Day (November 30th) and every Burns Night, celebrating the birth of our national poet

Robert Burns (born on January 25th 1759), British Caledonian would supply every Caledonian Society with a piper and highland dancer to entertain the Scottish and British community together with their guests. This was a great opportunity. Africans seldom see Europeans doing anything that is not "work": they see little of our families, never see our parents, and hardly know that Europeans have any culture apart from business. In those days I was director of The Gambia's biggest rural development for the NGO ActionAid, one of West Africa's cutting-edge programs. I used to book a table for each Scottish event so that ministers, officials and my senior Gambian colleagues could discover our home culture and the weird and wonderful ways of the Scots. And they got to see me dance in the kilt! I wear African national dress when I am in Africa and Scottish national dress when I am in Scotland. For Burns Night, I was back in Scotland for the evening.

The bagpipes are familiar in Africa. The Gambia had military pipers who were trained in Scotland. I used to arrange my Gambian guests in pairs for the Banjul Grand March: they adored marching around the dance hall in time to the pipes, turning left and right alternately when they reached the top of the hall, rejoining in fours and then in eights. The dancing was less familiar: indeed for Gambians, it was astonishing. While their children and their wives dance all the time, the social rule is that Big Men don't dance. When visiting projects up-country, my staff never allowed me to get up and dance during village celebrations. I sometimes used to drive off in my car to stay the night in villages by myself, without Gambian colleagues, so that I could dance with the village women and have a fun evening. At St Andrews Night and at Burns Supper I was free to dance, revealing to my Gambian friends a wild streak of Celtic *joie de vivre* normally hidden under my professional decorum.

We Caledonians provided food and lodging for the professional piper and the champion dancer who had been sent out for our entertainment. Margaret Fell, our RSCDS teacher in The Gambia, trained teams for a dance demonstration at each event. She also kept Edward dancing the highland steps between visits from the world champions, and taught his sister. After Billy Forsyth, on several occasions we received the Mitchelson brothers from Dundee: Deryck and Gareth were both wonderful athletes, Highland Dance junior and senior world champions. They stayed in our home, and to fill in the time between visits to the beach, they taught our kids to dance. For the first time, Edward and Catherine heard the Dundee accent: they took Gareth down to the beach to see the Atlantic rollers crash onto the African coast, and he declared that they were "Bug Waves" which our children found hilarious. Edward—your father—learned his highland dance (and his Scottish accent) from world champions, and Catherine Leïla as well.

One of the benefits of highland dancing, Liam, is that it developes your calf muscles. I learned quite late on in life that women love men with strong calves. Good to know! This is the sort of thing that a grandson needs to learn from his grandfather: if you wear the kilt and have fine calves, the women will flock to dance with you. In fact a man who dances well is generally admired by women for his athletic skill. Good dancing is more admired than good football.

In the 18th century, a man would salute a woman by pushing one stockinged foot forward and bowing, at the same moment turning his foot in order to show off the strong calf muscles developed by dancing and fencing. This was called "Putting your best foot forward" which has become a proverb. If you want admirable calf muscles, highland dance is the way to go. Or fencing. Wearing the kilt allows men to display their muscular elegance.

I myself have had a dozen different highland dance teachers over the years— starting with my mother, of course. My most important teacher was a lovely man called Bill Clement MBE, who later became Chairman of the RSCDS. He taught highland classes at St Andrews Summer School. A June 2012 obituary in *The Scotsman* described Bill as "a virtuoso of piping and Scottish country dancing. He was an inspirational figure who spent his adult life educating young people in the finer points of these pursuits. In his spare time, he was a full-time teacher of technical education."

Bill Clement was most famous as a piper, finishing his official army career as Pipe Major of the 10th Battalion of the Black Watch. His dancing style was therefore military, which greatly improved my highland steps since my mother's style was balletic. Having left the Black Watch to become a teacher in civilian life, Bill Clement joined the pipe band of the Atholl Highlanders in 1947, becoming a member of Europe's only remaining private army. Based at beautiful 700-year-old Blair Castle, its colonel is the Duke of Atholl. Bill Clement served with the Atholl Highlanders for 52 years. I have fond memories of him and of his wife Atsuko— and I have his 33 rpm vinyl record of pipe music with a grand picture of Bill on the cover in full highland military uniform.

My dancing friend Frank Joyce told me a lovely story about Bill that also reveals a lot about Japanese culture and Scottish dancing. One year at St Andrews, Bill Clement asked if anyone had already been taught highland dance, and a few people raised a hand. Then a man who had not raised his hand, executed a perfect *Highland Fling*. "I thought you had not had any teacher?" asked Bill.

"I never have teacher," replied the Japanese dancer: "I learn Fling from video pictures."

Bill Clement in his country dancing used to insist on the beauty of the pas de basque traveling step (as in Hallo-Goodbye setting, for example): you must drive your energy into the horizontal movement, and avoid jumping. To illustrate the progressive pas de basque, Atsuko remembers her husband dancing huge pas de basque steps across their sitting room .... with a glass of whisky balanced on his head. It never spilled. You could try this at home kids; but please use your father's whisky and not mine.

One summer holiday during the 1980s when we were in England visiting your great-grand parents, I found a private teacher who could train Edward and

Catherine to win official Highland Dance medals. It so happened that the RSCDS dance teacher in Chichester, where my father (your great-grandfather) lived after his retirement from doctoring Africa with the World Health Organisation, was a lady whose son had been seriously injured in a motorcycle accident. Elisabeth Dean was interested when I told her I wanted my children to try for highland dance medals because her son Brendan was a highland dancer. Every afternoon for two weeks, I drove my kids over to the Dean household and read my book while the highland dance lesson cum rehabilitation session took place. Elisabeth's 17-year-old was recovering his physical abilities, his dance skills and his self-confidence while he taught my young kids how to pass their medals. Catherine Leïla was too young even to know her right from her left. She danced pretty well, but her turning was not yet very reliable.

Then one Saturday your grandmother Michelle and I drove our children to Wimbledon, where we had located an official licensed examiner of the Scottish Official Board of Highland Dancing. We went off for an hour to drink coffee and read the newspaper while a private dance examination took place in the examiner's sitting room. Catherine Leïla duly emerged with her silver and bronze medals while Edward, your father, was wearing the silver and the silver-bronze-bar version, just one step shy of the gold medal. Very proud they were; and very proud we were. Highland Dance muscle memory is a wonderful skill to have, and it can only be acquired when you are young. I was especially proud that young Edward had shown the determination needed to reach almost the gold standard in such a short time. He would have needed extra time to learn one more highland dance. Mind you, he showed his stamina in other ways. Edward and his cousin Paris Innes decided one year that the funniest joke was this: "A man walked into a bar and said 'Arrgh!' It was an iron bar." They told this joke every single day at lunch time during the summer holidays, for a whole month.... Except on the day when I walked them both to the top of Ben Nevis. That day they were too exhausted to repeat their best joke of the year.

Margaret Fell is one of many dance teachers over the years who have been happy at our arrival in their class. At the Caledonian Society in The Gambia, your grandmother and I both danced every week. Meanwhile our kids—who were 4 and 7 years old at the time—quickly learned to dance. Margaret used a personal recipe, a three-step technique for teaching the pas de basque—the reel-time setting step— that I have adapted myself with great success. This progression succeeds very nicely in teaching the change of weight from one foot to the other, and illustrating the change of speed. Changing weight is the key to dancing, before becoming lighter and faster:

- E-le-phant
- Kan-ga-roo
- But-ter-fly

Kids love chanting and stamping out the E-le-phant rhythm. It is easy to imagine how the slow plod of the initial E-le-phant can morph into a sprightly Kan-ga-roo on the balls of the feet, taking the kids into a lighter rhythm with hops off the floor. Finally the best dancers can produce the light and lively Butterfly with a jetée at the end of each step and the toes of each foot neatly pointed downwards to the floor. I have translated the method into French using *Eléphant, Kangourou, Papillon.*

It also works with French adults at parties. It is amusing to have half-a-dozen guests laughing their way through the steps and stamping like six-year-olds as they chant *é-lé-phant*, then *kan-gou-rou* on their toes, before totally massacring the pas de basque step as they dance *pa-pil-lon* like a Charlie Chaplin cartoon with their toes in the air and their arms flailing. Dancing the pas de basque correctly on the spot and with toes pointed in an elegant *jetée* takes practice, though children learn more quickly than their parents. Scottish dance is generous, simple and healthy. Scots are popular the world over, and people love our dancing.

20

BLUE BONNETS AND STEP DANCING
WITH RUBY

Ruby Wilkinson was Director of Summer School in 2014–2015 after assisting her husband John, who was Director for a couple of years before Ruby. I remember her standing up on the first evening to welcome us all and saying, "Some of you will not know who I am."

"Oh yes we do," I cried maliciously: "You are Ruby, and you're John's wife."

Very wisely—for Ruby is nothing if not wise—she ignored me, while other old-stagers chuckled at my insider's joke. Ruby carried on talking as if I was not there. Strangely, women often do that when I crack a joke. Oh well, children, some women do not understand my wit. Certainly after 45 years of marriage, your grand-mother no longer seems to understand my jokes. In fact I think she is getting hard of hearing: she only hears me when it suits her, and that is usually when she wants me to do something for her.

Ruby Wilkinson is a great dancer of course, and over the years in St Andrews she has taught a lot Step Dancing in the afternoons. I went along one year to learn *Blue Bonnets* because that particular tune *Blue Bonnets over the Border* is the most beautiful in the whole of the Scottish canon (that means "beautiful to me" of course for nothing is more personal than love of music).

Blue Bonnets is a tune used by more than one Scottish dance. I have danced both the Country Dance and the Step Dance taught by Ruby Wilkinson. The country dance is an old one (RSCDS Book 3), pretty and easy and suitable for advanced beginners or for including in a ball (but it does end with a poussette, so dance it fairly early: maybe to start Part 2 of the ball program).

DoSiDo, children, is a dance notation based on the English mis-pronunciation of a French expression *dos-à-dos*, or back-to-back: which means that you dance forward around your partner passing right shoulders, and backwards passing left shoulders to your original position. I have told you that many (most, actually) dance instructions are French in origin: the poussette and allemande are obvious examples. Almost all ballet instructions are French.

BLUE BONNETS country dance

Jig 8 x 32 bars for 2 couples in a 4-couple longwise set. Anon. RSCDS Book 3.

Blue Bonnets were the symbol of Scotland after 1745, when kilts and tartan were outlawed by the English.

Bars 1- 8 : 1st Lady + 2nd Man Advance & Retire and dance DoSiDo;

Bars 9-16 : 1st Man + 2nd Lady Adv&Ret and dance DoSiDo;

Bars 17-24 : 1s lead down the middle and back;

Bars 25-32 : 1s+2s dance Poussette. End 2,1 ready to start again (twice: with 3s then with 4s).

Incomparably the best arrangement of the *Blue Bonnets* that I know is on the *Memories of a Scottish Weekend* CD with Dan Emery on the pipes, directed by Liz Donaldson. Dan's playing makes my very bone marrow tremble with emotion. Scottish Weekend in the wooded foothills of West Virginia is the best party after St Andrews. But September is my wife's birthday: I seldom get to attend because the dates clash and Michelle does not wish to dance.

Blue bonnets made of wool were the "typical" Scottish headwear in the late Middle Ages and beyond, becoming a symbol of Scotland after 1745 when wearing tartan in Scotland was forbidden. The "Young Pretender" Charles Edward Stuart, who nearly conquered England in 1745, is said to have plucked a white rose and pinned it to his blue bonnet: this may be the origin of the "White Cockade" which, like blue bonnets, became a symbol of the Jacobites. Jacobite is the Latin adjective from "James" and describes people (including all the Irish) who supported the claim of the dethroned James II and his son James III—Charlie's father the "Old Pretender"—to occupy the throne in place of the Protestant William of Orange and his wife Queen Mary: she was the Protestant sister of James II and daughter of Charles I who was beheaded in 1649. The split between the Church of Rome and the Church of England cost Bonnie Prince Charlie and his father the throne because they were staunch Catholics and followed the Pope. Charlie fled *Over the Sea to Skye*, ending his life as a sad and sozzled old exile in Paris. He lies buried in the chapel of the Scottish College near the Sorbonne. Meanwhile his father, after a period of French exile living in St Brieuc, went to Rome where he was buried in the crypt of The Vatican. James III ("James de Turd" as my friend Alasdair likes to say) is the only non-Pope lying in that hallowed space. Such trivial details are great for showing off cultural and historical knowledge in adult life: free advice from your grandfather on how to impress people.

English repression of the Jacobite rebellions was harsh. There were bloody massacres of Highland folk perpetrated by Butcher Cumberland after he defeated Prince Charles Edward Stuart's army at the Battle of Culloden; and the English government outlawed Highland dress. The Gaelic language went into decline. Ambitious Scots like Robert Burns realized that the English language was a path to advancement and promotion. In 1822, King George IV made the first visit of a reigning monarch to Scotland since King Charles I's Scottish coronation in 1633. David Wilkie's flattering portrait of the portly king in full highland dress tactfully edited out much of his obesity and the hideous pink tights that George IV actually wore beneath his red kilt and hose. Sir Walter Scott created a tartan pageant, turning the regimental "small kilt" into fashionable Scottish dress in place of the highland plaid that had been outlawed since 1745. Some purists criticize as artificial this action, which I consider a brilliant innovation. The primitive dress of mountain thieves and rebels became the national dress of Scotland.

George IV (the Prince Regent) was succeeded by his brother William IV (the Sailor King), whose title was Duke of Clarence and St Andrews. In 1837 William died and his niece Victoria became queen. Victoria visited Scotland in 1842, loved the country and purchased Balmoral Castle which has seen plenty of Scottish dancing in the lovely ballroom. The Victorian era restored tartan to its position as the key element of Scottish dress. I am sure that the young Victoria learned reels, strathspeys and some Scottish step dancing.

Ruby's step dancing class is charming and gentle. Step dancing in general is less demanding on the ankles than highland dancing. The best way to learn it is at the Summer School; or you can search for the illustrations on YouTube, a wonderful tool that did not exist when I learned to dance. For my grandchildren, YouTube may be your best source of instruction. If you search for *Blue Bonnets* on the internet, you will see a beautiful Russian teenager showing you how to dance the steps. In case you are in any doubt, children, about the world-wide reach of Scottish dancing, I bet you never imagined there would be a Shady Glen dance school in Moscow! The music is from the *St. Andrew's Collection of Step Dances* by Muriel Johnstone (piano) and Keith Smith (fiddle), one of the iconic musical partnerships of the RSCDS.

BLUE BONNETS step dance

The Blue Bonnets Step Dance uses the following specific steps: coupé over—coupé under and balance; pas de basque and a circular turn; hop-hop-down; assemble and change.

These and other steps can be found in 'Basic Scottish Dance Movements A-Z' playlist, all of which are based on descriptions published in the St. Andrew's Collection of Step Dances (RSCDS 2009-2013).

YouTube voice-over is provided by the book's editor and RSCDS examiner Helen Russell from Scotland. All movements are filmed by teachers and students at the Shady Glen School of Scottish Dancing in Moscow, Russia.

This is a great moment to salute the RSCDS Summer School staff and some of the other amazing dancers who have made life magical for us all over the years: key people like Moira Thomson, Cécile Hascoët (who comes from Crozon, where my Breton in-laws live), Jim Stott, Helen Russell, Pat Houghton, Jean Martin, Janet Johnson, Ruby and John Wilkinson, Anne Taylor, Anne McArthur, Marilyn Watson, Angela Young, Atsuko Clement, Mervyn Short, Jeremy and Grace Hill, John Johnson, Jimmie Hill, George Meikle, Robert Mackay, Muriel Johnson, Jim Lindsay and the Brady brothers ... and generations of other teachers and musicians who came before them and prepared the way. Thank you all for giving us so much pleasure.

Ruby Wilkinson's Farewell To Cranshaws—(a 32-bar strathspey for 4 couples in a set of 4) was devised by Alasdair Brown to honor Ruby, with music written by George Meikle. The dance was published in the RSCDS Book 52 in 2018 with an excellent CD recorded by Jim Lindsay, and was dedicated to Ruby Wilkinson on her retirement as Summer School director.

RUBY WILKINSON'S FAREWELL TO CRANSHAWS

Strathspey 4 x 32 bars for 4 couples all dancing in a 4-couple set. Devisor: Alasdair Brown.

2 chords—on the 2nd chord, 3s and 4s cross to the opposite side.

Ruby Wilkinson is a famous RSCDS dance teacher in Scotland, a former Director of Summer School

Bars 1- 8 : 1s+4s set, cast down/up to 2nd/3rd places (2s+3s step up/down bars 3-4). 1s+4s turn ½ LH and dance ½ LH across to 1M facing 3L, 1L+3M, 4M+2L, 4L+2M;

Bars 9-16 : 4s+1s dance diagonal interlocking reels of 4 with corner positions (LH across ½ way in middle)while 2s (in 1st place) and 3s (in 4th place) dance reels of 4 across. End with 4s+1s facing eachother, nearer hands joined with partner, (4s face down, 1s face up);

Bars 17-24 : 4s+1s Set&Link and dance circle 4H round to left;

Bars 25-32 : 2s+4s also 1s+3s dance the all-around diamond poussette. 2, 4 (1) (3).

If you read these instructions, my darling grandchildren, because you are not experienced dancers you will probably understand not a word nor a symbol; yet the pattern of this dance is actually quite obvious to experienced dancers. Better than any description by me you should watch a demonstration to see how the dance is clever and subtle, flows perfectly ... but only when you understand how to dance it. The YouTube video taken at a Summer School ceilidh shows the dancers Alice Stainer, Angela Young, Jean Martin, Debbie Roxburgh, Adam Brady, Alasdair Brown, Jim Stott and Eric Finley. They give you a wonderful feeling for perfect

Scottish dancing without fuss or over-elaboration, a relaxed example from experts with an average age of around 50. The RSCDS demo teams at Younger Hall are wonderful, but their average age is usually around 25. They are therefore more athletic than most of us. This may be the most difficult dance I describe in this book. I hope you will both be good enough dancers to enjoy dancing it one day.

21

JOIE DE VIVRE IN THE FRENCH SPIRIT WITH HUGUETTE

I think I should tell you some more about these Summer School ceilidhs, children. There are a lot of professional musicians and entertainers, so it is important not to try to rival them. My friends Trish and Laurel from Virginia demonstrated Hawaian hula dancing one year, wearing flowery garlands, and their hip movements kept the audience spell-bound. Jim Stott especially, who had the best view because he was sitting behind them. My friend Pete Campbell produced an impressive New Zealand Haka for one ceilidh. I do not have a professional party turn and so I usually keep quiet. I could tell funny stories about France, but I am not a good stand-up comic. When I make people laugh, it is more by surprise than "on stage" and often by using one-line absurdities such as: "I'd kill for a Nobel Peace Prize" (appropriate wit for a professional peace builder like me). Or advice: If you ever need to borrow money, children, borrow from a pessimist—they don't expect it back. (That is a joke).

My father based his financial savvy on the much safer rule that does not lose friends: "Never a lender, nor a borrower be." In West Africa sharing—rather than lending—is the culture. That means that if you pass something across to someone else, you should not necessarily expect to get it back. Patricia Cummins in Virginia loaned her husband's winter coat to the visiting mayor of Ségou, and naturally—because it was cold and still winter—the mayor kept it when he traveled on to New York. My very intelligent professor friend Patricia was philosophical about it when I explained that 'lending' is not a West African concept. If you do ask to get something back, you will probably find that it is not longer there because it has already been shared with someone else. The concept of individual property so dear to our

Protestant Northern European culture is collective in West Africa. If you have it, share it. If you don't have it, tough luck.

Life, my lovely grandchildren, is easier and more fun if you take a sunny view of life, sharing what you have and being grateful for what you have left. Smile your way through life! There is plenty of poverty in Europe and America, of course. Yet poverty in Africa and Asia is so much more intense that—by comparison—we all seem rich. Our northern cultures suffer particularly from spiritual poverty. In Africa for example, no old person is ever alone or homeless. In Africa children take care of their parents, and the whole extended family participates. They may not have much, but they share what they have. You lucky grandchildren live in a favorable climate and in a wealthy country. Everything looks good for you. So live an optimistic life, laugh and enjoy it. What is a pessimist? A pessimist is someone who, if everything seems to be going well, is sure that you must have overlooked something. So be optimists: keep smiling (smiley people are nicer to look at than grumpy people), and keep dancing in order to maintain a healthy physical and mental balance.

I admit that I was tempted to tell the following story about French cuisine to a St Andrews ceilidh audience; but my interior voices imposed wisdom and I kept quiet.

Once upon a time, there was a family having evening dinner, as French families tend to do, all grouped around the table together and eating well. Three roast chickens had been cut up, everyone of the eleven family members had been served, and all had eaten well. On the dish there remained a single chicken leg. The dish was passed around, and no one wanted to take the final piece of chicken.

Just as the dish was placed back in the middle of the table, there was an electricity cut and out went the lights.

An anguished scream split the darkness. Before the noise had died down, the lights came back on again. On the dish in the middle of the table lay the chicken leg, and one hand pierced by ten forks.

The funniest joke I ever heard at Summer School came from a German music teacher. Brits tend to think that "A German joke is no laughing matter" but this one was hilarious. Beate (I am not certain that was her name) sat down at her piano and announced in deadpan tones that she was going to play a piece of music called: "Nice Hands; pity about the face."

There was a pause as one hundred dancers in the ceilidh audience remembered their Scottish dance teachers repeating, time after time: "I want to see Nice Hands." A few nervous titters were emerging from the audience as they began to think about other dancers' facial features when Beate continued: "This is, of course, a tune about an old clock," at which instant one hundred people erupted into shrieks of laughter. Beate had to wait a full two minutes before she could start playing—which she did beautifully as a professional pianist.

Instead of trying to be funny myself, I came up with the idea in 2016 of creating a French dance skit that would make people laugh. What should we present to the ceilidh? Because Mary Queen of Scots created the genre, Scottish dance is full of French expressions. One year a group of Anglo-French dancers presented a ceilidh quiz based on mispronunciation by English speakers of these French words. One woman walked across the floor in her stockings, with no shoes. This referred to the pas de basque step adopted from Basque country; if pronounced "pas de bas" by a poorly-educated English speaker, it means: "no stockings" or possibly "no shoes"— because dancers only dance in their stockings if they have lost their shoes.

Somewhat in this same spirit, we decided to present a dance with a French title: *Joie de Vivre*. By happy chance, ours was the only humorous skit in the ceilidh: otherwise there were songs, poems, musical pieces, and amusing stories and songs from William Williamson the compere, who also danced the Sailor's Hornpipe, an energetic dance that my mother taught me when I was six. We decided to present: "Scottish dancers in France know what *Joie de Vivre* really means." You grandchildren will appreciate this story because your culture is half French. You have been to British weddings and to French weddings, and you know weddings are much better in France where we sing and dance and the party lasts for three days. And you know how much I enjoy a good party.

Joie de Vivre is a well-known Scottish dance, a cheerful and easy jig that had already appeared on one of the evening dance programs earlier that week. If you are going to play with something and change it around to be witty, then choose something that is well-known.

JOIE DE VIVRE

Jig 8 x 32 bars for 3 couples in a 4-couple set. Devisor: Irene van Maarseveen. RSCDS Book 39.

Joie de Vivre is what you should all aim to achieve in your lives; and dancing will help you achieve it.

Bars 1-8 : 1s set, cast, lead down between 3s and cast up to second place on own sides; 2s move up bar 3;

Bars 9-12 : 2s 1s 3s turn by the right;

Bars 13-16 : 2s1s3s chase halfway round clockwise;

Bars 17-20 : 3s 1s 2s dance dos-à-dos or DoSiDo;

Bars 21-22 : 3s1s2s set on the sides;

Bars 23-24 : 3s 1s 2s turn partners halfway by the right into allemande hold;

Bars 25-32 : 3s1s2s allemande, finishing 2s1s3s.

Huguette and I danced as first couple. We set and cast to meet in the middle, where I produced a rose. You may not know my friend Huguette, children, but she has wonderful facial expressions and no one in the audience could doubt from her face that she had fallen in love over that rose! By the time Huguette reached second place, the audience was already laughing.

Now as the first three couples all turned, the other two men produced roses for their partners. More laughter .... laughter that continued as the women turned their partners, chased round the set kissing their roses into their Do-Si-Do. We finished our first round with the allemande (which—by the way—comes from the French dance instruction "*à la main*" and has nothing to do with the Germans) and everyone thought we were finished. But not at all!

The 4th couple—who had been awaiting their turn—suddenly produced a bottle of wine, glasses and Breton biscuits on a tray. As the audience screamed with laughter and our cheerfully unperturbed pianist continued to play the music as if we were still dancing, we greeted each other with *la bise* on both cheeks, served each other glasses of wine and elegant Albane wearing a dress in *bleu-blanc-rouge* offered Breton butter biscuits to the audience. After which the pianist received his glass of wine. More laughter, as Jeremy Hill said, "Ah, thank you very much, I would love a glass of wine," and we all toasted La Belle France and the Scottish dancing community.

As we came back into lines for the third round, one of the ladies raced into the audience to grab Jim Stott, the Summer School Director, who now became one of our dancers. To general hilarity, Jeremy struck up *La Marseillaise* so we danced *Joie de Vivre* one last time to the French national anthem, disappearing off into the audience with the allemande. Jim Stott is a great sport, but I had secretly tipped him off that he would be called upon. Winston Churchill used to advise people: "The best impromptu speeches are those that have been very well prepared."

And now, lovely grandchildren, I want to introduce a special favorite of mine to celebrate your multiple Celtic heritage and the Irish identity of your maternal grandfather, as well as your new Irish passports: post-Brexit, every Brit needs a second European passport. *The Irish Rover* is a dance with fabulous music that every experienced Summer School dancer knows and loves. I can also sing the song (about a ship called the *Irish Rover* and its motley Irish crew which included an English shipmate from Dover ... conveniently rhyming with Rover). I am sure you will sing it yourselves one day as you dance the Irish Rover and come to love it as I do. My favorite memory of this dance was one evening in St Andrews when the legendary pianists Robert Mackay and Muriel Johnson sat down together at the piano around midnight in the party room of University Hall and we danced an impromptu *Irish Rover* partly out into in the kitchen because the dance space was too constricted.

THE IRISH ROVER

Reel 8 x 32 bars for 3 couples in a 4-couple set. Devisor: James B. Cosh. 22 Scottish Country Dances (and 2 more).

The Irish Rover was a mythical 27-masted sailing ship with improbable amounts of cargo and crew that sank in a storm leaving only one survivor: the singer. Written by J. M. Crofts, the song was made famous by the Dubliners.

Bars 1-2 : Taking nearer hands, 1s lead down below 3s;

Bars 3-4 : 1s cast up on own sides to 2nd place;

Bars 5-8 : 2s1L and 1M3s right hands across;

Bars 9-12 : 1s half diagonal reel of 4 with first corners;

Bars 13-16 : 1s half diagonal reel of 4 with second corners, finishing by taking left hands;

Bars 17-24 : 1s turn about ¾ by the left into reels of 3 across, 1L with 2s, 1M with 3s, starting with left shoulder to first corner positions and finishing 1s in 2nd place on own sides, 3s at the top on opposite sides, 2s at the bottom on opposite sides;

Bars 25-28 : 3L with 1s and 2M half diagonal rights and lefts;

Bars 29-32 : 3M with 1s and 2L half diagonal rights and lefts, finishing 2s1s3s.

Dance Notes

Bar 1 If you do not start at once and with long steps, you will be late on bar 5 for the RH across.

Bar 8 Holding onto the hand of your first corner to set the diagonal correctly helps intermediate dancers.

Bars 12-13 1s should pass left shoulders even though some people like passing right shoulders.

Bars 16-17 1s take left hands as they approach, turning by the left to enter the reels of 3 across the dance.

Bars 23-24 1s must slow to finish in 2nd place on own sides, facing W up and M down for the R&L.

22

FAMILY DANCING WITH RORY AND MAUREEN

You kids know that a good ceilidh deserves one of our family dances. The French and Irish are numerous enough to handle their own national image, but only the family will look after its own. The best of our family dances is *A Reel for Rory*, which has the same diagonal rights and lefts as *The Irish Rover*. You would not want to put both of these dances on the same dance program, because a dance program needs to vary the formations that we invite people to dance. I would put *The Irish Rover* on my March 17th St Patrick's Day dance sheet and use *A Reel for Rory* at Burns Night on January 25th, or for a St Andrews Day Ball on November 30th. Written for my brother Rory by RSCDS teacher Margaret Fell and published by my father's old friend George Swirles, *A Reel for Rory* turns out to be very popular in Japan where there are no fewer than 80 Scottish dance groups.

A REEL FOR RORY

Reel 8 x 48 bars for 3 couples in a 4-couple set. Devisor: Margaret Fell. Island Cottage Collection Vol 6.

Written for Rory Poulton by Margaret Fell to say thank you for his teaching in The Gambia, March-Sept. 1985

Published in volume 6 of the Island Cottage Collection edited by George Swirles.

Tune: Ladies of Dingwall: use "Ladies of Dingwall" music on R Gonnellai RSCDS 13.

Bars 1-4 : First couple with right hands turn each other down center of set to face out on opposite sides in second place, while second couple step up on 3-4;

Bars 5-8 : First lady casts up and first man casts off to finish lady between second couple facing down and man between third couple facing up; all set;

Bars 9-10 : Lady casts off to own side and man likewise;

Bars 11-14 : First couple turn with left hands to own sides;

Bars 15-16 : All set with nearer hands joined;

Bars 17-20 : Dance three right hands across, lady with second couple and man with third;

Bars 21-24 : First couple passing left shoulders dance left hands across lady with third and man with second;

Bars 25-32 : First couple dance right shoulder half reels of four with first corners and then with second corners, finishing in second place own sides;

Bars 33-40 : First couple dance half rights and lefts diagonally with second and third couples (as in Irish Rover) lady dancing up to begin and man down;

Bars 40-48 : Dance six hands round and back. Repeat having progressed one place.

Dance Notes:

All casts are to the right.

Half diagonal reels, followed by diagonal rights and lefts are confusing for some beginners. It can be helpful to explain that these are movements that bring them back to their own sides, with beautiful phrasing.

This reel was often danced in Chichester by the whole family, which by then included Maureen whom Rory had met dancing. One icy evening in winter, Rory was very kindly driving Maureen home from a Scottish dance when he slid off the road into a ditch. With the car tilted at an acute angle, Maureen rolled out of her seat and landed on top of Rory. I do not need to give you more details, children: I have no idea how long they were stuck in the car in the ditch, but it was sufficiently enjoyable that they got married. Their older son Tim just qualified as a doctor like his great grandfather, while his brother Matt is earning lots of money in the City. The best dancers in our family are definitely Rory and Maureen.

It was great having my brother living next door in The Gambia. Rory was running the restaurant of the Novotel while we were working in humanitarian development projects. We were able to dance together and play tennis together. Rory organized our Scottish dancing while Margaret Fell was away for several months, and he proved something that a lot of RSCDS teachers refuse to believe: that dancers (and especially beginners) dance better and better when they know and love the dances. Learning new dances is stressful for beginners, who make mistakes as they try to understand new formations and our strange vocabulary. Dancing well motivates them to dance more and to dance better. Rory decided that the whole Gambia group would master the very exciting and pretty complicated square jig *Ian Powrie's farewell to Auchtarardar*.

Auchterarder is a small town in Perthshire, home to the world-famous Gleneagles Hotel where Rory worked when he was young. Ian Powrie (1923-2011) was a Scottish musician, a fiddler who gained national recognition in the 1960s by appearing with Andy Stewart on the wildly popular BBC Scottish dance program *White Heather Club*. I adored watching the *White Heather Club*. After touring Australia and New Zealand with the BBC, Ian and his wife Leïla decided in 1966 to emigrate to Australia, which was the occasion for the writing of this dance by the

Edinburgh Demonstration Dancers for whom he often played. Bill Hamilton was their teacher. Originally the two promenades were written to go clockwise, but Bill Hamilton agreed that the second promenade works better counter-clockwise. He did not like a popular variation on the last circle: people I dance with like to finish by circling all the way around to the right.

Ian Powrie is one of those dances that feels obvious and natural once you know the moves and the music, which fits the dance so perfectly that it tells you what to do next. The dance starts with a circle round-and-back. Then I usually cry out: "Ladies away!" which reminds the women to dance in front of their partner and out around the next man, meeting for a right-hand wheel; and they repeat the sequence to rejoin their partner for a first promenade. The 1s and 3s keep going out of the promenade and have four bars to dance around into lines across the dance, the lady following her man, to face 2s and 4s: man facing man, and woman facing woman. Everyone sets to the person in front of them and does a quick 2-bar turn, to start the reels across. If you do not complete this turn quickly enough, you can find yourself starting in the wrong direction ... with predictable chaos. Dancing couples then dance a complete figure of eight around their standing "gateposts" before a left hand wheel allows them to leave the set by the way they came in: the women dance between the standing couples while their male partners pass the standing men by the left shoulder and follow their lady back to place.

The pattern is repeated by 2s and 4s; after which, the ladies' chorus is repeated by the men, who pass in front of their partners going right, and create two left-hand wheels. As the men dance out of the second wheel, they join the circle with a change of step, flowing into slip-step right all the way around (if you come from my village!) or round and back if you are Old School. When briefing the dance, it is important to tell people in advance whether they are doing a final circle-and-back, or the complete circle to the right.

Our beginners in The Gambia used to clamor to dance *Ian Powrie*, often as the final dance of the evening and we all became so confident that it was unnecessary to brief the dance (although Rory or I would call out instructions if needed). Dancing *Ian Powrie's farewell to Auchtarardar* always reminds me fondly of my old friend Jim Washington, the most regular dancer in the Richmond group when I joined in 1999. Jim—a widower—later married his childhood sweetheart Marya Dull at the age of 70 and announced that instead of a honeymoon they had decided to arrange cardiac appointments! It was really a joke: Jim had a great and strong heart. We danced at their Delaware wedding, and Marya took up dancing in order to spend Tuesday evenings with her husband. Jim passed away after five years of marriage, and I am one of many people who miss his humor and his dancing. Dancing *Ian Powrie's farewell to Auchtarardar*, Jim and I always seemed to meet facing each other for the important set-and-turn (bars 37-40), and we shared a special grin as we turned because Jim was a very big man and it helped him to have a strong partner to get around in time for the reel.

Repeating dances anchors them in the minds of dancers. It brings them greater confidence, increases pleasure and improves both footwork and timing. Celia Belton in Charlottesville is one teacher who makes sure that new dances are repeated once they are learned, and usually she repeats them again the following week so as to cement the memory and to bring dancers into "dancing better" mode. A successful club will establish a core set of (say) thirty dances that everyone knows and likes, so that each can be danced two or three times per year. This seems common sense to me even though some teachers say it bores them to repeat dances.

This poses the question who "owns" a dance class? Should RSCDS teachers be the only people who choose dances? Of course they know more about the dances and they will create a teaching plan based on specific formations and dances; but other intelligent adults should also be allowed to express preferences. Old School RSCDS teachers often believe that they own the class. I believe that in a class of adults, the teacher is *primus unter pares* or "first among equals." This implies a different relationship than you find in an elementary school, where Teacher is Boss. RSCDS teachers—like Miss Jean Milligan of blessed memory—can sometimes be too dominant. Perhaps RSCDS certification should include communication and participation skills that encourage teachers to avoid bossiness. If teachers refuse to listen to their students or consult with their dance friends, they are not good leaders (and possibly not good teachers).

IAN POWRIE'S FAREWELL TO AUCHTERARDER

Jig 1 x 128 bars for 4 couples in a 4-couple square set. Devisor: Bill Hamilton and Edinburgh demo dancers.

Ian Powrie was a famous Scottish musician who left Auchterarder and emigrated to Australia.

Bars 1-32 : Ladies' Chorus.

1-8   All 8 hands round and back;

9-12   Ls dance in front of partner, behind next M and meet in center;

13-16   Ls right hands across;

17-20   Ls dance in front of M standing opposite partner, behind next M and meet in center;

21-24   Ls right hands across;

25-32   All promenade clockwise around the set to places (the music tells you to promenade!)

Bars 33-64 : 1s and 3s solo.

33-36   1s release hold and, 1M leading, chase clockwise behind 2L, 1L dancing between 2s, 1M dancing around 2M, (finishing 1L facing 2L, 1M facing 2M) WHILE 3s dance likewise around 4s (finishing 3L facing 4L, 3M facing 4M);

37-40   1L2L 1M2M 3L4L 3M4M set and turn by the right, finishing with 2s 4s still in original places;

41-48   2L1L3M4M 2M1M3L4L reels of 4 across the dance, finishing with 2s 4s back in original places;

49-56   1s cross between 2s to start figures of 8 WHILE 3s cross between 4s to start figures of 8;

57-60   1s3s left hands across;

61-64   1L dance out between 2s and cast anticlockwise to place WHILE 1M dance out around 2M and cast anticlockwise to place WHILE 3L dance out between 4s and cast anticlockwise to place WHILE 3M dance out around 4M and cast anticlockwise to place.

Bars 65-96 : 2s and 4s solo.

Repeat the 1s and 3s solo with 2s dancing as 1s, 3s as 2s, 4s as 3s and 1s as 4s.

Bars 97-128 : Men's Chorus.

97-104 All promenade anticlockwise around the set to places (the music tells you to promenade!)

105-108 Men dance in front of partner, behind next L and meet in center;

109-112 Men left hands across;

113-116 Men dance in front of L standing opposite partner, behind next L and meet in center;

117-120 Men left hands across, coming back to place (with a change of step) into .....

121-128 8 hands round to the right and back ; OR : 8 hands all the way round to the right (optional).

Dance Notes

Bars 39-40 Complete this quick turn, or you may find yourself starting the reel facing in the wrong direction

Bars 49-56 Require a FULL figure of eight, leading then into the left hands across

Bars 61-64 Lady passes between the couple, where she came in on bar 36: go out the way you came in!

Bars 121-end When briefing the dance, tell people whether they are doing a final circle-and-back, or the (optional) complete circle to the right. It works better if everyone chooses the same option.

23

FLYING THROUGH THE REEL OF THE ROYAL SCOTS WITH MAIKE

W *ritten one April 29th on the International Day of Dancing (who knew?)*
I am in the Younger Hall once more, at the St Andrews Summer School, and we are going to fly through *The Reel of the Royal Scots*. There are 180 dancers on the floor this Saturday evening at the "Olympic Games of Scottish Country Dancing" and I have invited a young intermediate dancer for one of those rapid classic reels with fabulously great music. "The Reel of the Royal Scot was named for a great old railway engine," I tell Maike with confidence; later I find out that I am quite wrong. I should have known, because the train has no 's' on the end. In fact Roy Goldring composed this dance in 1983 to celebrate the 350th anniversary of the Royal Scots Regiment—formed in 1633 when King Charles I granted a Royal Warrant to raise a body of men to serve in France (Hepburn's Regiment). Until the regiment was merged with other Scottish infantry regiments in 2006, The Royal Scots was the oldest Infantry Regiment of the Line in the British Army. The regimental museum is in Edinburgh Castle. I expect Maike will forgive me for my railway mistake (she probably does not even remember the event).

This is July 2016, and I spot a set forming with some exciting couples: William and Helen from Inverness in the Highlands are tall and elegant, Lars and Riekje from Oldenburg in Germany are dynamic and (come to think of it) Lars is even taller than William. Both men danced in the RSCDS Demo Team, and with those long legs they will travel far and fast. This will be a great set for a dance like *The Reel of the Royal Scots*. The third couple I also recognize as experienced dancers: Ludmila is a good dancer from Cologne, although I do not know the man's name. With such a group to help her, my hesitant young partner will be fine.

"Have no worries," I tell Maike: "This set will be great and the dancers will all take you with them. Dancing with excellent dancers is the way to progress. Just watch me and follow what I say. We are fourth couple, so the first time around you can watch what the others do."

It can be daunting for a beginner when the vocabulary seems weird and new formations follow fast one upon another; yet it is easier for a beginner to dance with seven great dancers, than to dance in a set where others are floundering. With dancing partners like these, Maike will get to feel what we are trying to achieve. One day she will dance as well as Helen and Riekje and Ludmila. I smile encouragingly at my partner (or at least that is what I think I am doing: perhaps she thinks I am leering). The band strikes its chord, we bow and curtsey to one another, and immediately the kilts are flying.

"Watch carefully!" I tell Maike: "When we are first couple, you will half-turn the person beside you so that we are back to back, and set, then half-turn the next person so that we set again. And now the first couple is OFF, flying up to the top of the set as the third couple follows them. That third couple will be us next time through, and I will be holding your hand before we cast down to the bottom of the set and IMMEDIATELY turn up into place ready for the CORNER TURN NOW as first man comes flying in to turn you." I smile more encouragement (or another leer) as William turns the third lady Ludmila with his right hand. Next time William will turn Maike. I will make sure she is ready, and she will swoosh around with him.

"Watch now: after the two corner turns there is a circle. And after the circle, it is our turn. Are you ready?" I beam excitement, and Maike smiles back nervously.

The music changes to part B, and immediately here come William and Helen for their second act. As I take William's hand to set and turn myself into triangles, my free hand directs Maike to turn and set. I smile over my shoulder as I see her join me in the back-to-back setting. Then as William and Helen turn us around to follow them up the set, my right hand stretches out to catch Maike's left hand. "Now we FLY!" I cry joyously and the music carries us to the top, around the corner and we follow the Crawfords back down the outside of the set.

"READY for William's turn?"

William swoops in and turns Maike with ease, then makes a wide loop past his wife who is flying across the set in perfect balance to take my hand as her second corner, and I am ready to catch and turn her. And now we are all moving into the circle: "Here we really fly!" I tell Maike as I check my speed for a micro-second to catch her hand. "Just stretch your legs and let it go."

And our circle flies!

These young, long-legged and highly skilled dancers carry the circle 30% farther than any normal circle, and then we fly back again ... and as we soar around at top speed I swear that I never have I felt such excitement ... except for the last time ... and then of course there will be the next time ... and the joy on the faces of the other dancers shows how we are sharing a moment of pure ecstasy. It is true that you need either young legs (Maike has them) or excellent technique (I have it after 50 years of dancing) to carry off a circle powered by William and Lars ... but they provide the momentum and all we have to do is to allow our toes to take off and find the floor again as the music tells us.

"Ready, Maike? Now we are third couple again." William and Helen step down to the bottom of the set, and here come Lars and Riekje turning into their triangles as our new first couple. Again, with my spare hand, I show Maike the timing. With my eyes I tell her she can do it; and she can, of course, because everyone else is taking her with them.

Now Lars and Riekje are flying up to the top, and we follow as third couple. Holding Maike's hand again, I turn her outwards into the cast down to the bottom of the set and IMMEDIATELY show her how to turn up into place ready for the "CORNER TURN NOW!"as Lars comes swooping in to turn her.

Maike's eyes are shining. She is feeling what this dance is supposed to be, and now yet again we are off in the circle, Lars pulling us around ... but with William and Helen standing out as fourth couple, the circle's power is less than before. We have one more chance to watch as third couple goes through their paces, and then it will be our turn to lead the dance.

"You have seen it, you have danced it, and now you KNOW we can do it," I smile to Maike as I raise my hand for her to start on the right beat. And here we are half-turning back-to-back, half turning again, setting, and "NOW IT IS OUR TURN" I cry as I seize her inside hand and whoosh her up to the top of the set, cast her down the outside and turn her outwards again to look upwards toward the first man's position where her corner is ready. "Are you ready for William? NOW!"

And Maike is ready, following my direction as she dances out to meet William Crawford who is now her first corner back at the top. William turns Maike towards me, and with my hand I describe Maike's curve as she dances round to face Lars— second corner turn, and now I slow Maike down as I whisper the word "Circle" and place her in second position between Helen and Riekje. Oh! How we fly, and how Maike's eyes shine as our circle powers around and back again. First time around her eyes showed panic. This time around they show joy.

"One more time through," I tell Maike as we turn into the triangles. "Make the most of it," I laugh as we turn out to the side and set to each other. "Now let us fly!" I cry as I take her hand and race her to the top of the set to cast off once more. Another corner-and-swoop-and-corner-and-circle, but this is bigger and better than all the others because all four couples are powering our final circle. As the band stops, we bow and curtsey in a state of angelic heavenly bliss, and raise one hand in the air to request an ENCORE! Because who would not want to go through that fabulous experience once again?

REEL OF THE ROYAL SCOTS

Reel 8 x 32 bars for 3 couples in a 4-couple longwise set. Devisor: Roy Goldring. SCD Leaflets.

Written for the Royal Scots Regiment in 1983 to celebrate their 350th anniversary.

Bars 1-2 : 1st Lady and 2nd Lady turn by the left halfway WHILE 1st Man and 2nd Man turn by the right halfway, finishing back-to-back in double triangles position;

Bars 3-4 : 2s1s3s balance (set) on the sides;

Bars 5-6 : 1L3L turn by the right halfway WHILE 1M3M turn by the left halfway, finishing back-to-back in double triangles position;

Bars 7-8 : 2s3s1s balance (set) on the sides;

Bars 9-16 : WHILE 3s cast to follow, 1s lead to the top, cast, lead down and cast up to 2nd place (3s finishing in own places);

Bars 17-20 : 1s turn first corners by the right and pass partner (right shoulder);

Bars 21-24 : 1s turn second corners by the right and pass partner (right shoulder) to finish in 2nd place on own sides;

Bars 25-32 : 2s1s3s 6 hands round and back.

Dance notes: Each couple must be sure to cast back to their correct place in the set, notably third couple.

24

CROSSING THE TAY TO DANCE HOOPER'S JIG WITH RSCDS TEACHER STELLA

W e are in St Andrews and the sun is shining on the tennis courts of University Hall where I stretch out in the warmth before leaving to dance in Perth. The year is 2006 and I am living in a matriarchy run by Stella, our famous and brilliant teacher from Richmond, Virginia and originally from Gourock, on the Clyde. After 40 years of marriage to an American sailor and engineer, Stella Fogg's West of Scotland accent bears not a trace of America. She is Scots from her bone marrow outwards. After teaching us through the winter and spring, Stella comes to dance in Scotland during the summer. Half a dozen of us are here from Virginia, and Stella has decreed that this evening we shall dance in Perth Town Hall.

One of our Summer School musicians, the wonderful Mo Rutherford, is playing for a dance in Perth. We shall support her and enjoy her husband Neil Copeland's band. A mini-bus arrives, we all pile in, and drive off through the Kingdom of Fife. Macbeth was once the king of these sand dunes and fields of gorse where a dozen golf courses have been created in and around St Andrews. Macbeth ruled over the rich farmlands that lie between the Forth and Tay rivers where we drive north past Leuchars Air base with its Royal Air Force super-sonic fighters and bombers hidden away in plain sight, and cross the bridge over the River Tay. It is impossible to cross the Tay into the marmalade, fruit-cake and jute city of Dundee without thinking of William Topaz McGonagall, the worst-ever poet in the English language whose greatest quality was his total indifference to the opinions of others. He was a 19th century Scottish weaver and actor, who petitioned Queen Victoria to make him Poet Laureate. Here are a few lines of his terribly bad poem about the *Beautiful Bridge over the Silvery Tay,* which we used to read aloud for laughs during dinner when I was a student in St Andrews.

> *Beautiful Railway Bridge of the Silvery Tay !*
> *With your numerous arches and pillars in so grand array*
> *And your central girders, which seem to the eye*
> *To be almost towering to the sky*
> *The greatest wonder of the day,*
> *And a great beautification to the River Tay,*
> *Most beautiful to be seen,*
> *Near by Dundee and the Magdalen Green.*
> *Beautiful Railway Bridge of the Silvery Tay!*
> *The longest of the present day*
> *That has ever crossed o'er a tidal river stream,*
> *Most gigantic to be seen,*
> *Near by Dundee and the Magdalen Green.*

In 1879 there was a disaster. Violent winds came whipping in from the North Sea, racing up the Tay valley, that caused the high girders in the middle of the bridge to sway, and then to give way entirely. In the initial design, the engineers had not taken sufficient account of wind resistance. MacGonagall reacted immediately with a new poem. *The Tay Bridge Disaster* is one of the most famous in his list of terrible poems. My friend Ewan recites this poem regularly in ceilidhs in America, getting the whole audience to join in the chorus. It is utterly hilarious. Dearest grandchildren, if you want a party turn that will bring laughter, then learn to recite this horrible poem by William Topaz McGonagall, the worst poet of the English language. The first stanza will suffice to illustrate its awfulness!

> *Beautiful Railway Bridge of the Silv'ry Tay!*
> *Alas! I am very sorry to say*
> *That ninety lives have been taken away*
> *On the last Sabbath day of 1879*
> *Which will be remembered for a very long time.*

When Ewan recites the poem, he has the whole audience chant in unison the line "Which will be remembered for a very long time"—a line which comes at the end of every stanza. The audience loves it! The Poet Laureate under Queen Victoria was Alfred Lord Tennyson, of whom MacGonagall was jealous, convinced that he himself was the superior poet. Tennyson, by the way, was a very gifted poet, the first and only person to be enobled for his poetry. When Tennyson died, our William immediately wrote to the Queen to apply for his position. In support of his claim, MacGonagall penned yet another appallingly bad poem:

Alas! England now mourns for her poet that's gone
The late and the good Lord Tennyson.
I hope his soul has fled to heaven above,
Where there is everlasting joy and love.
He has written some fine pieces of poetry in his time,
Especially the May Queen, which is really sublime;
Also the most gallant charge of the Light Brigade –
A most heroic poem, and beautifully made.

I am not sure that it is any better to laugh at a dead person than to speak ill of him; but anyone who laughs at MacGonagall must be excused. If only this was supposed to be comic .... but alas! WTMacG believed he was writing poetry. I wonder what McGonagall would have written about the world's first all-plastic footbridge, built over the Tay in 1992 for the Aberfeldy golf club: another Scottish First! Because the site and the budget were too tight for traditional cranes, a team of engineering students at Dundee University designed a fiber-reinforced bridge using recycled plastics. It lasted without problem until 2017, when £15,000–worth of repairs were needed for safety, partly from wear-and-tear but also from weight abuse. The bridge was designed for men and women pushing golf carts, but some vandal drove a vehicle over the plastic footbridge in 1997 causing serious damage that required patching.

Oh! You great and amazingly orginal plastic bridge spanning the Silv'ry
Tay
Some ghastly fat idiot in a Range Rover has got in your way
By over-stretching the glass-reinforced multi-cellular planks of your deck
And causing massive weight damage needing to be repaired like heck!

Such were the happy and inconsequential thoughts that passed through my head as we crossed the Silv'ry Tay, drove up through Tayside's rich green meadows with dark Aberdeen Angus beef cattle grazing peacefully, and approached the rolling countryside around Perth, gateway to the Highlands. Elfrida Hamilton Maclean, your great great grandmother, was born on the beautiful Glen Earn Estate, beside Bridge of Earn, on the way to Perth.

"The trouble with dancing in places like Perth," I told Stella and my other friends, "is that they do not give briefings. My youthful dancing in Scotland was spoiled by the stress of having to remember all the dances and get them right. We will have to study each dance before we dance it, and we have not even seen a list of the dances on their program."

"Och, noo," said Stella. "Everyone gives briefings nowadays. Your memories are too distant, Robin. Modern dances always have briefings. The old dance programs were all more-or-less the same. There are so many new dances nowadays that we always have briefings."

We stopped in front of the grand classical entrance of Perth City Hall. I was excited, I imagined my great grandfather Charles Maclean of Glen Earn, with his Hamilton wife, dancing in this very hall, on the same floorboards and under the same elegant ceiling. Complete rubbish of course: my great grandfather was dead 20 years before this hall was built in 1911. The elegant Edwardian building—where Margaret Thatcher made her first speech as Prime Minister—was happily saved from demolition by a lobby that included the Prince of Wales, sparing Perth from an ugly concrete shopping center spoiling the heart of the city. We walked into the building just as the band was playing the opening bars for the first dance.

"Come on!" I called to Stella. "If we are quick we can join in at the bottom of a set." And so we did, slipping in as fourth couple. "What are we dancing?" I asked my neighbor.

"This will be *Hooper's Jig*," came the response in the soft undulations of a Highland accent.

"That's fine," I smiled at Stella. "We can manage *Hooper's Jig*." Whereupon the chord sounded, everyone bowed, and *Hooper's Jig* began with the famous "all clap"—a noise that sent shivers down my spine. No briefings then? I raised my eyebrows at Stella, and she rolled her eyeballs. I was in for a stressful evening. Over the past thirty years, dance briefings have attuned my brain to following patterns on the floor, following the dance rather as water follows a pipe. I am out of the habit of transferring detailed written instructions to the dance floor, which involves imagining words as feet moving across the boards. I would need some intensive reading if there were dances on the program that I had never done before. Thank goodness that Stella and I both knew *Hooper's Jig*!

Just to be sure, I focused hard as the first couple crossed, cast around into a wheel with the 3s, and clapped as they crossed back up to first place for left hands across with the 2s. Aha! I remember that the 2s must step up, and then step down again, or the wheels won't work.

Now first man and third lady—and then the first lady and third man—sped diagonally across the set, changing places and then back again. It is a wonderful dancing moment, but Aha, yes! I must remember that the final cross is with the left hand, to help the third lady back into her place. Another point: the 2s must remember to step up, ready for rights-and-lefts with the 1s. And they are off again, and now we must be ready for our turn on the wheel: 1s and 3s right hands across. After that, the dance was easy. But I swear that it was one of the few easy dances of the evening.

HOOPER'S JIG

Jig 8 x 32 bars for 3 couples in a 4C longwise set. Anon in Miss Milligan's 99 More Scottish Country Dances.

A hooper makes the bands that hold whisky casks together: an important man in Scottish culture and history.

Bars 1-4 : All clap, 1s cross (giving right shoulder, no hands) and cast;

Bars 5-8 : 1s and 3s right hands across;

Bars 9-12 : All clap, 1s cross (giving right shoulder, no hands) and cast up;

Bars 13-16 : 1s and 2s left hands across;

Bars 17-18 : 1Man & 3 Lady cross diagonally by the right;

Bars 19-20 : 1L3M cross diagonally by the right;

Bars 21-22 : 1M3L cross diagonally by the right;

Bars 23-24 : 1M casts WHILE 2s step up and 1L and 3M cross diagonally by the left. 1L ends in 2nd place;

Bars 25-32 : 2s and 1s rights and lefts.

Dance notes: 2s must step up on 3-4 and step down on bars 11-12. Then 2s step up again on bars 23-24.

Bar 24 cross LEFT hand.

Actually it cannot be quite true that there were no easy dances because I remember at the beginning of the second half of the evening that I invited a Chinese student to dance. I would not have invited her unless it was an easy dance that I could guide her through. There was a small group of Chinese students at the far end of the hall. Since I guessed (rightly) that they must be in Perth to learn English, I went across to chat to them during the interval. I am a supporter of students wanting to learn English. In 1971 I shared a UN office in Kabul with an Afghan who had spent a year in Tennessee studying English, and during that whole year he found not one single American student willing to talk with him and become his friend. Abdul Yari's English became fluent only because he happened to meet a pair of Jehovah's witnesses. They were willing to talk to him every week for an hour or two while they explained their religion and their desire to convert Abdul. Abdul used them to improve his English. He learned a lot about American religion and culture. Eventually the missionaries wanted to lead him to baptism. Abdul did not want to stop the English conversation lessons, so he fixed a date for his baptism in early July. His plane left Tennessee for Afghanistan on June 30th.

Abdul's story of American unfriendliness made a deep impression on me. Every semester when I was teaching, I told this story to my American students and begged them to make a point of befriending foreign students. Here in Perth were some Chinese students; naturally I went to talk to them. They knew some English, and were eager to practice. I asked them if they wanted to dance? They said they were only here to watch. Excitedly they posed for photos with me wearing the kilt. Now that I think about it, I was the only person wearing the kilt who went over to chat with these student visitors. Finally one of the Chinese girls said she would like to try dancing, and so I invited her for the next easy dance (the first dance of the second half is usually an easy warm-up). I led her through the dance, to her great pleasure, and she felt she had achieved a new level of Scottish understanding and social acclimatization.

25

A MORE USER-FRIENDLY RSCDS: A NEW GENERATION OF JEANS

I n the minibus back to St Andrews that evening, Stella gave me a lecture on dance etiquette.

"When you are at someone else's dance, you do NOT invite a beginner onto the dance floor because it might offend some of the other dancers."

I laughed off the fact that Stella—a wonderful teacher and a good friend—was treating me like a child even though I was past the age of 50. I replied that the only way to introduce new people to dancing is to bring them onto the dance floor. We need to teach young people—including children, whom many teachers keep out of their class. Students learning English could be future Scottish dancers, and they also want to learn about our culture—of which dancing is an important part. I had no regrets whatever about inviting the young Chinese girl to dance, and I disagreed with Stella's interpretation of dance etiquette. The incident caused me to reflect on a different aspect of Scottish culture: why did Stella think that she could and should give me a lecture as though I were a schoolboy?

As an Old-School RSCDS qualified teacher, Stella is part of the old matriarchy: one of those people who apply the model inherited from Miss Milligan, the Queen Victoria of Scottish Dancing. I am old enough to remember that Summer School under Miss Jean Milligan was like Boarding School under Miss Jean Brody. Miss Milligan would preside over lunch like a Head Mistress at High Table, a table where none outside her close circle was allowed to sit. Even speaking to these people was discouraged. In his lovely book of dance stories *Miss Esther Scott's Fancy* Lorn Macintyre (who lives in St Andrews) describes Miss Milligan's generosity to her students, her caring for people as well as for their dancing and how Glasgow and Scotland have benefited from her untiring quest for excellence. Her legacy is one of generosity, but also of rigidity. RSCDS Old Schoolers are sticklers for rules. Rules are more important than having fun. Old Schoolers do not mix children with adults; a lot of them do not even like children. Beginners are allowed to dance only the very easiest dances and may be expected to sit and watch their "betters" for long periods during class. No wonder so many of the people who attended Stella's class for the first time never came back.

I am not saying it is easy to combine dancers of different levels, but teachers need to adjust the class structure or take care of the beginners separately. The trick is to find ways to include them in the dances. Different teachers use different methods to include beginners, often using simpler dances to include everybody in the action. Intensive step-practice is great for workshops, but it is boring for people attending a weekly dance class. Teachers of the Scotia Dancers in New York City manage to introduce the basic steps to beginners in two or three minute sessions within the set lines, in such a way that the beginners learn as they dance and more experienced dancers do not have time to become bored.

There is a strange contrast here: the same Scottish women who are brilliant teachers, huge personalities and authors of the wittiest one-line jokes, are often profoundly insecure and unwilling to change their ideas. Their bossiness conceals their uncertainty. Stella herself, when I first met her, seemed unwilling to believe me when I told her that she was a brilliant teacher. Was I the first person to tell her she was great? Scots and Brits in general are sparing in praise and are afraid of expressing emotion. That is a problem we need to overcome. If you do not tell people you love them, children, they may never know it. I say: "Share the love!" At St Andrews, I told my class teacher, Jean Martin—at that time the Society's Chair —that her teaching was as good as Stella Fogg's. Jean Martin of Aberdeen is the stellar opposite (yes, there is a clever pun in here) of the fearsomely rigid, though highly admirable Miss Jean Milligan. Jean Martin is kind and friendly, a dance leader for the 21st century. Jean Martin is a part of the modern, reforming, user-friendly RSCDS.

Obviously, Jean Martin went off to find out who Stella Fogg might be. Only after this did Stella begin to teach workshops around America. Stella was a great teacher, but she did not believe in herself. I have found the same in many Scottish women. Perhaps women in the 21st century feel more secure? There have been four female Moderators of the General Assembly of the Church of Scotland and Scottish women are very well represented in politics: we have the SNP's leader Nicola Sturgeon as First Minister and Ruth Davidson as her Conservative opponent. And yet .... I have discussed this question with plenty of talented Scots women of my own generation who admit to their own internal insecurities. Does Scotland now have the problem of insecurity sorted? What is it in the Scottish make-up that has made many of my women friends—equal or superior to men in every respect—feel insecure?

I blame John Knox, the horrid little man who persecuted Mary, Queen of Scots from his Protestant pulpit in St Giles Church, Edinburgh. Was Knox a woman-hater, a mysogynist? The evidence suggests that he was: his dislike of Mary was personal, not constitutional because Elizabeth I was on the throne of England and proving that a woman could be Head of State. Knox had returned to Scotland in 1559 from Geneva, and had already crossed swords with Marie de Guise who was the Regent in her daughter's absence. Mary Stuart, like her mother, was a beautiful and impressive educated woman. She danced, played tennis and golf and was a French Catholic. The Protestant Knox had been captured in St Andrews and punished for 18 months as a galley slave after the murder of Cardinal Beaton: rowing French ships was hard labor, so he had no love of the French. The misogyny of John Knox infected Scottish society and Scottish religion for centuries. The Scottish Presbyterian Church was male-dominated. This has changed: my friends Lesley and Phil Hanlon are both Elders of their church in Paisley, something that would have been inconceivable when we were all young.

The front end of a Scottish church was dominated by a pyramidal wooden structure that placed church officials way above the congregation: minor officials (men) sat in raised pews; the Elders (men) sat above the officials; and the Minister, a man dressed in black, climbed a narrow stairway until he was seated above them all, like a justiciar placed between Man and God. And women? They sat in the audience. Women were controlled by the Scottish Church hierarchy every bit as severely as women are controlled by male hierarchies in the Roman Catholic, Orthodox, Jewish, Hindu or Buddhist faiths and by Sunni or Shia Muslim Imams. If you doubt it, watch the violent-but-memorable Scottish film *Breaking the Waves*. Organized religion was designed by men to control women, and Scots women have suffered like the rest. And yet Scots women are so smart, so sexy, so quick, so witty! They can also be severe.

RSCDS Old School teachers are horrified when someone like me teaches beginners how to dance, for I threaten their hegemony. Old Schoolers have their way of doing things. They were trained by Miss Milligan in the Headmistress School of Management. I learned my management skills in business and in sport. I have been dancing for half a century. I dance as well as anyone, and I happen to be very good at teaching children and beginners: but I have never wished to go through the stressful teacher certification processes that the RSCDS imposes. I am not Old School. I dance for pleasure, not for pain.

One of the men in my Advanced High Impact group at Summer School put it pithily: "Our Branch sent three of our brightest, charming, and enthusiastic young dancers to St Andrews to gain their certification," he told me, "and when they came back, they behaved like arseholes."

I agree that RSCDS training improves some teachers' technique and pedagogy. Samuele Graziane from Bologna told me that studying for Unit 2 of the teacher's certificate "provided the best week of my life: I danced eight hours per day with some of the very best dancers. It was heaven!" But even he feels that Unit 5 was twice as long as it needed to be. I support the RSCDS and its teaching role. I own all the books and music. Despite being a paid-up Life Member since 1967, I regularly pay annual branch subscriptions and make additional donations to the Society. I have funded youth scholarships at Scottish Weekend in West Virginia and at the wonderful St Andrews Summer School where people from all over the world gather to celebrate Scottish dance, music and culture. I love my international network of dance friends, but I deplore the rigidity of the Old School RSCDS teachers, their frequent rudeness and unfriendliness to beginners, and the lack of welcome to children that—in the past—has so often accompanied the RSCDS method. No children today = no dancers tomorrow.

Raphaëlle Orgeret and her mother Christiane in Lyon provide a 21st century model for enthusing RSCDS youth in France, providing pleasure and motivation as well as dance instruction. The Orgeret model combines inspiration for new dancers and simple fun dancing for beginners, with quality demo dancing. Some of their beginners have become top-quality dancers even selected to take part in St Andrews RSCDS demonstration teams. Aberdeen provides a similar model for Scotland, where Jim Stott and his supporters are taking dancing into the schools and are unafraid to say that Ceilidh dancing is also Scottish dancing. Jack Pressley and his wife Jamie do the same in North Carolina, and they are living proof that it is more important to love kids and teach them well than to have an RSCDS paper qualification. Over the years the Pressleys have provided scholarships for more than twenty of their dancing youths to attend St Andrews Summer School. They raise funds by creating exciting dance demonstrations and charging $200 to each institution that hosts them. Jamie says it is hard work, but she and Jack cannot think of a more wonderful way to spend their retirement than bringing music and dancing skills to children. Young people all over the world will love Scottish dancing, music and culture if we give them the opportunity to discover them.

These words were written in St Andrews, after seeing the RSCDS children's class in action, meeting the teachers and chatting to happy parents spending a week dancing in Scotland with their kids. These parents are having a great dancing holiday in Scotland, while giving their children a gift that will enrich the rest of their lives. Roísín has parents who dance, and I know she will be a great Scottish dancer. I hope the same will be true for Liam and Isabelle.

How is it possible that the children of RSCDS teachers often do not dance? What is wrong with our RSCDS teachers? If you motivate young people, they will follow you. Dancing should not be a personal hobby, but a collective and shared joy. Dearest grandchildren, I remember young Edward your father, at the age of 8, standing in the setline between me his father, and Billy Forsyth, the former World Highland Dance Champion. My son was so proud I thought his chest would burst. I believe that no teacher should be RSCDS certified unless they are willing to teach children. Like the Hippocratic Oath for doctors, the RSCDS should insist on every teacher taking a vow that they will teach children, or arrange for someone else in their dance group to teach children while they are teaching their adult classes. Blasphemy for Old Schoolers, but I believe that teaching children to dance and enjoy it is more important than achieving the perfect pas de basque—even though no lesser people than Jean Martin, Stella Fogg and Atsuko Clement, three of the Society's best teachers, have complimented me on my perfect pas de basque. So there you have it, Liam and Isabelle, and Roísín as well: I confess to blasphemy. I believe that enjoyment is the first and principle purpose for dancing.

Some RSCDS teachers are committed to popularizing joyful dancing. I received this email from Jimmie Hill, one of the top teachers in the RSCDS. Although Jimmie is famous for his perfect footwork, he also believes that enjoyment is more important that rules: "One Monday night here in Edinburgh I was asked to teach the first class of the local 'reel' club. We did the Gay Gordons, The Canadian Barn Dance, The Dashing White Sergeant—twice!, the Eightsome Reel, the Kingston Flier and the last figure of The Lancers. There were 48 beginners in the class and I can guarantee they will be back next week—and probably with a friend. If I had started with skip change round the room and pas de basque practice and foot positions, I would be lucky if 12 turned up next week!"

I am a strong supporter of new approaches in the Society. We now find ceilidh dancing acceptable and Scottish and fun. At last we are welcoming children to Summer School, 50 years later than I would have liked. More relaxed relationships have developed in recent years between THEM (the elite teachers) and US, the rest of the membership who love to dance but who are not part of the inner clique. The inner clique is becoming less exclusive. Partly thanks to internet communications, there are now working groups that do not have to meet in Edinburgh: members who live in America or Germany or New Zealand can discuss together by internet. Jim Stott and the Wilkinsons and a generation of fine, forward-looking women like Jean Martin, Helen Russell, Janet Johnson, Rachel Shankland and others are responsible for introducing a new atmosphere at Summer School and for encouraging young people to participate. I applaud them and their teams, and all their supporters, for modernizing the Society and making it user-friendly. In the matter of comparative Jeans (I am not talking about denims with jagged holes ripped through them), I prefer the modern Jean Martin RSCDS to the Victorian version left us by Jean Milligan.

26

THE REEL OF THE FIFTY-FIRST DIVISION, FAMILY DEMOS AND EMMA'S FLASHMOB

One of my precious memories is a dance demonstration with my son, father and brother on the cathedral green during the Chichester Festival. After twenty years serving as a United Nations doctor in Africa, children, your great grandfather Teddie (Dr Edward Maclean Poulton) retired in the 1970s to the cathedral city of Chichester, where he joined the local RSCDS class—in those days taught by Mary Corelli, whose Italian father had emigrated to Britain before the second war. Rory and I danced too, and Mary adored the young Poulton brothers (we were young then). Mary was definitely Old School, but my brother Rory and I flirted with her mercilessly and she melted before our dancing, our energy and our youth. Mary was a very good teacher and she improved our dancing which—apart from my time in St Andrews—had largely been learned in Africa, in British colonial club houses that all had the same smell of beer and sweat soaking into the floor boards since they were built back in the 1920s. Scottish dancing in Africa was fast and furious and fun, but it was not precise.

We worked in development projects—your grandmother Michelle was West African Director for Save the Children, and I was a director of ActionAid and later worked for USAID and the UN. Michelle's career took her to Virginia where she supervised the programs in 40 countries of ChildFund International. I named her "the Mother of 12 million children" after our own biological children left home to start their own careers, dancing when they had time. We lived four years in The Gambia, but much of our life was spent in French-speaking countries (Mali, Senegal) where Scottish culture was unknown. Occasionally I used my Scottish dancing to entertain Americans; once each year I wore the kilt for United Nations Day on

October 24th; but mostly my knees and ankles were rested unless I was visiting Chichester.

By now my father had created his own group on Wednesday evenings in the games room of his home, The Island Cottage: a group largely composed of elderly and retired RSCDS dance teachers who shuffled around the floor with excellent phrasing, bickering with each other as they disagreed on interpreting the newest and most complicated RSCDS dances. It was hilarious dancing around them while they argued. One of the less disputatious members was dance devisor George Swayles, a taciturn Scot and family friend. In addition to this group and the weekly RSCDS class in Chichester, Father attended Saturday dances from Brighton in the east to Portsmouth and Bournemouth in the west. My mother's bad ankles and knees, alas! kept her at home watching Coronation Street on television while Father went dancing.

One evening during tea break, I was chatting to an older lady called Christina who mentioned that she lived in St Andrews during the war where she was evacuated in 1942 with her three small children. Where did she live, I wondered politely? When Christina told me she was at No 49 South St, it turned out—most improbably—that she had rented the same apartment in 1944 and from the same Miss Tanner where I lived 25 years later in 1969 with my friends Peter Martin and Sandy Scott ... and Christina had slept in the same front room as me. I swear that Miss Tanner had not changed the mattress since Christina slept on it. Sandy (Dr Alexander Scott) was researching the pituitary gland of the lobster for his PhD. We established a grand system. Fishermen caught lobster for the Gatty Marine Laboratory, Sandy extracted the pituitary gland, and —since the rest of the lobster was considered waste—Sandy brought lobsters home for supper every week. I have never eaten more lobster than when I was a penniless student.

Family parties brought together Us-Poultons on the dance floor. If my brothers Rupert and Rory and sisters Alana and Lucie were all there, with me and Michelle and our kids the family could produce a complete set of eight dancers. Often we chose dances devised by George Swayles for his Island Cottage Collection, including *The Poultons' Pleasure; The Island Cottage Strathspey; Leïla's Lilt* (for my daughter); *Rory's Rant* (for my brother); *A Reel for Rory* (devised by Margaret Fell, who also created a two-couple demo dance called *Robin's Rant*, which we probably only ever danced once). *Leïla's Lilt* and *A Reel for Rory* are fun: both have diagonal rights and lefts .... But there are hundreds of other dances that are just as good, and which can be found on the Strathspey Server and the Scottish Dance Dictionary https://www.scottish-country-dancing-dictionary.com. We love the people who invest so much of their time into keeping these websites updated. I hope, my lovely grandchildren, Liam, Isabelle and Roísín, that you will have the time to explore them one day and to use these websites throughout your lives.

Some years our summer visit to Chichester coincided with the city's festival, when the Scottish dancers from all over West Sussex congregated on the cathedral green for a set of reel and jig and strathspey demonstrations. These were not "demo dances" in the formal sense that we use in Scotland, but a display of social dancing for our own enjoyment, showing other people how much fun we have. Time and again, people have said to me: "If only I had known how wonderful Scottish dancing is, I would have started years ago. I really regret that I have missed out on twenty years of enjoyment."

My fondest memory of Chichester cathedral green is the day that we danced the *Reel of the 51ˢᵗ Division* in three sets as a demo by twenty-four men wearing kilts, with my father Edward (Teddie), my brother Rory and my son Edward all in my set. What a precious moment of family history! The reason for a men-only and kilt-only rendition is that *The Reel of the 51ˢᵗ Division* was devised in a German prisoner of war camp during WW2, where of course there were only soldiers, including a lot of Gordon Highlanders wearing the kilt. Dancing was a way for the men to take exercise, to celebrate their culture, their discipline and their regiment. This reel also recreated the St Andrews Cross (the saltire, the national flag) under the noses of the German prison guards, who did not realize the symbolism and defiance that was present on every occasion when the prisoners danced *The Reel of the 51ˢᵗ Division.*

THE REEL OF THE 51ˢᵗ DIVISION

Reel 8 x 32 bars for 3 couples in a 4-couple longwise set. Devisor: J.E.M. Atkinson. RSCDS Book 13.

Written for solders in a German prison camp during WW2 for exercise and secretly to reproduce the saltire.

Bars 1-2 : 1s set;

Bars 3-8 : 1s cast two places, meet, take left hands and lead up to face first corners;

Bars 9-12 : 1s set and turn first corners by the right, finishing 2M1L1M3L in line on the first corners' diagonal;

Bars 13-14 : 2nd Man and 1st Lady and 1st Man and 3rd Lady balance in a diagonal line;

Bars 15-16 : 1s turn by the left;

Bars 17-20 : 1s set and turn second corners by the right, finishing 3M1L1M2L in line on the second corners' diagonal;

Bars 21-22 : 3M1L1M2L balance in a diagonal line;

Bars 23-24 : 1s cross by the left to own sides in 2nd place;

Bars 25-32 : 2s1s3s 6 hands round and back.

Dance Note: 1st couple meet at the bottom on bar 6, allowing 2 bars to lead up and face 1st corners on bar 8.

Obviously the use of "Man and Lady" in this description uses the RSCDS convention even though the dance was written to be danced by eight men, as we danced it for the Chichester Festival. Scottish dance is actually pretty gender-neutral: men or women can lead equally well. I remember the pleasure—I would say even the excitement—of setting and casting off opposite my twelve-year-old son Edward, meeting him at the bottom of the set on bar 6, and leading him up to place him opposite his grandfather for the set-turn-balance figure. My father, bless his heart, was always more enthusiastic than elegant: his pas de basque had a rather high knee movement while young Edward's pas de basque was exquisite. Since my son was trained both as a highland dancer and as a country dancer, he can produce a perfect two-beat highland setting step and a perfect three-beat country dance setting step. When, ten years later, Edward spent a year in Lyon on a European Union Erasmus fellowship, we danced together at the RSCDS Lyon Branch. After one dance, Christiane Orgeret had seen enough to invite Edward to join her demo team for their presentations during the soccer World Cup in France —in those days her delightful daughters Emma and Raphaëlle were still teenagers, but already wonderful dancers, and Christiane's son Axel had not yet reached his teens. As you know, children, your father has both French and British nationalities, so France hosting the World Cup was a big deal in our family. That was the year— 1998—that France won their first World Cup and Zinedine Zidane scored two goals in the final. Zidane, as the departing manager of Real Madrid, has just led his club to three successive European Cup victories. He is a French and a family hero. Meanwhile France have just won their second World Cup in Russia in 2018.

After all the joyous setting and balancing, *The Reel of the 51st Division* finally ends with all eight kilts joining hands for a fabulous circle round and back. Our circle did not turn very fast on the cathedral grass, but we had finished yet another triumphant *Reel of the 51st Division*: just one of so many fabulous reels in the RSCDS repertoire.

Unlike my severe, wee-free paternal grandmother Maclean, my biological grandfather on my mother's side, Ian Monteith Hamilton—no wee-free he!— would have enjoyed our dancing. He was a Gordon Highlander, and my grand- mother's lover. You will learn the *Gay Gordons* one day, children, as a standard ceilidh dance. This regiment served in the First World War version of the 51st (Highland) Division, known as "HD" for short. At the beginning of WW2, many soldiers of the HD were taken prisoner in 1940 at the time of the Dunkirk evacua- tion, and they were the ones who created our Reel. The division served under Montgomery in North Africa, then in France and Germany. Other British Army units called them the "Highway Decorators" because of the HD insignia marking the route of their marches across France: British humor! German soldiers in 1916 called them "The Ladies from Hell!" as they charged screaming through the smoke of battle with bayonets set, kilts flying and bagpipes wailing. Grandfather Hamilton was in Gallipoli, so he was not one of the Ladies from Hell although it was he who trained them to shoot straight. Born in 1853, he would have had to live to be almost 140 to witness our social dance demo on the cathedral green: but as a keen social dancer himself, he would have enjoyed our reel.

Some people, the bagpipes abhor:
Quite a few .... among many more!
I believe in the past
That bagpipes were classed
As an inhumane weapon of war.

Bagpipes are an ancient Celtic instrument (whatever the name "Celtic" means, this is a musical truth) for it seems to have been an Indo-European instrument and it was a very useful way to exploit the stomach of a sheep, particularly for shepherds who had eaten enough haggis, thank you. There are only four things you can do with a *panse de brebis*: stuff it for haggis, blow it up to use as a football, turn it into bagpipes, or wear it on your head to keep off the rain. The bagpipes are widely distributed over southern and western Europe. One academic historian has suggested that the bagpipes only reached the Scottish Highlands in the 15th century. This means I suppose, that (s)he found a written reference to them in the 1500s or late 1400s. But some academics are sadly lacking in imagination: do they think the pipes disappeared between 1500 BC and 1500 AD? Of course not! Picts and Scots played the pipes before Jesus Christ was born, and the pipes developed multiple variations through the ages. No one can know how, nor at what moment, or indeed WHERE in the Highlands the *biniou braz* (the Big Pipes) emerged as specifically Scottish whereas the Celtic *biniou coz* (the Old Pipes) has a single drone —I am using the Breton language terminology since the Scottish Gaelic uses only one expression *A' Phìob Mhór* "The Big Pipe". I am sure the bagpipes were used as a weapon of war throughout Scottish history; but perhaps they only developed their lethal sound when additional upright drones were added in the 15th or 16th century. If you ever learn to play the pipes, children, your lives will be changed forever— and your parents' lives as well.

The greatest of all RSCDS "social dancing demonstrations" took place in Aberdeen on Saturday 5th September 2015 when Emma Allsop organized a fantastic FlashMobDance at the Union Square shopping center, filmed by RSCDS member Mike Greenwood. You should watch the video on YouTube. The "mob" started with one group of eight dancers, and ended with five full sets circling to the music of Frank Thompson's accordion. When you watch it, kids, Emma is the one with fabulous footwork dancing in the initial set and wearing a blue skirt.

By the time the tune *Blue Bonnets* is played for the first time, four sets of eight people are all dancing the same choreography. Soon a fifth set arrives and forty dancers now fill the vast space of the shopping center while hundreds of shoppers take photographs and watch in amazement at how much fun everyone is having. It is a great display! Mike's lovely film-takes show people watching and filming with their cameras, children trying to imitate dance steps and—at one precious moment —an unsighted man with a white stick walking across the concourse and right through the middle of a set of dancers, enjoying the music no doubt, but oblivious to what is happening because he cannot see. Perhaps the most important moment of the whole event comes at the beginning, when Emma tells her dancers: "The purpose is to enjoy yourselves."

At the Younger Hall during Week 1 of Summer School 2016, I happened to invite Emma Allsop for a dance. She seemed vaguely familiar but so do a lot of dancers, for obvious reasons. My partner Emma was a wonderful dancer, clearly a teacher, and I had to raise my dancing level to match hers. When I dance with a beginner or an intermediate dancer, my muscles relax and I focus more on organization than on precision. When someone like Emma comes along, the emphasis changes and the enjoyment increases as we match perfect phrasing and timing. The following week I was touring Royal Deeside with Breton friends and we stayed over in Aberdeen. We knew there was a dance at The Curl, the Aberdeen home of the ancient sport of curling. We entered the dance hall and paid our small dance fee. Looking around the room, I saw my partner of the previous week and suddenly I knew who she was. So I walked across the hall and shook her hand.

"I danced with you at the Younger Hall last week," I said, "and now I remember that you are the lady who organized the wonderful Aberdeen FlashMob that I have enjoyed on my computer and recommended to hundreds of people. Thank you for dancing with me last week." After which, I flashed her my winningiest smile, and fled.

The Poultons are known for a slightly awkward and abrupt style of speaking, and I suspect I gave Emma an example of the genre! You grandchildren already seem to be socially smoother than me. My Maclean grandmother was an introverted Scots Presbyterian who disapproved of too much jollity; but she was a totally devoted mother and grandmother. Her manner was abrupt. Her daughters-in-law said that Granny was never seen to hold or cuddle a baby. I suspect she may have had Asperger elements in her personality, but this syndrome was unknown when I was a child. Her father Charles Maclean had a heart attack or a stroke while sitting on his horse. He fell off the horse, was seriously injured, and dragged around for months until he died in 1893 when Granny was only eight. Her mother died of cancer when she was twelve. She and her sister Aunt Olive (Mrs Packe) had a sad childhood, living with people in Oxford during term time, and spending holidays in Ayrshire with "Aunt Adie" who was actually the cook of their official guardian, a certain Mr Parker who was the local Westminster Member of Parliament. Their Christmases were spent with "Aunt Em" and her unmarried sisters in London: the rather severe Honorable Emily Kinnaird, a generous, very Christian and pious (and terribly snobbish) founder of the Young Women's Christian Association (YMCA). [It was at one of Aunt Em's Christmas parties during the 1930s that my parents met when ... they were playing sardines, an intimate form of hide-and-seek.] My Granny's early life was not easy. Life as an orphan being shunted "from pillar to post" is not conducive to developing the warm and cuddly elements of a person's character.

I can illustrate Granny Maclean's toughness with stories told by my father. As a small boy reading in bed, his mother came into the bedroom to wish him good-night. They were holidaying in the Stables at St Helens Cottage, Sir Edward's Victorian holiday home in the Isle of Wight. As she opened the door, the curtain by the open window blew into the flame of the candle beside his bed, and caught fire. Granny crossed the room in two strides and crushed the flame with her bare hands. Of course she was burned, but the fear of fire was so great in those days of candle flames and wooden houses that she never hesitated. Fire, children, is a terrible enemy. Beware of fires, floods and landslides. After she died, her children discovered that Granny Maclean had had one breast surgically removed. Three of her five children were doctors, yet none of them ever knew that she had lost a breast when my father, her first-born, was an infant. She had an abcess, a breast was removed and she told no one. Such toughness is admirable, even if it is not endearing.

If Emma Allsop was surprised at my approach, she was pleased with my enthu-siasm for her Aberdeen FlashMob. She turned to her neighbor, Jean Martin (former RSCDS Chair, then about to be elected President of the Society) and asked, "Who was that?"

Jean had been my teacher during a previous Summer School. She replied: "I think his name is Robin." Amazingly, I was so focused on congratulating Emma about the FlashMob that I had not even noticed Jean Martin sitting beside her. Elements of my Maclean grandmother's character definitely influence my own behavior. My spirituality is less severe than hers, however, and I am very warm and cuddly. I dance, and I allow modest alcohol consumption. That evening in Aberdeen turned out well for me: both Jean and Emma asked me for a dance, the Aberdeen crowd was large and friendly, and the dancing was great.

27

A PAEAN TO THE DANCING OF CARRIE AND THE SCOTTISH STRATHSPEY

THE SENSUAL SANDS OF MORAR

I am attending Washington D.C.'s springtime Snowdrop Ball. I have invited a young lady with beautiful feet for the *Sands of Morar*. She is an excellent dancer. I watched her feet during the previous dance. A beautiful woman must have beautiful feet. As a dancer, it is a lady's feet that I see first (although my father, a dancing scientist, would say it is really the pheromones). If a woman is not a good dancer, I am not interested. Other men may watch the hips, stare at the buttocks, goggle at breasts, but I start with feet and posture. What use is a good posterior without good posture? Movement is everything in a beautiful woman. A good dancer moves with elegance. After the posture, I check out the eyes and the smile. Our dance teachers are always telling us to make eye contact when we dance. I try to make eye contact before I ask a lady to dance .... But only after I have made eye contact with her feet.

I should tell you, children, that good posture is important for good health as well as for looking good. Your stomach and diaphragm muscles need to be kept in good shape to protect your spinal column in middle age and to keep your whole body upright. Isabelle, Roísín: hold yourself like a dancer and you will look beautiful. Liam: hold yourself like a dancer and you will attract admiring glances. My mother always used to tell us that she loved the way my father stood straight and handsome like a soldier—unlike his brother stooping with osteoporosis.

I do not know the young lady I have invited to dance the *Sands of Morar*, but I have noticed that she has perfect timing and perfect posture. It is a joy to surge through our double figure-of-eight and meld perfectly into the reflection reels, touching fingers at every chance. The smoothness of the music, the strength of her steps and the delicate touching of fingers remind me of happy days in the 1960s when I was camping and in love beside the *Sands of Morar* on the west coast of Scotland: a stunning string of white sandy beaches, with amazing views out to the Small Isles of Rum, Eigg, Muck and Canna. The Silver Sands of Morar are spectacular. So are the rainstorms. You need a good tent. We had one, and a good sleeping bag. This is the country of MacDonald and Maclean, my grandmother's part of the world. Dolphins, seals and golden eagles share the Morar beaches that embellish the Arisaig peninsular. We sang to seals in the Sound of Arisaig, and they swam over to listen. Around the corner lies the mysterious and misty Loch Morar, Scotland's deepest loch. On nearby Ardnamurchan you can walk in the Sunart Oakwoods, Scotland's rainforests lush with ferns, mosses and lichens, and (in summertime) with dragonflies, butterflies, bees and birds. And midges. Don't forget the midges! Who can forget the midges? This is a remnant of the ancient oak woods that once covered the Atlantic coastline from Norway to Spain—oak woods with the spice of Highland midges.

From the reflection reel we move into the powerful double-handed turn that will bring us down the center to set, and then cast up to the top. Now for our final movement, the dramatic *tourbillon* that echoes Atlantic storms coming into Morar from the west: those "mists rolling in from the sea" celebrated by Paul Macartney when he lived on the Mull of Kintyre. We twist in the stormy winds, breathe in the sea mist and pull each other around the set, using our strathspey step technique to stretch out as we reach the opposite side, then crossing over on the final bar. I bow thanks to my lady, she smiles her thanks, and we part—another dance, another partner, another pleasure.

SANDS OF MORAR

Strathspey 8x32 bars for 3 couples in a 4-couple longwise set. Devisor: Barry Priddey. RSCDS Book 45.

Celebrating of of the most beautiful spots in Argyle close to Scotland's deepest and most mysterious loch.

Bars 1- 8 : 1s dance Fig of 8 round 2s giving hands when possible;

Bars 9-16 : 1s dance reflection reels of 3 on own sides (1s dance down between 2s to begin);

Bars 17-24 : 1s turn 2H and dance down middle to 3rd place as 2s+3s continue reel and dance down behind 1s, all set and 1s followed by 2s+3s cast up to original places;

Bars 25-32 : 1s+2s dance the Tourbillon:—

25 1s and 2s turn partners 2H ½ way;

26 1M and 2L lead partners on 1 place clockwise to end 1s on Ladies' side and 2s on Men's side;

27-28 1s set to 2s;

29 1s and 2s ½ turn partners 2H;

30 1L and 2M lead partners on 1 place to end 2s in 1st place and 1s in 2nd place;

31-32 2s+1s cross RH to own sides (using long strathspey steps).

"Please take your partners for the final Strathspey, *Minister on the Loch.*" I look around and I see my partner from the *Sands of Morar*. A happy memory. What was her name? Did it begin with K? Three strides bring me to her side: "May I invite you for a second Strathspey? This is one of my all-time favorites." Her smile shows that she also remembers our earlier dance, with pleasure. No words pass. No words are necessary. She places her hand in mine, and we move into the setlines.

The excitement of strathspey lies in the power of the music and the precision of every step. For this dance, its beauty is enhanced by my memory of the Reverend Robert Walker skating on Duddingston Loch, whose portrait inspired this dance. I went again to see Henry Raeburn's painting of "The Skating Minister" last summer in the National Gallery of Scotland in Edinburgh on my way to dance at St Andrews. I never learned to skate, but it looks fun when the Reverend does it, sliding elegantly across an ice-skape shrouded in winter mist. The dance echoes the skating. I cannot dance *Minister on the Loch* without a secret smile for the "The Skating Minister."

Every Scottish ballroom dance begins elegantly with a bow—what the French call *une révérence*—and we step out into the strathspey all-around poussette. This is one of God's (or Miss Milligan's?) greatest gifts to dance. Angels in heaven dance the diamond-shaped all-around strathspey poussette. Some partners require a firmness in their rounded arms to twirl around 180 degrees into a perfect diagonal with the other dancers; angels do it simply with their fingers. Did-it-begin-with-K? generates enough momentum with her own perfect steps that we skate around 180 degrees with barely a tightening of our fingers. Then comes the solo. Eyeball to eyeball with radiant smiles because we are enjoying ourselves so much, we skate down the middle for two, turn for two bars and and return to the top where the second full turn sends us peeling off in opposite directions as my partner twirls away to leave me, casting off my fingers with a last lingering glance ... with the elegance of an ice dancer ... and we sweep into the double figure-of-eight.

Some ladies (especially the older ones) force me to slow my crossing steps, or adjust my angle of dance to let them pass. Did-it-begin-with-K? surges out of the turn and straight across the middle with such exactitude that I know I am free to do the same, as if I were surging across the ice. The excitement of this move comes from the precision: one inch either way and we could both trip and fall heavily. In perfect control of our feet and phrasing, our toes pass inches apart as we cross in the middle and the music brings us flowing round for the repeat cross in the opposite direction.

Facing out, my left hand comes up for second man, and we begin the "barn-door-turns" that will skate us to the bottom of the set. Each turn brings us shoulder-to-shoulder, wrist-to-wrist as we swing around. I seek my partner's eyes. Our eyes lock together and our arms brush on every turn of the barn doors. Our eyes share passion. Our smiles have the radiance of lovers, and—at that precise moment—we are truly in love. Not with each other, of course: did her name begin with K? No, we are in love with dance and music, with the blessings of Scottish Country Dance, and with the perfection of the Scottish strathspey.

THE MINISTER ON THE LOCH

Strathspey 3 x 32 bars for 3 couples in a 3C longwise set. Devisor: Roy Goldring. *24 Graded and Social Dances.*

Inspired by Henry Raeburn's 1790 portrait of the Reverend Robert Walker skating on Duddingston Loch.

Bars 1-8 : 1s & 2s dance the all-around **Diamond Strathspey Poussette:**

1   1L 2M advance with the right foot, giving left shoulder, to finish back-to-back on a diagonal line at right angles to the line joining their original places WHILE 1M 2L (starting with the left foot) advance to face partners;

2   Taking both hands, 1s 2s set to 1M's 2L's right, turning 1⁄6 on the third beat (1M 2L turning on the spot in their own side lines) to finish on the other diagonal line as compared to bar 1;

3   1s 2s set to 1M's 2L's left, finishing on the center line, with permanent smiles and intimate eye contact;

4   2s 1s turn 5⁄6, finishing on the original diagonal having almost exchanged places (from the end of bar 1);

5-6   Repeat bars 2-3, 2s dancing as 1s, 1s as 2s;

7   1s 2s turn 2⁄3, finishing on the center line between original places;

8   Releasing hands, 1s 2s set retiring to places, keeping eye contact and maintaining straight lines.

Bars 9-12 : 1s lead down (nearer hands) and turn both hands;

Bars 13-16 : 1s lead up (nearer hands) and turn both hands, finishing facing out;

Bars 17-24 : 1s and 3s dance double figures of 8 around 2s, 3s crossing up to start;

Bars 25-28 : 1M2M turn by the left 1½ times WHILE 1L2L turn by the right 1½ times;

Bars 29-32 : 1M3M turn by the right 1½ times WHILE 1L3L turn by the left 1½ times.

Footnote : A couple of years later at a contra dance in Glen Echo, Maryland, I noticed an attractive young woman wearing an amazing multi-colored skirt who was a fantastically good contra dancer—one of many, I must say, but her skirt and her dancing and her multiple spinning skills caused her stand out even among the 200 dancers on the floor of Glen Echo, where some of America's best dancers congregate. During one dance we met, and as we balanced the circle, this lady performed a pas de basque.

She may have done so because I was wearing the kilt. Whatever the reason, I knew immediately that she was my strathspey partner of two years earlier. I do not believe she remembered me (why would she?) or the strathspeys we danced together. No matter! The joy is in the dancing. The name of this talented musician and dancer, I discovered, is Carrie. It does not begin with K.

This has anything to do with Carrie or with dancing, kids, but Nonsense is a British literary art form of which Limericks are just one example. The most obvious source of this humor is Edward Lear's *A Book of Nonsense* (1846) although the most famous Nonsense was in Lewis Carrol's *Alice in Wonderland* (1865) and

Through the Looking Glass 1871). I wonder whether Does-it-begin-with-K likes Nonsense. Our favorite nonsensical family limericks:

> *There was a young man from St Bees,*
> *Who was stung on the arm by a wasp,*
> *When asked "does it hurt?"*
> *He replied, "Yes it does,*
> *And I'm glad that it wasn't a hornet.*

> *There was a young man from Japan,*
> *Whose limericks never would scan,*
> *When he was asked why,*
> *He said in reply,*
> *"It's because I always try to cram as many words into the last line as I*
> *   possibly can".*

> *There was a young man from Tyree,*
> *Whose limericks stopped at line three,*
> *Like this one.*

28

BRITTANY'S BILINGUAL BALLS WITH MARTINE AND RAPHAËLLE

omme vous le savez bien, les enfants, je dance en France—oops! Sorry! Wrong language! Your Mamie Michelle and our own children were all born in Brittany. After Africa and America, we came back to live in our Breton house on the cliffs overlooking the English Channel. Now I dance mostly on the southern shores of the English Channel = *La Manche*. Brittany is a good alternative to Scotland: a Celtic nation like a miniature Alba without mountains or haggis, but the bread is as good as Scottish bread and there are plenty of oats. And honey.

The main difference really is that France specializes in *haute cuisine*, while Scotland's expertise is in *oat cuisine*. Oat biscuits, oat cakes, cheeses rolled in oats, haggis, Atholl brews, porridge, or what I usually eat for breakfast: uncooked rolled oats with milk, honey and fruit.

I dance on Tuesdays with *The Scots Bonnet* in St Quay Perros where Martine Guilbert teaches a RSCDS dancing group founded in 1990 by Malcolm MacGregor and his family. We have some excellent dancers trained in St Andrews—the footwork of Marie-Jo and Marie-Laure immediately stands out, the grace of Viviana and Marie-Mad, but our best dancer is Céline Le Bongoat who learned her dancing and phrasing in Edinburgh while working as an *au pair*. Well done, Edinburgh! Then on Fridays I often dance with *Echanges et Savoirs* in Lannion, where people enjoy good Scottish dances in a friendly ceilidh atmosphere. Christiane Louvet and André Squeren choose the dances, everyone there dances for fun and no one worries about perfect footwork. Occasionally Christiane asks me to improve their pas de basque or specific formations, but in a relaxed fashion. I also travel to dance in Rennes, Vannes, Josselin, Lorient, Paris, Lyon and St Andrews as well as Brussels, New York and Richmond. The Cercle Celtique in Rennes has two teachers Françoise Gréau and Anne Christine MacLennan who are great dancers and who deserve a bigger class to teach. How can we tell more people about our dancing and how much fun it is? Maybe the creation of an RSCDS Branche Bretagne will help.

Another of our Brittany teachers, Roland Telle told me: "I share your enthusiasm for dancing, Robin. My only regret is that I was 58 years old before I discovered Scottish dance. Now that I am retired, I travel across Europe as much as I can to attend as many dances as possible." His story reminds me of Julie Duke, a Virginian around the same age as Roland who was sitting in the audience one year as we were dancing in the Richmond Highland Games. This lady's shining eyes told me that she would love to dance: so I stepped down from the stage and persuaded her to come and dance with me. Julie was a "quick learn" who managed to get through her first dance, joined our Tuesday class and became a member of our Silver Thistle Dancers demo team within a couple of years. She is a great person, a valuable member of our group. I often wonder when I dance with Julie, how many other thousands of people out there are missing the joys of dancing with which Julie has been blessed.

At the end of June every year we organize the Scots Bonnet Ball in St Quay, with the wonderful music of Ian Robertson and John Dudley. Dancers join us from around France and across the Channel: a delightful annual migration to a bilingual ball. It helps if we also have a bilingual teacher for our Saturday morning workshop, someone like—in 2018—the amazing Raphaëlle Orgeret from Lyon whose dancing, language and teaching skills are exceptional.

On Friday evening we have a mainly-English language rehearsal, walking through the tricky dances before eating soup for supper. On the Saturday before each dance, we give a briefing in English and in French. Halfway through the ball, we all sit down for dinner (around 10.30 pm with wine included, of course) and then dance until 1am or 2am. What a delightful evening!

Translating is not an easy skill even though you kids have been raised bilingual. Here is a test: try rendering into French the double-meanings of this quote from Eleanor Roosevelt that exposes multiple cultural, colloquial references: "A woman is like a teabag: you never know how strong she is, until you throw her into hot water."

Impossible? No, but can you produce a pithy translation as wittily colloquial as the original? British jokes based on puns, or regional accents, are especially hard to translate. So are Scottish names. When our teachers announce a dance in Brittany, I often need to look over their shoulder at the paper to understand what dance they are trying to pronounce. If I pronounce the name, they are often unable to copy me because adults are strangled by writing. French children repeat my English (or Scottish) words perfectly because they ignore spelling. Children hear sounds; adults imagine written words and sound horrible.

In primary schools I teach a favorite Scottish children's song and French kids produce very clear pronunciation. We introduce other family (granddad, cousin, uncle, auntie) and transport vocabulary (train, plane, boat) as the singing lesson progresses:

> *O you canna shove yer Granny off a bus,*
> *O you canna shove yer Granny off a bus,*
> *O you canna shove yer Granny*
> *'Cos she's yer Mummy's Mummy*
> *O you canna shove yer Granny off a bus.*

Translation can sometimes be needed between Scots and English. The charmingly-named dance *"Twa Sparkling E'en"* (two bright eyes) was heard by some Americans as *"Swashbuckling Iain."* This caused so much hilarity in the Society that one of the RSCDS San Francisco devisors wrote a dance to fit the new name. To many Americans, Scots and English sound like two different languages. To amuse them, I sometimes switch accents. The poems of Robert Burns, my lovely grandchildren, will give you hours of reading pleasure: whether it be *To a Mouse* (amusing), *My Love is Like a Red Red Rose* (romantic), *Tam O'Shanter* (great story-telling) or *Address to a Haggis* (gastronomic and hilarious). But you will need a glossary to understand some of the words Burns uses in the La'land (Scottish Lowlands) vernacular, which is largely based on old German brought in by Saxon tribes fifteen hundred years ago. If you pronounce the old Glasgow slogan that is used to see if a man is drunk, you can hear the German: "It's a braw bricht moonlicht nicht tonicht a'richt." If you want to hear it in the Glaswegain original, listen to Sir Harry Lauder, that great music hall performer, sing the song

> A Wee Deoch an Doris.
> *There's a good old Scottish custom that has stood the test o'time,*
> *It's a custom that's been carried out in every land and clime.*
> *When brother Scots are gathered, it's aye the usual thing,*
> *Just before we say good night, we fill our cups and sing...*
> Chorus
> *Just a wee deoch an doris, just a wee drop, that's all.*
> *Just a wee deoch an doris afore ye gang awa.*
> *There's a wee wifie waitin' in a wee but an ben.*
> *If you can say, "It's a braw bricht moonlicht nicht",*
> *Then yer a'richt, ye ken.*
> *Now I like a man that is a man; a man that's straight and fair.*
> *The kind of man that will and can, in all things do his share.*
> *Och, I like a man a jolly man, the kind of man, you know,*
> *The chap that slaps your back and says, "Jock, just before ye go..."*

Glossary
aye: always
but and ben: a two-roomed cottage
deoch an doris: a drink at the door (Gaelic)
gang: go
ken: know

Back to dancing! I met *Swashbuckling Iain* for the first time in Virginia shortly after the 2001 demolition of the Twin Towers in New York. My friend Bern Runk and I devised a third iteration of the dance: from *Eyes* to *Iain* to a version we called *Bonny Ben Laden*, to be danced by women in veils and men with their knives drawn: the *sgian dhu* (black knife) we wear in our stockings. I tell curious Americans that my knife is for saving Scottish virgins from dangerous dragons. Few men actually dance with a knife in their stocking. I may follow the example of my friend Jay Andrews who prefers a black bottle opener: more useful now that dragons are almost extinct (and virgins too). My own *sgian dhu* was confiscated when I visited the Scottish Parliament building in Edinburgh: apparently the not-very-Scots police of Holyrood are promoting plastic *sgian dhu*. They say all fixed blade knives are now forbidden, which was news to me. An insolent young police officer threatened to arrest me, a 70-year-old man, for wearing a traditional piece of Scottish dress that I had handed to security asking to collect it on my way out. Our satirical dance would look silly waving plastic knives, but if you master the moves of *Swashbuckling Iain*, you can easily envisage a man with his *sgian dhu* leading his partner, especially in an Arab or Afghan culture where the woman always walks behind her man. We are not approving that habit: just noticing that *Swashbuckling Iain* follows the pattern.

SWASHBUCKLING IAIN

Jig 8 x 32 bars for 2 couples in a 4-couple longwise set. Devisor: Carolyn Hunt. San Francisco Collection 2.

Inspired by an American misunderstanding of the meaning of the dance *Twa Sparkling E'en*.

Bars 1- 8 : 1st Man dances reel of 3 on opposite side with 1st Lady and 2nd Lady (Right Sh to 2L);

Bars 9-16 : 1M followed by partner dances Tandem reel of 3 across with 2s (RSh to 2M);

Bars 17-24 : 1M followed by partner dances down the middle and leads her up to top;

bars 25-32 : 1s+2s dance the Allemande.

Here is my interpretation in Franglais of Iain swashbuckling his way across the dance floor with a touch of Frenglish—the languages of French Scottish dancing. "Feerst we 'ave cross-over reels en miroir, on ze opposite side, épaule droite to beegeen. On bar neuf, ze first coopole weel dance un reel en tandem avec le second coopole. First coopole zen zey dance down ze meedell, revenir en première position, et ze first two coopoles—premier et deuxième coopoles—dansent une Allemande."

Somehow our bilingual ball works. There are dancers who speak both languages and there are people who know the dances. A few people like me—and you, my lovely bilingual grandchildren, will come into this category—understand not only French, but also Frenglish and Franglais (though I would not want you to speak either). The teaching walk-through on the Friday night allows us to review the dances: we walk-though the more difficult dances, practice strange formations like the Targe or the Espagnol (both pretty easy) or the slightly more difficult Tourbillon, and make people feel confident. We avoid putting into our Breton program tricky formations like the Tournée and the Spurtle that terrify intermediate dancers. The dances on our program have to be interesting and varied, but not over-challenging—to illustrate these rules, our excellent 2018 ball program is included at the end of this book. We allow one or two couples to dance each dance on the Friday evening, and this should (it SHOULD) prepare everyone to dance well on Saturday evening.

Saturday morning our visiting teacher runs workshops, improving dance technique for some people. Raphaëlle was asked to teach in English, which she did. A few French people were miffed; but Martine argues that we should emphasise English because this (or Frenglish) is the language of Scottish dance. We rest on the Saturday afternoon before dressing for the ball. Quite a few Brits come over and spend a whole week in Brittany, reserving a hotel or camping or staying with dancing friends. For our 2018 ball, my friend Michel Monfroy drove up all the way from Grenoble in his camping van to enjoy our dance and spend a couple of weeks with his wife Aline traveling around Brittany, visiting Morgat beach and watching the Tour de France arrive in Quimper. We spent one gorgeous day kayaking along the coast in the Breton sunshine.

By Saturday evening we are rested and ready for the Scots Bonnet St Quay Ball. Martine and Sylvie are the compères, briefing the dances in two languages as quickly as possible so that the band does not get stiff, or bored. There is always someone who is too old, too deaf or too monolingual to understand the briefing, but somebody else in their set can usually pull them through the dance.

The thing that stands out for the Brits is our sit-down dinner for 60 dancers. The food and wine are always wonderful, and we usually have far too much food. One year a lady ordered 60 portions of cold meats from the *charcuterie*. We received enough meat to feed four hungry rugby club teams, or 150 Scottish dancers. Dancers do not eat like 20-year-old rugby players. Some of us are over 70, more than half of us are women, and we all need to lose some weight .... There was so much food left over that we were begging Scots Bonnet members to take meat home to freeze. The meal and wine and cider are, of course, always fabulous. Foreigners adore the fact that the French are happy to finish a dance at 2am or even 3am in the morning, so long as the meal is not rushed. We provide plenty of French cheese and fruit, and wonderful home-made desserts. After the ball, we have all Sunday afternoon to clean the hall and so we can sleep until lunch—which is eaten in a restaurant on the Sunday, after Huguette (our lovely tour-specialist) has led visitors on a walk around a piece of the coast with a jewel of a chapel or some pre-historic standing stones to admire. Brittany guarantees a weekend of fun and good dancing.

A delightful twinning arrangement has evolved over the past 20 years between St Quay Perros and the town of Bridport, in Dorset. Every second year, *The Scots Bonnet* members travel to dance in Bridport, and the following year we receive a number of dancers from Bridport to our annual ball in Brittany. On this last weekend of June, they are joined by dancers from Cornwall, Devon and Dorset, from Guernsey and Jersey, and from all over France. One year we had visiting dancers from Dunblane in Scotland, and Lübeck in Germany; another year we had people from Grenoble in the Alps, Rome in Italy, and Prague in the Czech Republic. We also have occasional visitors from America: Celia and Bob Belton came one year to dance at our bilingual ball in Brittany; followed by Linda and Alasdair MacDonald the next year. All are welcome!

I was excited that the 2017 Bridport trip provided my first visit to Dorset. Twinning breeds friendships. I stayed with Caroline and Philip in a 200-year-old house with a very special walled garden. Philip took me to his croquet club where he thrashed me (at croquet), and then we toured long narrow lanes where the workers of Bridport used to twist ropes thick and thin for fishermen sailing to Iceland and for the naval ships that defeated Napoleon Bonaparte, the man who wanted to conquer Europe. Boney was defeated by the Iron Duke of Wellington in 1812 at the Battle of Waterloo, outside Brussels.

My lovely grandchildren, war has blighted Europe for centuries and I should tell you that your English-Scottish-Breton-French-Irish heritage symbolizes a recent period of peace in Europe, largely thanks to the existence of the European Union and the United Nations. Like the UN, the EU was created between former enemies in order to avoid a Third World War started by Europeans. Our political and maritime history has been one long story of conflict. The reason that Admiral Lord Nelson stands atop a column in Trafalgar Square, in London, is that in 1805 he defeated the French fleet at Trafalgar (off Portugal) and spoiled Napoleon's plan to invade Britain. You will visit his flagship one day in Portsmouth Harbour. Your grandmother and I took your father to visit HMS Victory when he was ten years old and Edward discovered that the ship's boys who carried the gunpowder for the cannons, the "powder monkeys" as they were called, were the same age as him. It came as quite a shock, a wake-up call at the age of ten about the grim reality of war. French and British and American cultures glorify war, but soldiers and sailors know that war is dirt and guns, blood and bad food, pain and death.

While this was my first visit, Martine and Sylvie were visiting their friends in Bridport for the 30th time. Sylvie brought her whole family. Caroline Templeton generously invites people every year in mid-July to her beautiful Garden Dance and many of our Breton dancers over the past twenty years have crossed the Channel for this charming event. Dorset hospitality is lavish. Within a few hours I felt I had known Caroline and Philip for years, and they will surely visit us in the future in Brittany. Caroline is the author of a great strathspey called the Lannion Link, which she wrote for her Breton friends and which has entered our regular dance schedule.

THE LANNION LINK

Strathspey 4 x 40 bars for 4 couples all dancing in a longways set. Devisor: Caroline Morgan-Smith.

Composed for dancing friends in Lannion who are a part of the Dance Twinning with Bridport in Dorset.

Suggested music: "The Ship of Grace" (Highlander Music, Scottish Dances Volume 4) BSD CD # 13/6

Bars 1-8 : 1s cast to foot, followed by 2s, 3s and 4s…. As each couple reaches the foot of the set they take promenade hold and dance up the center with 1s and 3s casting down while 2s and 4s dance up.

Order: 2, 1, 4, 3 2s need to curve back on themselves to join the Right Hands Across;

Bars 9-16 : 2s & 1s, 4s & 3s RHA and LHA. Finish with 1s & 4s back to back facing their corners diagonally in cross formation (as in a saltire, or St Andrews cross);

Bars 17-24 : Full double diagonal reels of four, beginning with center couples passing their corners right shoulder and turning towards the middle (briefly touch left hands in the center to cross) and then pass right shoulders again while other couples cross the center with a brief half wheel. This is quite fast, and should be timed carefully;

Bars 25–32 : 1s & 4s (in center) turn their corners Both Hands for 4 bars, then all 4 couples turn their partner BH for 4 bars to finish in sidelines;

Bars 33–40 : Leaving the 2s in top place 1s, 3s & 4s dance the Knot. Repeat three times.

Three couple Knot

1-2 1s, 2s and 3s turn partner half-way by the right hand to finish facing down in allemande hold.

3-5 3s, followed by 2s and 1s, curve round and dance up the women's side, releasing RH on bar 5.

6 Men dance up, passing their partners in front of them with LH, and Women take a long step towards the center.

7-8 All continue to turn by the left hand to own side: all 3 couples turn in the middle of the set.

Dance Note:

Bars 17-24 Dancers merely touch hands in the middle as they cross, and should not to allow this move to slow their phrasing in the reels. Sometimes people arrive late in position for the following turn with both hands, which they are then forced to rush.

29

CLEVER REELS FOR LEGO LOVERS, ENGINEERS AND FOR SYLVIE

As I watch you both playing with ever-more-complicated Lego constructions, dearest Liam and Isabelle, I wonder whether you may become mechanical engineers like your other grandfather who spent his distinguished career with the Ford Motor Company at Dagenham; or maybe computer wizards like Roísín's dad? I cannot hold a screwdriver straight, but I admire your embryonic technical skills. You will love the clever engineering dances like *Shiftin' Bobbins*, which imitates the Spinning Jenny and the Flying Shuttle machines that revolutionized thread and cloth production during the Industrial Revolution, and *Nottingham Lace* which cleverly reproduces on the dance floor the intricate patterns of lace-making.

Many engineers enjoy Scottish dancing because of its logical structures and interweaving patterns; but if they impose too much rational logic they can miss the artistic joy of dancing. Everyone has their own way of seeing things, and engineers have their own perceptions. For example: to the optimist, the glass is half-full, while to the pessimist, the glass is half-empty; but for an engineer, the glass is twice as big as it needs to be. Not true in dancing: I always wish that a great dance would go on longer. And longer. And since it was so much fun, why should we not dance it again now at once? When Michael and his wife Su from Kendall bade me "Farewell" in St Andrews, they said they had never met anyone dance with as much *joie de vivre* as me.

SHIFTIN' BOBBINS

Reel 8 x 32 bars for 3 couples in a 4-couple longwise set. Devisor: Roy Clowes. Ormskirk Scottish Dances. Inspired by the machines that transformed textile manufacturing during the industrial revolution.

Bars 1-2 : 1s cross down to face out between corners, while 2s step up on 1-2;

Bars 3-4 : 2s 1s 3s set on the sides, 1s have their backs to each other;

Bars 5-8 : 1s cast up, meet, dance down nearer hands joined and offer your free hand for...;

Bars 9-12 : 1L 2M 3M right hands across WHILE 1M 2L 3L left hands across, on the sides;

Bars 13-16 : 1s from second place, followed by 2s 3s, dance down;

Bars 17-20 : 3s, followed by 2s 1s, dance up and cast, 2s end in 1st place, 3s finish in 3rd place;

Bars 21-24 : 2M 1L 3M left hands across WHILE 2L 1M 3L right hands across, on the sides;

Bars 25-28 : 1s dance to the top and cast;

Bars 29-32 : 1s half figures of 8 round 2s, finishing 2s 1s 3s, ready to repeat the dance.

Dance Notes

Bars 1-2 2s must be awake to move up on bar 1.

Bars 13-20 Take nearer hands to dance down and up: a right-hand-in-right lead works less well.

Bars 20 & 24 3s must complete their moves to 3rd place before and after the hands across, allowing room for 1s to pass through second place on bar 28 and to finish there on bar 32.

My father and I always adored this *Shiftin' Bobbins* reel and the way in which it fits together—not just with the wonderful music, which is a distinctive feature of every great dance, but also the clever movements by which the wheels interlock in a design that mirrors machinery. We loved the artistry, for neither of us was the least bit mechanical. My principal tool is the hammer.

If you do become engineers, dearest kids, you will have to put up with engineering jokes.

- What's the difference between Mechanical Engineers and Civil Engineers? Mechanical Engineers build weapons; Civil Engineers build targets.
- The job of a Design Engineer is to make things difficult for the manufacturer, and impossible for the service agents.... And so on. The jokes never stop. Laughter is one important aspect of *joie de vivre*, helping to deliver the greatest happiness to the greatest number of people.

One way to deliver happiness is by dancing in places where people appreciate you: like fund-raisers, schools, or homes for elderly or handicapped people. These can be very informal demos. For my German dance group in America I have done *Schuhplattl* demos alone with an Oompapa band, or with just one other costumed partner. Scots prefer to hunt in packs: but instead of always choosing 3-couple or 4-couple dances, I favor 4-person dances for demos because they are so clear to watch. It can be difficult for the audience to see what is going on when there are eight dancers, especially on a raised stage. It is easier to see, follow and identify four individual dancers. There are plenty of dances around, and Sylvie Le Charpentier has a collection of 4-person dances for demos. Engineers love their clarity. One demo we presented this year was a delightful 5-person strathspey called *Dragonflies*, which translates into my very favorite French word: *Libellules*. Feel how the word rolls off your tongue. The dance moves from figures of eight through a circle to set-and-link, and finally into half diagonal rights-and-lefts twice. Two of our demo dancers, Brigitte Génie and Gaël Jegu, had been dancing for less than a year when Sylvie's team presented our *Libellules*.

DRAGONFLIES

Strathspey 5 x 32 bars for 5 dancers. Devisor: Jane Lataille.

Published by the Santa Fe Scottish Country Dancers in their book *Always Enough to Dance*.

Music: Susie Petrov's 5x32S set from her vinyl album *Hold the Lass Till I get Her* or any good strathspey.

We danced this *Libellules* (in France) at the *Forum des Associations* in St Quay Perros in September 2018.

Stand in two lines as a Trapezoid formation: 2 in one line (dancers 1 & 2) opposite 3 dancers (3, 4, 5) so that dancers 1 & 2 face the spaces created between 3, 4 & 5.

---

1   2

5   4   3

Bars 1-8 : 1 & 2 dance a left shoulder figure of eight around two people, going to their left;

Bars 9-16 : Circle (10 hands) round and back;

Bars 17-24 : Set and link twice: 1 & 2 back in orginal places, while others finish in line 354;

Bars 25-32 : 1 & 2 dance half R&L going to their right;

Bars 33-40 : 4 & 5 (now in the places of 1 & 2) now dance half R&L going to their left.

The dancers finish:

---

3   1

2   5   4

This little dance is a neat feat of dance engineering, as you can tell. Take no notice of mockery. It is important to keep a sense of humor and the capacity to make fun of yourself. Whatever your profession, that will help you get through life. Engineering jokes are less vicious than the lawyer jokes your parents have to put up with. Lawyers have been mocked at least since the days of the ancient Greeks. Example: A bad lawyer can let a case drag out for several years. A good lawyer can make it last even longer.

Or this one: A lawyer dies and goes to Heaven. "There must be some mistake," the lawyer argues. "I'm too young to die. I'm only 55." "Fifty-five?" says Saint Peter. "No, according to our calculations, you're 82." "How'd you get that?" the lawyer asks. Answers St. Peter, "We added up your time sheets."

What is our family attitude to lawyers? My dad's advice was: "The law benefits .... lawyers." My great grandfather Sir Edward Bagnall Poulton was a famous lecturer in his day, known for building wonderful wooden models to illustrate his natural science lectures: for example he built an articulated model illustrating the flight of the albatross. 130 years later a copy of his wooden model flies in the sitting room of our friend David Cameron Kirk. EBP delivered the 1915 Romanes Lecture on the theme of science and government. He argued—as many argue still today—that too many ministers are lawyers or political scientists, and too few are scientists who might understand certain issues better than the average politician. He also observed, with the deepest sorrow, that one of his nephews had decided to take up the law. "As a scientist, I have spent all my life trying to discover the truth. As a lawyer, my nephew will spend his whole career trying to conceal it." Very witty.

Winston Churchill is the man whose pen and wit fashioned many of the best sayings in the English language: "Lawyers occasionally stumble over the truth, but most of them pick themselves up and hurry off as if nothing had happened."

Industry, engineering and the law are parts of our culture, like literature, music and dancing. I want to place Scottish and other dance traditions like Morris, Irish or Breton dancing into their broader cultural context. When I describe Scottish dance, I am also describing 3000 years of culture and music. You told me, Liam, that the world's most famous dance is *La Macarena*; and you gave an amusing demonstration of *La Macarena* while your multi-talented father sang in Spanish the song for your dance. It was fun. You were very entertaining: but was it really any more than aerobics, like the *Zumba*? Is *La Macarena* any more popular than the *Chicken Dance* (*La marche des canards* in French)? We dance the *Chicken Dance* every hour during Oktoberfest celebrations, but no one would claim that the *Chicken Dance* is a part of German culture. Line dancing is popular, often called *Disco Dancing* in France, but it is an import. I can enjoy *The Electric Slide* during an evening fund-raiser for our local school, but it is not a part of Breton or French culture. In France, American line dancing is also called *Country*. At the 2018 French Film Festival in Richmond, one short film presented *Country* in Toulouse and astonished Americans screamed with laughter as hundreds of French people danced their night away dressed as cowboys. The German dance *Anton aus Tyrol* is the equivalent of *La Macarena*: "*Ich bin so schön, ich bin so toll, ich bin der Anton aus Tirol*" is a fun line dance, but no one would call it a German cultural icon. I came home from Tübingen in 1965 carrying a 45-rpm vinyl record of the new dance craze *Let Kiss*, which I introduced to family parties. The fad lasted a couple of years. How about the *Lindy-Hop* rage introduced to Britain by American GIs after the war? Who remembers it now? The TV bonanzas *Strictly Come Dancing* (UK) and *Dancing With The Stars* (USA) at least combine traditional forms of European dance with their showbiz razzmatazz. What I personally love are the historical roots of dance. Waltz is a "new" dance from this point of view. Scottish and Irish and Breton dancing have lived and developed during more than 1000 years.

Will you become engineers? Your father tells me that now in 2018 you have a long-term plan for Isabelle (aged seven) to become a full-time writer, while her brother Liam (now ten) will be an environmental engineer earning enough money to keep his sister in comfort and provide a three-story house for her to live in: Isabelle and her family on the top floor, Liam and his family on the middle floor, with communal cooking and eating facilities on the ground floor. Apparently you have chosen Toulouse in France, because it has a warm climate. A great plan. I won't be around to see if it happens, but I can warn you about families. Once you fall in love, communal living in Toulouse may not suit your partners.

Toulouse was known for lace making, like Nottingham in England. One of the favorite dances of our Lannion dance group *Echanges et Savoirs* is *Nottingham Lace*, a reel danced in a square set. It is not difficult (if this dance was really difficult, the Lannion group would never be able to dance it), but its patterns do seem as complex as lace making.

NOTTINGHAM LACE

Reel 96 bars 4-couple repeat with all couples dancing in a 4C square set. Devisor: Jenny Bradley.

This dance reproduces the patterns and mechanisms of Nottingham craftswomen making lace.

Bars 1-24 : Chorus.

1-4   All half grand chain;

5-6   All set to partners;

7-8   All turn by the right ¾;

9-10 Ladies left hands across halfway WHILE Men dance clockwise one place round the set;

11-12 All turn second corner (on partner's side) by the right halfway;

13-14 Men left hands across halfway WHILE Ladies dance clockwise one place round the set;

15-16 All turn partner by the right halfway;

17-24 Repeat previous 8 bars, finishing in original places.

Bars 25-26 : 1L3M 1M3L cross by the right up and down;

Bars 27-28 : 1M 3L cast to the left WHILE 1L 3M cast to the right;

Bars 29-30 : 3L1M cross by the right up and down behind 2s WHILE 3M1L cross by the right up and down behind 4s (finishing in lines with 1L4M4L3M on the Man's side facing 1M2L2M3L);

Bars 31-32 : All set on the sides;

Bars 33-36 : All advance and retire;

Bars 37-40 : 1s4M2L 2M4L3s four hands round to the left (finishing in lines across, 2L1M1L4M facing down, 2M3L3M4L facing up);

Bars 41-44 : All advance and retire;

Bars 45-48 : All eight hands round to the left halfway, finishing opposite original places in the square set.

Bars 49-72 : Repeat bars 25-48 with 2s 3s 4s 1s dancing as 1s 2s 3s 4s, respectively (and treating the 2s position at bar 48 as the "top" of the set), all finishing in original places.

Bars 73-96 : Repeat chorus, bars 1-24.

Dance Notes: The secret is remembering where in the set you are. Tell dancers to look and see where they are in the hall (for example, are they next to a window?) so that they can hurry back to place if they lose their way.

Square sets are popular because they are different. Different from what? Different from the *contredanse* longways sets used by French dance masters. Whereas many of the dances in the early RSCDS dance books are relatively simple and relatively similar, over the past fifty years devisors like Hugh Foss, John Dewry, Roy Goldring, Derek Haynes and Moira Turner (to name only these five) have been creating new formations and new dance structures which modern RSCDS members find more exciting. There are more than 15,000 dances in the Scottish repertoire. Let us say that Scottish country dances have been re-engineered. The Strathspey Server and the Scottish Dance Dictionary show hundreds of new dances that require more concentration that the dances of Mary Stuart's day. Some of the most popular recent dances also involve changing the music, so that dancers perform a medley.

30

MACDONALD OF KEPPOCH, MACLEAN OF DUART AND CATHERINE CAMPBELL

F or the St Quay Ball in 2018, we had to master an amusing medley called MacDonald of Keppoch (a place name), written by Chris Ronald who dances with your aunt Catherine Leïla in New York. He knows several of my American dance friends, and many UN friends with whom he and I have worked on peace and disarmament and economic development over the years. Chris Ronald (originally Clan MacRanald from Islay—a Sept, or branch of Clan Donald) like all the MacDonalds, claims a theoretical descent from their common ancestor Somerled, a Viking chief. Sommerled's grandson Donald gave Clan Donald / Ronald their name.

DNA analyses show that 76% of the MacDonald chieftaincy family members are descended from this single male ancestor. Somerled was the 12th century Norwegian Lord of the Isles. Anyhow, that is the legend. Roísín's father and Gaelic scholar Professor Michael Newton offered me the following comment: "Somerled / Somhairle had Norse ancestry, but he was culturally a Gael. He and his progeny wanted to be counted as Gaels culturally. Ethnicity is not the same thing as genealogy / genetics, and all manner of historical errors and political evils result from this confusion."

I agree with Michael that Ethnicity is a very doubtful concept. It is our education, our language and our dialect / accent, our parents and our culture (music, dance, beliefs, fears, loves, stories) that compose the most important parts of our identity. Stuff like genes, blood, skin, eyes, hair and religion make up a very small part of who we are. We all have multiple identities. I consider myself a Scot, a Brit, a European and a West African all at the same time (or perhaps at different times, depending on where I am); I have the identities of grandson, son, brother, nephew, cousin, husband, father, grandfather, dancer, entertainer, manager, researcher, writer, teacher, peace worker, rural economist and so forth. When asked on United States government on forms for my "ethnicity" I usually decline to answer. For religion, I write "monotheist."

One of the major events of Scottish history was the Massacre of Glencoe in 1692. In Scotland that seems like yesterday. At 5am on 13th February 1692, Campbell troops paid by the king, who were quartered and had been fed and housed by the MacDonald clan for the past twelve days, received orders from London to put to the sword all the Glencoe MacDonalds under the age of seventy. They treacherously killed their hosts while they slept. This gave rise to the Great Feud: and in this Great Feud the Macleans (who are descended from Gillean of the Battle-Axe) stand with Clan MacDonald. This means, children, that you should never marry a Campbell.

This advice is confirmed by my favorite Maclean story, that I call *The Lady Rock*. Lachlan Cattanach Maclean, 11th Chief of the Clan Maclean, had a very tiresome wife. He was called Cattanach because his mother was from Clan Chattan; but it also means "rough and hairy" and so he was known on Mull as Lachlan the Shaggy (1465–1523). Cattanach was driven to distraction by the shrill nagging of his wife Catherine Campbell, sister of the 4th Earl of Argyll. Her cooking was so terrible, people said she was trying to poison her husband. One day when he could stand her no longer, the Chieftain took action. Lachlan the Shaggy tied his wife to a chair, placed her in a skiff, rowed out into the middle of the Sound of Mull and marooned her on a rock that is visible at low tide but disappears at high tide. Our gallant Chieftain then rowed back to Duart Castle, broke open a flagon of whisky (*uisge beatha* = the water of life in Gaelic) and settled himself on the balcony to enjoy the sight of his nagging wife disappearing slowly beneath the rising tide. Up came the tide and Catherine Campbell's feet were delightfully covered by water. The tide rose to her calves .... then her knees .... Did she dance? Yes, the lady danced. She danced the best jig she could manage while still tied to her chair on the Lady Rock.

Unfortunately a sea mist came down and the Lady Rock disappeared from sight. Lachlan did not see a fisherman pass by, who heard the lady's cries and rescued her. Lady Catherine landed on the mainland and rejoined her brother in Inverary Castle. Revenge was taken when Lachlan Maclean was visiting Edinburgh in November 1523. He was stabbed (*dirked* in his hotel bed while he slept) by his brother-in-law Sir John Campbell of Calder, a treacherous murder that confirms you should never trust a Campbell (my story's conclusion in Scotland). For the French I change the ending by telling them that the moral of the story is: "You should never trust .... a woman." This never fails to raise laughter.

I wear my Maclean dress tartan when I am telling this story or when demonstrating dances on stage, because the red sparkles between the mainly greenish tartans of other dancers. I notice in photographs that the famous Scottish actor Sir

Sean Connery also wears the Maclean of Duart tartan, although he favors the dark green hunting version that my brother Rory prefers. Like our grandmother, Connery's mother Effie was a Maclean of Duart from the Isle of Mull, although she was born in Fife. She was a Gaelic speaker, and obviously a remarkable lady who transmitted human qualities of determination and creativity to her son Thomas Sean Connery. Several times when I was working in Cambodia, I was asked by young women serving me dinner or drinks in big hotels: "Are you a famous film actor?" In order not to disappoint the girl looking at me with excited admiration, I always placed my finger over my lips and whispered, "Sssshhh!"

It must be Sean Connery with whom they were confusing me: not because we share Maclean DNA (which apparently we do) but because to Asians in Indochina, all ugly *barang* with long noses and big nostrils look much the same. When we also wear gray beards, ugly white *barang* are indistinguishable one from the other. Except for our voices. I have a deep baritone voice that sometimes reveals a Scottish lilt, while Sir Sean Connery—on Cambodian dubbed films—talks in squeaky tonal high-pitched accents that make me laugh out loud. I expect Connery laughs too, every time he receives a royalty check.

In New York I enjoyed dancing the MacDonald of Keppoch medley with my daughter Catherine Leïla (a great dancer whom you kids call *Tata* in the French jargon for an Auntie). Chris Ronald's dance starts with strathspey and switches to reel time: two rounds of each. Engineers enjoy the way in which the vertical and horizontal reel directions interact. I discovered when I took a bus from Richmond to New York to visit Catherine Leïla and Pierre Claude that the bus put me down just three blocks from the church where Leïla dances. Since I had 90 minutes to spare, I found the church and a delicious Thai curry to eat close-by. The church sits on a street corner beside a hideous chaos of noisy freeways and concrete highways filled with grinding traffic and lines of honking buses. It is the perfect location: stepping into the peaceful church was like walking out of New York Hell into Paradise. A paradise of Scottish dancing.

MACDONALD OF KEPPOCH

Medley (S64+R64) for 4 couples in a Square Set. Devisor: Chris Ronald in New York. RSCDS Book 49.

Written to honor the Clan and Sept from which the devisor is descended.

Bars 1-6 : 1s+3s dance 6 bars of Rights & Lefts (Men end with polite turns) to finish in center Back-to-Back with partner facing side couples across the set (1L+2L, 1M+4M, 3L+4L, 3M+2M);

Bars 7-8 : All set;

Bars 9-16 : Reels of 4 across. Dancing couples 1 & 3 finish in line up/down with Ladies facing each other in the middle of the set, 1st Man facing down, 3rd Man facing up;

Bars 17-24 : Reel of 4 in the middle of the set (1L+3L pass RSh) all pass LSh at ends, RSh in middle. Finish in original places facing partners;

Bars 25-30 : All set for 2 bars, all turn partner RH 1¼ into promenade hold for 4 bars; and

Bars 31-32 : All dance 1 place anticlockwise.

Repeat from new positions in Strathspey then twice in Reel time back to original places.

Dance Note: On bar 16, 2s and 4s must be back in place horizontally across the set, as the 1s and 3s take up positions vertically up-and-down the set with the Ladies in the middle ready to pass right shoulders. This combination is the high point of the dance.

So MacDonald of Keppoch begins with 6 bars (not 8 bars) of rights and lefts that end with a fun-turn, placing partners back-to-back for setting to the other couples in lines across the set on bars 7-8. Two parallel horizontal reels of four across the dance are then followed (a neat and clever idea) by a vertical reel for 1s and 3s, who dance their reel up-and-down the dance to finish in their original places. All couples then set for two bars, turn their partners for four bars with the right hand, and promenade one place counter-clockwise, ready for the original 2s and 4s to dance as 1s and 3s. Once you have the pattern, even beginners can enjoy MacDonald of Keppoch, dancing twice in strathspey time, and twice in reel time; and the change of tempo gives everyone a delightful opportunity to "Hooch" as the reel music begins. I never miss the opportunity to let my excitement show with a "Hooch."

When I am not around, I hear that many of my dancing friends miss my whoops of delight! My father called me a "noisy dancer" but I want my grandchildren to know that noisy dancing is OK in Scotland. A loud "Hooch" is an excellent way to wake up partners who seem to be day-dreaming, without having to humiliate anybody or call out their name. Very often, just one "Hooch" or one word will keep a set straight. If I say the word "Reel" at the right moment, I know that we will all be dancing the same movement. Especially in demos, the whole set feels stronger when there is a guiding word to keep them strong.

In our Lannion group where some of the dancers tend to lose their way on turns, we often dance *A Trip to Bavaria*. This dance—another of my father's favorites—has a central wheel-movement that makes it a great demo dance. We use it in France for demos because it is easy for the audience to see the repeated wheeling patterns. As the audience watches, the wheels look interesting. *A Trip to Bavaria* has turns in the middle and on the corners with everyone dancing all the time, and we all love the music. The four dancers in the middle dance a right-hand half wheel, which places them in front of a person on the corner who has just crossed the set with their right hand. This leaves everyone's left hand free, and all dancers do a left hand corner half-turn which puts the original corners into the middle for the next right hand wheel. Keep wheeling and crossing until you get back to place. The dance finishes with a double lacing figure "set and cross" that brings first couple to the bottom on opposite sides. All then advance and retire, the dancing couple in 4th place switching with a sharp two-hand turn on bar 31: an exciting piece of trickery with which to end each round of this fine dance.

While this dance is easy enough for any demo team, I know from experience that the dance works best for beginners in Lannion if I call out "Droite, Gauche" every two bars, to remind dancers to use their right hand and then their left. If one confused dancer misses a change or stops, the whole dance can break down. Without this reminder, there is always the risk that a dancer will stop or hesitate, and put everyone out of phase with the music. Such calling is not RSCDS standard practice, but it works. It is the fruit of experience.

A TRIP TO BAVARIA

Reel 4 x 32 bars for 4 couples in a 4C set, all dancing. Devisor: James MacGregor-Brown. Guide To SCD (ex-Collins Pocket Reference Book). Inspired by the large number of Scottish dancers in Bavaria and in Germany.

1-2 : 1s cross and 4s cross RH, WHILE 2s and 3s turn right hands across halfway;

3-4 : 2s and 3s s half-turn corners by the left, finishing 3s1s4s2s, all on opposite sides;

5-8 : repeat bars 1-4 from new places, those in 1st place dancing as 1s and so on, finishing 4s3s2s1s;

9-16 : repeat bars 1-8 from new places, those in 1st place dancing as 1s and so on, finishing in original places, 1s facing down, 2s facing up;

17-18 : 1M and 2M also 1L and 2L set;

19-20 : 1s cross down to face 3s;

21-22 : 1L and 3M also 1M and 3L set;

23-24 : 1s cross down to face 4s;

25-26 : 1M and 4M also 1L and 4L set;

27-28 : 1s cross down to 4th place on opposite sides;

29-32 : 2s3s4s advance and retire WHILE 1s advance, turn both hands and retire, finishing 2s3s4s1s.

Dance Notes

All dancers are using Right hands then Left hands alternately and non-stop for bars 1-16.

1-16 Beware of going too far in the right hands across halfway; if you pull the left shoulder back slightly at the end to face the corner up or down, everyone "theoretically" can turn on the side, although in reality it is a corner turn that finishes with both on the side. 2nd and 3rd couples must end in the corner positions, in order IMMEDIATELY to cross RH, while the 1s and 4s are now completing their RH across in the middle. The most common mistake is the people in the center reach the corner position, and and fail to cross RH.

19-20 1s should take right hands while crossing down.

23-24 1s should take left hands while crossing down.

27-28 1s should take right hands while crossing down.

29-32 The first step of the advance should be long so that the 1s can more easily turn both hands on bar 30; the first step of the retire on bar 31 should be short so that the 1s can more easily join in.

We used this dance as a demo in Josselin one year, a stunningly beautiful

Breton medieval city where Dr Penny Gibbs invited a bunch of Brittany's Scottish dancers to participate in a British weekend. Your Mamie refused to attend, children, because she doesn't like the way certain British expats behave overseas. The demo went well until two English DJs made schoolboy jokes about kilts and Scots, showing your grandmother's prescience—her foreknowledge of natural English coarseness proved that the English are less amusing than the Scots.

Some of the ladies in our dance group became angry about English stupidity concerning "true Scotsmen" and "flying kilts"—rightly so; but I know from experience there is no point in talking to deaf people, or to stupid people who are not listening. I went along with my angry ladies and, to take the sting out of this confrontation, I produced a couple of old jokes that you may also use one day if needed. "If you want to know the answer to your question," I told the childish Englishmen, "you must send your wife for a private meeting with me to discover what I have under my kilt. Does your wife know Braille?" That response embarrasses any man who is with his wife, and amuses those who are not. The English DJs liked my joke, even if I did not much like them.

"Anyhow," I continued, "there is nothing worn under my kilt: everything is in perfect working order." They loved that worn old chestnut. They have very simple minds, these English.

It is a fact that certain Scottish regiments did require soldiers to wear kilts without underwear. That of course is how Highlanders wore the plaid and the kilt in centuries past. During WWI this was sometimes known as "going regimental" or "military practice" but I have no idea if it is still current. It is certainly comfortable, at least in summer: although, my dear grandson, you must remember to keep your legs down and try to avoid strong winds. Wearing underwear is more hygienic because it is easier to keep clean. Kilts will last a lifetime—or two—but you cannot simply throw a kilt into the washing machine.

THE CUMBERLAND REEL

I use a really simple wheel dance when I teach Scottish dancing in elementary schools. I am usually allowed too little time to get the kids to practice steps. My best experience has been teaching a course of 3 x 90 minutes every second year to the CM1+CM2 class of Marie-Pierre Bernadac, a clever teacher who uses my native English pronunciation and my Scottish singing, acting and dancing as an aid for teaching English. *The Cumberland Reel* is so simple that I do not need to write down the list of dance moves for you. This is a 4 x 32 bar reel for a set of four to six couples. The top two couples do a wheel right and left (right hands across, then left hands across) for the first eight bars. Then the first couple goes down the middle, back up and they cast off or "peel the banana" down to the bottom, followed by all the others. Then is lead up to the top. Everyone makes an arch, and the first couple goes through the arch down to the bottom of the set. I used this same idea once when I choreographed the musical *Brigadoon*, creating an arch so that the bride and groom could dance towards the audience.

You can also have the first couple make the arch at the bottom, and allow all the others to dance to the top of the set, passing under the arch…. But since most young kids do not listen to the music and most are not doing dance steps, they usually finish far too quickly and I need more activity to use up the music. Ideally it takes three lessons for this dance to become respectable: kids remember what they learned from one week to the next and they dance better each time. When I have three weeks, I can teach them the pas de basque and the change of weight (using the recipe "elephant, kangaroo, butterfly") and the traveling step or *pas chassé* which a few of them will then use instinctively when they hear the music in 3:4 time.

I believe you grandchildren could learn *The Cumberland Reel* in three minutes because you have heard the rhythms of Scottish music all your lives and you know what it means to dance. But most of your friends at school have never danced. They may think that jumping around and pumping their arms is dancing, but they are wrong! Marching is a form of dance, as I explained earlier, because it is controlled movement synchronized with music. Boys jogging around the floor while waving their elbows incoherently, do not fit the definition of dance.

31

CLAUDINE & ANNE SUPPORT SCOTLAND'S
HISTORY AND CEILIDH TRADITIONS

How can I learn to dance properly?" Claudine asked at the end of our riotous Burns Night in Vannes. She could feel that she had learned only a simplified version of something better.

"The best solution," I replied, "would be to attend the RSCDS Summer School in St Andrews, the most beautiful city in Scotland, where you will find the best teachers, the best dancing and the best music. In St Andrews you will have the time of your life."

Claudine believed me. She and her husband Eric went to dance in St Andrews. Claudine became a teacher, and in 2018 she led a dozen dancers from South Brittany to enjoy Summer School. Even speaking no English, they all loved it. The Vannes example provides a brilliant example of how ceilidh dancing can lead people into more exciting forms of dance.

That does not diminish the benefit of the ceilidh as a pleasurable activity itself. Claudine Auriacombe runs good ceilidhs in Vannes. Anne MacGregor organises a great ceilidh at Lannion each year for her birthday and often I get to dance with her delightful young granddaughters Orlane et Abigael. Anne's husband Yannick is our "official regional piper" and we are so lucky to have them. Anne and Claudine use *The Gay Gordons* and *The Dashing White Sergeant* as well as simple round-the-room dances like *The Circassian Circle*. This is really a simple "barn dance" and is different from the reel of the same name that appears in RSCDS Book 1. To avoid confusion, the Scottish Dance Dictionary therefore calls our ceilidh version the *Circassian Big Circle*. It goes as follows:

CIRCASSIAN BIG CIRCLE

Reel n x 32-bars around the room in a circle with partner on Man's right. Traditional.

Circassia is a region of the Caucasus between the Black Sea and the Caspian Sea. So what? You may ask.

Bars 1- 8 : All dance in 4 steps and out, and repeat;

Bars 9-12 : Ladies dance in 4 steps, clap and out again;

Bars 13-16 : Men do the same but turn to face partner as they dance out;

Bars 17-24 : All swing partners and end facing anti-clockwise round the room;

Bars 25-32 : All Promenade counter-clockwise for 8 steps.

Dance note: To make it progressive, men can face the lady behind them as they turn on bar 16.

You can see that the RSCDS version below is more complicated: like *The Waltz Country Dance*, it is danced by couples progressing in opposite directions around the room using a series of elegant reel formations: rights-and-lefts, setting and turning with two hands, followed by a ladies' chain and the pas de basque poussette, which both need considerable skill to look nice.

The most perfect way to enjoy the poussette is to dance it without hands, using the full width of the set and still getting around perfectly: an exercise for the young and fit. Jeremy and Grace Hill danced it this way one evening in the Younger Hall, alongside their teenaged daughter Zoey and her friend Emma. It was delightful to watch, reminding me of my athletic youth. Few dancers can manage it well, so taking hands is usually better and the man can help lift his partner in the turn if his hands are below hers. Recently at a ball I invited a Russian semi-beginner for a dance with a poussette. I recited the words to help her: "Out to the side and quarter-turn; up or down with quarter-turn; into the middle and turn right round; back and back." She seemed to be furious with me at the end, told me I had pushed her around which—of course—is what the word *poussette* means. I do not believe that I did push her; I simply danced with her. If she didn't enjoy it tough luck, *tant pis*. The solution will be for me not to dance with her again—not too difficult since I shall probably never meet her again.

CIRCASSIAN CIRCLE

Reel n x 32-bars around the room with couples facing in twos (2 facing 2). Traditional. RSCDS Book 1.

Berthold Brecht's play *A Circassian Chalk Circle* describes a Judgment of Soloman Caucasus-style: what a delightfully irrelevant piece of information. I acted in this play when I was at school aged 16.

Bars 1- 8 : All dance Rights & Lefts;

Bars 9-16 : All set to partner twice and turn 2 Hands;

Bars 17-24 : All dance Ladies' Chain;

Bars 25-32 : All dance Poussette to change places and progress to face next couple.

Ladies' chain

The two ladies cross right hand, then turn their partner left hand before repeating the move in the opposite direction. The men describe a loop on the side each time to meet the lady's hand. Finish on own side opposite your partner.

The best-known barn dance is a Canadian version of an original French country dance. Similar dances have Scandinavian and other names—the Swedish *Hombo* for example. Some Breton couple dances are not very different. We used to dance the *Canadian Barn Dance* at family parties throughout my childhood. Whole families can visit a ceilidh to discover that dancing is really not difficult. I took my French neighbor Sebastien Ellis and his family to one of Anne Macgregor's ceilidhs, and they danced every single dance. Eowyne was around eleven and her sister Aileen six years old. It was a perfect evening for them both, and their mother Sophie loved it. Ellis is a Scottish name. Seb knows his great grandfather settled in Paris when he left the British army. Ceilidhs are in his blood.

CANADIAN BARN DANCE

Reel or Jig n x 16-bars around the room. Couples facing anticlockwise with Ladies on partner's right. Traditional.

Canadian evolution of traditional French folk dance, ideal for dancing in a barn when, Baby, it's cold outside.

Bars 1- 4 : Starting with outside foot walk forward for three steps and hop, walk backwards for three steps and hop;

Bars 5- 8 : Skip or chassé sideways away from partner (Men towards the center, Ladies outwards) for two steps and clap, return two steps to take partner in waltz hold;

Bars 9-12 : Skip or chassé sideways to the Man's left for two steps and back for two steps;

Bars 13-16 : Polka (one-two-three-hop) counter-clockwise round the room.

In a ceilidh with dances like these, families can enjoy dancing and have a sing-along that builds Scottish culture at a community level. Every family party during my childhood was a form of ceilidh. My mother's mother, known by the affectionate name of Mumsmum, loved all these ceilidh dances and others like the *Boston Two-Step* and the *Valeta*, which are easy to dance even when the lady is seventy and her partner is seven, or seventeen. We mixed dancing with games like *Are you there, Moriarty?* (a viciously skillful game that involves hitting people over the head with a rolled-up newspaper) and bobbing for apples (picking them out of a bowl of water using your teeth, which gives an advantage to young people without dentures) and picture quizzes of many varieties. One of our favorite games has always been cutting the flour cake: you pack flour into a pudding bowl and leave it in the fridge to consolidate overnight. At the party you turn out the flour-cake onto a large platter, place a grape or a raisin on top, and start cutting thin slices. The person who finally causes the grape to drop has to pick it out of the flour with his or her teeth—and (s)he can then eat the grape. Most of our favorite games required a towel. Then my father would always recite a few limericks—as many as he was allowed to recite. What sweet memories!

There was a young man from Nepal
Who went to a fancy dress ball.
He said: "I will risk it,
And go as a biscuit."
And a dog ate him up in the hall.

There was a young man born in Cosham,
Who took out his eyeballs to wash 'em.
His wife exclaimed: "Jack,
If you don't put them back
I shall tread on the darn things, and squash 'em."

The other standard dance for a Ceilidh—especially in America—is the Virginia Reel, which has variations dating back to the 17th century or earlier. Multiple versions were used by traveling dancing masters in the 1700s and 1800s to entertain second-generation Scottish settlers in America who had forgotten much of their parents' heritage and culture. I have taught the Virginia Reel to kids in schools as well as in ceilidhs. It is easy to learn and fun to do.

VIRGINIA REEL

Reel 4 x 40 bars in a 4-couple longwise set (or 5 or 6 or even 8 couples in a set). Traditional 19th century.

Version of a dance re-introducing their grandparents' traditional dances to Scottish migrants in Virginia.

Bars 1- 8 : All Advance & Retire 2 steps, and repeat;

Bars 9-16 : All turn partner RH and turn partner LH;

Bars 17-20 : All turn partner 2 Hands;

Bars 21-24 : All dance DoSiDo (back to back passing right shoulders);

Bars 25-32 : 1s slip step down the center and back;

Bars 33-40 : 1s followed by 2s+3s+4s cast to bottom and 1s form arch as 2s+3s+4s

dance under arch and up to top to finish 2341.

Dance note: When beginners or children are not listening to the music, or are running excitedly down the room instead of dancing, couple 1 may race down back up to the top of the set by bar 36: in which case you can have couples 2+3+4 make the arch, and couple 1 can dance down to the bottom to finish 2341.

Ceilidh dancing is a great path towards the introduction of more advanced dances, if you create the right ambiance. Even Lannion's beginners adore John Dewry's unusual *Ramadan-ce* with music by Franz Schubert and Wolfgang Amadeus Mozart—a clever adaption of Franz Schubert's *Moment Musical* No. 3 in F minor and Mozart's *Marche turque* (*Rondo alla turqua*) from piano concerto No 11 (K331)—in an arrangement played by the fabulous Marian Anderson and her band. This clever idea is enormous fun to dance precisely because the music doesn't really fit a reel. The title combines exotic music with *dance* and the Muslim holy month of *Ramadan*. Dédé Squéren and his wife Rosie are particularly good at getting uncertain people through this dance. Overcoming the challenge gives them all huge satisfaction—rather as my brother Rory taught *Ian Powrie* to beginners in Banjul. Beginners struggle at first with the double cross-over Inveran reels; with the partner pass-and-twirl; and with the directions for the three half reels: diagonal, then across the set, and finally on the side. Once they understand the positions they need to reach, it moves and then finally the dance flows and they become excited. A great dance challenge with lovely music to carry you through.

RAMADAN-CE

Reel 8 x 32 bars for 3 couples in a 4-couple longwise set. Devisor: John Drewry. Turkish Set.

Ramadan is the Muslim holy month of fasting, when no food or liquid is imbibed from dawn until dusk.

The music borrowed from Schubert and Mozart gives this dance an oriental feeling. To be danced seriously.

Bars 1- 8 : 1s dance Inveran Reels with 2s+3s (1s cross down, then cross back up);

Bars 9-16 : 1s cross RH, cast 1 place & turn RH to face 1st corners ;

Bars 17-20 : 1s dance RSh round 1st corner, pass RSh & dance RSh round 2nd corner to end 2nd place opposite side WHILE 1st corners dance in, 1/2 turn RH, twirl & dance out to each other's place;

Bars 20-24 : 2nd corners dance similarly. (3)(1)(2);

Bars 25-32 : 1s dance 1/2 LSh reels of 3 across (Man at top with 3s & Lady at bottom with 2s), 1s dance 1/2 RSh reels of 3 on own sides (Man Down, Lady up).

32

ELISABETH'S PEACE DANCING AND BREXIT'S THREAT TO PEACE

D earest grandchildren, your grandparents were children of the Peace and Love Generation. Our parents grew up in war-torn Europe and they came of age during the Second World War. Everything changed thereafter. Soldiers returning from war demanded better living conditions in Europe, while Indian and Pakistani independence in 1947 began the unraveling of the European empires. America's Marshall Plan rebuilt Europe as a market for US products, launching a 30-year period of unprecedented peace and prosperity in Europe, *les trente glorieuses* and encouraging moves towards European unity. The Marshall Plan and the United Nations organization were America's great legacy to the post-war world.

However, by the 1960s my generation would no longer tolerate American imperialism in Vietnam, racism in South Africa, hunger and famine in India and the Sahel. Your Mamie and I danced as students, but we also collected funds for medicines and food in Vietnam, contested nuclear weapons, marched in the streets against poverty, organized bank boycotts and helped lead a massive student protest movement in 1969 against South African all-white sports teams. Meanwhile France had the student revolution of 1968: students and workers brought down President de Gaulle and removed minor symbols like suits and ties and academic gowns in universities, although we can see—with the benefit of hindsight—that they changed little in French elitist society. At the Olympic Games of October 1968, 200-meter athletes Tommy Smith (gold medal) and John Carlos (bronze) made a Black Power gesture protesting racism in the USA: a problem that has not improved despite the civil rights movement and the work of Martin Luther King.

Love was the key to the 1960s: Peace, Love, Flower Power. The Russians invaded Prague in 1968 to crush "socialism with a human face" and Czech students climbed onto the Soviet tanks to place flowers in their guns. Some of the Russian soldiers cried when they realized how they had been manipulated by the Kremlin. While some in the hippie movement smoked pot, your Mamie and I embraced the peace and love philosophy without ever smoking drugs—in fact we never smoked anything at all. Ever. Why would we dull our humanity and our emotions with tobacco or drugs? I express love through my dancing, through my teaching, though my family and my work for peace. Music and dance work for me better than alcohol or tobacco (nicotine) or cannabis could ever do. Although I admit that I do love dark chocolate.

Notably in Britain and America the hippie generation changed attitudes to gay rights while the birth pill liberated women and sexuality, encouraged by the music and messaging of Elvis Presley, Chuck Berry, Bob Marley, Joan Baez, Bob Dylan, Leonard Cohen, Franco, the Rolling Stones and the Beatles. This atmosphere of freedom, peace and love I still find in the dance community today, and especially in the environment of American contra dance where people wear fun clothes. Plenty of men wear skirts. I wear the kilt. Contra dance retains many of the good elements of the 1960s and is tolerant of gender variation. Flower power is an alternative to weaponizing society. 50 years on I still work in the United Nations Institute for Disarmament Research, in the Peace Movement and with various peace networks including Transcend, founded by Professor Johann Galtung, "the father of peace studies." I taught at the European Peace University in Austria, where your aunt Catherine Leïla did her master's degree.

This peace and dancing is not the same as "Dances of Universal Peace," a Sufi-influenced movement in USA that celebrated its 50th anniversary in June 2018. My contra-dance friend Elisabeth Drumm told me about it and piqued my interest, children, because Mamie and I took your father Edward (when he was aged 14 months) to Konya, in Turkish Anatolia, to visit the shrine of the great mystical Sunni Muslim Sufi writer Jallaluddin Rumi. Known as the *Mevlana* or "Master", Rumi founded the Whirling Dervishes. He was born in Balkh, in northern Afghanistan where we were married. As a young man around 1216, Rumi fled with his family to avoid Genghis Khan the Mongol monster of destruction, the nuclear bomb of the 13th century. Rumi's father and his disciples settled in Konya, where Rumi taught and was buried. The Mevlana taught love and peace and dancing.

Elisabeth and her husband Tom frequented Sufi dances, as Dances of Universal Peace are usually called in Richmond and Charlottesville. They are simple circle dances, danced around musicians who sit in the middle. Everybody can participate. The dances emphasise singing; they are meditations set to music. Most songs/dances express love—to oneself, to each other, and to the world in general; they are beautiful and meaningful. Elisabeth and Tom enjoyed this loving and supportive community. A Sufi teacher taught the dervish spinning technique to initiated Sufis and by invitation only. Dervish whirling is a religious experience requiring intense concentration. At Sufi peace dance camps in America, the pinnacle of the evening is a performance of the *sema* dervish dancing in the space between the musicians and the audience. Sufi initiates circle on their own axis (like the Earth) and on an orbit (as if around the Sun) with one hand pointing down to the World and the other raised to Heaven. The dances can go on for 15-20 minutes, beautiful and powerful in tune with oriental music of mysticism. Four dances symbolize the four seasons, the four elements and the four ages of man. The *sema* ceremony has seven parts, each of which follows a distinct musical theme called a *selam*. With your Mamie I have attended dervish religious dance ceremonies in America, in Britain, in Turkey ... but I have never been to a peace dance camp. Sufi dance is more like ballet dancing (an activity for experts who create an artistic and mystical experience) than "dancing" in the participative sense that I usually understand the word. Peace dancing, on the other hand, is participative.

Elisabeth is actually German, as well as naturalized American, and she—like the rest of my American and European friends who dance for love and peace—is appalled that the English have voted to leave the European Union. If the EU disintegrates, you may be sure that we will have another European war. Elisabeth told me that both her grandfathers died in the battle of Stalingrad. Ethnocentric Americans and Brits often forget that ordinary Russian and Polish and German citizens suffered the most during the Second Would War (including, of course, Jewish citizens and the Roma = gypsies who were specifically persecuted by the Nazi regime and killed in the Holocaust). Defeating Nazi Fascism was necessary, but everyone suffers in war—especially women. War is terrible. Almost anything is better than war. Churchill famously said about diplomacy at the United Nations: "Jaw, Jaw, Jaw is better than War, War, War."

The cities that suffered the worst destruction in WW2 (1939–45) seem to have been the German cities of Jülich, Dresden, Hamburg, Cologne and Berlin; the Polish capital Warsaw; Stalingrad in Russia; the French cities of Brest, Caen, St Malo; Manila, the capital city of Philippines; Rotterdam in the Netherlands; the British cities of Hull, Coventry and London; and the atom bombed cities of Nagasaki and Hiroshima in Japan. It was truly a World War. Maybe 60 million people died during WW2, more than half of them civilians. Casualties from the First War (1914-18) are even harder to estimate: maybe 20 millions killed to which we can add related genocides and the WWI epidemic of Spanish Flu that killed 20 million alone. Probably 100 million people perished during the first half of the 20th century because of Europe's wars. That is Europe's recent history, children. The European Union was created to stop it happening again.

I have recommended living your lives to promote the greatest happiness of the greatest number. Two important books have been written recently by women called Kate, each of which should prove seminal for the happiness of your generation. Kate Pickett (with her husband Richard Wilkinson) has published *The Spirit*

Level (2009) showing how inequalities of income have made our society less happy, more divided, poorer in spirit. Bank corruption and the crisis of 2008 deprived millions of their jobs, their houses, their lives: yet no banker was held to account. Financial bonuses continued to be paid, mostly by the taxpayer. This example of elitism, privilege and impunity, more than any other factor (even including immigration), explains the Brexit vote. Kate Raworth's book *Doughnut Economics: Seven Ways to Think Like a 21st-Century Economist* offers an economic model that values human well-being and advocates for a "regenerative and distributive economy" and is the most important economics book written in the past 100 years. These two brilliant Kates, children, offer your generation new ways to reinterpret your lives within the limited ecological resources our planet provides.

Therein lie future happiness and peace.

When I was a boy I learned to speak German. In 1961 I stayed with the family of a greengrocer in Laböe-bei-Kiel, a coastal village in Schleswig Holstein near the Danish border. After leaving school in 1965, I worked for a charitable medical foundation in Tübingen and attended university beside the beautiful river Neckar. There was no German dancing, so I joined an American square dance club led by Germans. After American dancing in Germany, I was thrilled to find Bavarian *Schuhplattl* dancing in Virginia. For fifteen years I wore *Lederhosen* and danced with the Cheek and Britton families for Oktoberfest as a proud member of Richmond's *Hirschjaeger Dancers*. I think I look terrible in short leather trousers even with beautifully embroidered leather suspenders, but I have happy memories of slapping my shoes and thighs, of dancing Ländlers, Polkas and Waltzes with lovely women including Dale, Audrey, Trish and Su Boer. I danced with Leah Cheek when she was three years old, giggling as I swung her in my arms, and later as a beautiful young woman of 16—still giggling.

All my German friends' parents fought in (and some were killed in) the Second World War between 1939 and 1945. Germans told me their war stories. I have enjoyed the books of Hans Helmut Kirst about Gunner Asch, an honest German soldier surviving war and corruption in the non-democratic Nazi system. My father's generation of British soldiers and sailors and airmen risked their lives (or lost them) during that same war. Mamie's father fought viciously in the Burmese jungle, while her French family in Brittany suffered German occupation for four years until Americans launched the Normandy Landings in June 1944 that began the liberation of France. Nazi and Italian and Austrian Fascism damaged everyone. That war dominated our young lives and the lives of my many German friends. We must NEVER let it happen again.

Our *directeur de thèse* at the Collège de France, a Romanian anthropologist called Paul-Henri Stahl said: "Democracy will occupy a short time between the European wars, and I am grateful to live during the democratic period." It was in order to stop people making war in Europe that the United Nations organization and the European Economic Community were created. Our worldwide RSCDS dance community is one of many international friendship organizations that help avoid the future threat of war. Sister Cities International is a network of town-twinning friendships created by President Dwight Eisenhower to promote "citizen diplomacy" in the hope that people who know each other will not kill each other.

I do not know a single person in the dance community who supports the English decision to take Britain out of Europe. Scotland (66%) and Northern Ireland (58%) voted to remain inside the EU. Surveys in 2018 show that the Welsh (who voted to leave) and a lot of English regions are changing their minds as the true costs of Brexit emerge. Celts feel European, after centuries of English persecution. I deliver a lecture (in French) I call *Historical links between France and Scotland, and why everyone hates the English*. This is rhetorical over-statement, of course: but Celts suffered English repression since the 1200s. Edward I was called "The Hammer of the Scots" because of his brutality. I tell stories from Anglo-Scottish and French history, show pictures of beautiful Scotland and demonstrate Scottish dancing with Breton friends and bagpipers. At the end we discuss Brexit, which the French cannot understand. At the Josselin British Weekend, Dr Penny Gibbs told me to stand on stage as her dance spokesperson and denounce the Brexit vote in English and in French, telling the Bretons and the British why all thinking people support peace and unity in Europe. Like any organization the EU is bureaucratic: bureaucracy is a mechanism of governance. People will trade with or without the EU. The EU is about peace, which is why the EU won the 2012 Nobel Peace Prize.

The UK joined the European Communities (EC) in 1973. In the referendum of 5th June 1975, 67.2% of the electorate voted to stay in. In the Brexit referendum on 23rd June 2016 a very small majority voted to leave the EU. It was a close-run thing: 17,410,742 (51.9%) voted to leave; 16,141,241 (48.1%) voted to remain in the EU. Since only 65% of voters actually voted, was it a valid "democratic" way to change our unwritten Constitution? Britain's Electoral Commission has found that the Leave campaign lied, overspent and hid illegal funding. There are reasons to believe that Russian and/or other foreign elements ran covert campaigns to promote Brexit, in order to weaken NATO and the European Union. The Electoral Commission found "serious breaches of the laws put in place by parliament to ensure fairness and transparency at elections and referendums" and has referred the matter to the police. These facts justify invalidating the result of the 2016 referendum.

The Brexit referendum was a ridiculous attempt to placate angry men in Britain's Conservative Party (which it failed to do). Putting highly complex matters to a simple Yes-or-No vote is unintelligent. Every good leader and manager knows that good decisions are made after analysing multiple scenarios. It is not a question of "If" but of "Which?" Saying "In or Out" of Europe is absurd. The British Isles cannot put up a sail and float away to another place. The British are tied to Europe because we are stuck between the Irish Sea, the North Sea and the English Channel. Liam, my dear fellow, you were the person who produced at the age of seven the most cogent reason for refusing Brexit. "I think we should stay European," you told your parents: "I don't think we want to join with Asia or something."

Precisely! But your generation was not consulted. As a result, with less than 52% of British votes cast for Brexit, and with the Scots and Irish voting massively against leaving the EU, the French and the Celts have a new reason to hate those elderly English who voted to leave.

33

DANCING WITH LESLEY IN GLASGOW, CITY OF ART AND CULTURE

On 16th June 2018, as I was finishing this book, the Charles Rennie Mackintosh building in Glasgow was burned to the ground.

On Sunday 17th June 2018 I listened to the Sunday service on BBC Radio 4, coming from an Episcopal Church in the heart of Glasgow during the famous Glasgow Festival that I have enjoyed in past years. I am deeply saddened by the destruction of the beautiful School of Arts and the world-famous Charles Rennie Mackintosh building. What a tragedy for those who love the city and its arts, I have little artistic talent myself, but I admire Art Nouveau, the Arts and Crafts Movement and late nineteenth century Glasgow Style. Artistic creation—including music and dance—allows human beings to claim that we are a "higher order" of mammals: but we are animals nonetheless. Early reports suggest that the renovated Glasgow School of Arts building may have been destroyed beyond repair, even the stone façade. It is tragic.

I should also add for your benefit, lovely grandchildren, that Mackintosh migrated to Suffolk during the First World War, then to southwest France after the war where he became a painter of water-colors falling in love with the light and colors of the French countryside. He went broke, of course: water-color painting does not pay the rent as handsomely as architecture. The library at the Glasgow School of Art is no more; Glasgow's most important architectural building has been destroyed. I wrote a condolence note to my friends living in Glasgow. The disaster provides a sad but fitting end to the thoughts about Scottish culture that I have been sharing. In the end, everything is born to die. Even art and architecture do not last eternally, from dust to dust ... from ashes to ashes ...

Apparently there was a new sprinkler system in the arts building, but it had not yet been connected to a water supply. How sadly ironic. I always feel a little part of me lies in Glasgow. Because of my love for the wonderful Scottish String Orchestra? Because Miss Milligan, our RSCDS co-Founder, was a teacher at Jordanhill College in Glasgow? Because my great great grandfather William Maclean was a Baillie of Glasgow? Because of the wit and influence of Billy Connolly and Harry Lauder? Because J.B. Milne was a Glaswegian? Some of this dance and musical and comic influence draws me into the city's ambiance and so does my love of the work and style of Charles Rennie Mackintosh. This is his 150th anniversary: he was born 150 years ago on 7th June 1868. A part of me in Glasgow? I used to travel from St Andrews to Glasgow to carry out research in the Glasgow Public Library, using old-world micro-film technology to roll pictures of old newspapers across a huge magnifying screen. Only in Glasgow were these journal records available—a technology that makes me sound so 20th century!

Our Maclean ancestors moved from Mull to Glasgow, like so many Islanders. My paternal grandmother Frida Maclean was born in 1885 on the beautiful Glen Earn estate in Perthshire which was sold when the Bank of Glasgow went bust: great grandfather Charles Maclean must have been a stock holder, I suppose, although family legend claims that he lost his money when a Glasgow fire destroyed a gas holder and wiped out all who owned parts of it. Perhaps he was unlucky with both the bank and a gas company. Whichever, the money made by Charles' father William Maclean from shrewd investments in the construction of new-fangled 19th century railways, went up in gas smoke or disappeared in bad Argentine railway investments made by the bank. Willie Maclean was the owner of the Plantation estate in Glasgow (now the Plantation District) and Maclean Street was named for him. For my grandchildren these 200-year-old events are ancient, history, yet the birth of my grandmother 133 years ago seems an intimate part of my personal life. Curious how time changes perspective.

The other Scottish grandfather Ian Hamilton was raised at Hafton House in Dunoon on the Clyde just west of Glasgow in a military family. He fell in love with my grandmother Doris Iremonger, née Chamier and gave her a baby: my mother. Doris herself was born in India, to very religious Huguenot descendents of a family originally from Southern France. Daniel Chamier, one of her ancestors, appears on the Reformation Wall in Geneva, Switzerland. Doris' mother Alice Zélie Norton (or perhaps Alice Zélie's mother?) came from Quebec, which is why Alice Zélie spoke French and was called "Grandmère" by her grandchildren. That is where the family name Zélie comes from. If Alice knew about her daughter's "affair" with General Sir Ian Hamilton, she and everyone else kept silent—as the British always did. Every summer when my mother was small, Alice Zélie would rent an apartment in Dinard so that her grandchildren could play on the beaches of Brittany. Just to remind you, dearest grandchildren, that you have solid French ancestry as well as Scots and Irish.

The Mackintosh School of Arts is not the only fine building in Glasgow, of course. The RSCDS organized a worldwide Dance Aid in 1987, and we attended the Glasgow fund-raising dance with our friends Philip and Lesley Hanlon in Glasgow's magnificent City Chambers. Here, every room is built with glorious hard woods imported from different countries of the British Empire: a symbol both of the avaricious nature of the Empire and of Glasgow's role as a trading center that benefited hugely from imperial military conquest. Most of the ships of the British Empire were built on Clydeside. We explored the City Chambers. Catherine Leïla aged 8 sat in the grand chair of the Lord Provost, and told us that the seat fitted her perfectly. But while there are other splendid buildings in Glasgow, including the imposing Glasgow University, losing the Charles Rennie Mackintosh building is a tragic moment for the city: two terribly destructive fires in four years have attacked, and probably now destroyed, this artistic center of the city. Can it be coincidence? Two fires in four years seem suspiciously unusual.

Glasgow will recover. Death is only a passing and Glasgow is greater than any one building, however beautiful. The dance *J. B. Milne* was named after the owner of Glasgow's cinemas between the wars, and imitates both the rectangular shape of the movie screen and the moving pictures (illustrated by the meanwhile figure which has the dancing couple setting-turning in the middle while the corners cross-set along the sides and then across the dance.) The entrepreneur J. B. Milne was the heart and core of Glasgow's movie culture, and his dance is one of the very best in the whole Scottish dance repertoire. I have danced *J. B. Milne* with my dear friend Lesley Hanlon in Glasgow and also in Banjul. When I waltzed with her at the wedding of Catherine Leïla and Pierre Claude, everyone else left the floor in order to admire Lesley's grace and charm. Now that Glasgow is suffering, I am thinking of Lesley and Phil who both taught medicine at Glasgow University. When I cannot get to sleep, kids, I hum the music as I dance *J. B. Milne* inside my head. It does not put me to sleep, but it keeps me entertained. Dancing is so much better than counting sheep.

J. B. MILNE

Reel 8 x 32 bars for 3 couples in a 4-couple longwise set. Devisor: Hugh Foss. Angus Fitchett Album.

Dance inspired by the movie screens in J.B. Milne's Glasgow cinema chain.

Bars 1-4 : 1M2L set advancing and turn by the right;

Bars 5-8 : 1L2M set advancing and turn by the right;

Bars 9-12 : 1s set advancing and turn both hands to face out, while 2s step up;

Bars 13-16 : 1s cast and petronella turn, finishing 1L at top facing down and 1M between the 3s facing up;

Bars 17-20 : 1s set and turn by the right ¾ to opposite sides WHILE 2M3M 2L3L cross by the right on the sides and set;

Bars 21-24 : 1s set and turn by the right ¾ (finishing 1M at top facing down and 1L at bottom facing up) WHILE 3s 2s cross by the right to opposite sides and set;

Bars 25-28 : 1s set and cross (up and down) by the right WHILE 3L2L 3M2M cross by the right on the sides and set;

Bars 29-30 : is cast (L down, M up) through the ends of the set and curve right through their third corner position to 2nd place on own sides WHILE 2s 3s cross by the right, all finishing facing in;

Bars 30-32 : 2s1s3s set on the sides.

Dance Notes

Bars 1-12 pas de basque throughout.

Bars 13-14 require the traveling step, while bars 15-16 need pas de basque.

One of the greatest feelings in Scottish Country Dancing comes on bars 29-30 as you fly swooping out through the end of the *J.B. Milne* set, and turn the corner (passing through the corner position) to arrive with perfect phrasing for the final setting with the supporting dancers on bars 31-32. If one day I am no longer able to swoop out of the end of the set in *J.B. Milne*, I shall take it as an indication that my dancing days are past ... but NEVERTHELESS I intend to shuffle on until the very end.

Let me add this wonderful message that I found on my Facebook page from Laurel Hayward, who used to dance with me all the time until she moved from Virginia to Florida. "One of my happiest memories ever in my life was dancing *J.B. Milne* with you in Younger Hall." Thank you, Laurel. What a lovely tribute to dancing, to *J.B.Milne*, to St Andrews and to life!

Dearest grandchildren, I shall leave you with a blessing of Irish origin, showing respect to your beautiful Celtic genes.

> *May the road rise to meet you,*
> *May the wind be ever at your back.*
> *May the sun shine warm upon your face,*
> *And the rains fall soft upon your fields.*
> *And until we meet again,*
> *May God hold you in the palm of his hand.*

Sharing my love of dance is the best gift I can offer you, my lovely Liam and Isabelle and Roísín. Take care of yourselves. Very much love to you always.

Papy!

THE END

AFTERWORD

THANK YOU once more to the RSCDS and to its leadership and teachers, to the folks who run the Strathspey Server and the Scottish Dance Dictionary, to all our amazing dance musicians and to the writers of the cribs and diagrams; thank you to all the many lovely ladies who have danced with me over the years and to those who will dance with me in the future, Finally, a big thank you to everyone who contributes to the love of dancing in all its forms and in every country, and in the Younger Hall in St Andrews. We dance and therefore we are!

ANNEX I

DANCES DESCRIBED IN THIS BOOK

Category	Dance name	Dance type	Source	Chapter
JIGS				
	Blue Bonnets	Jig 8 x 32 bars 2 couples, 4C set	Trad. RSCDS Book 3	20
	Hooper's Jig	Jig 8 x 32 bars 3 couples, 4C set	Anon. 99 More Scottish Country Dances	24
	Ian Powrie's Farewell to Auchtaradar	Jig 128 bars all dance 4C squ set	Bill Hamilton	22
	Joie de vivre	Jig 8 x 32 bars for 3 couples, 4C set	Irene van Maarseveen. RSCDS 39	21
	Muirland Willie	Jig 8 x 32 bars for 3 couples, 4C set	Anon. RSCDS Book 21	16
	St Andrews Fair	Jig 8 x 32 bars	Roy Goldring	15
	Swashbuckling Iain	Jig 8 x 32 bars for 2 couples, 4C set	Carolyn Hunt. San Francisco Collection 2	28
REELS				
	Cumberland Reel	Reel 4 x 32 4C set	Trad. RSCDS Book 1	30
	Irish Rover	Reel 8 x 32 bars 3 couples, 4C set	James B. Cosh in: 22 Scottish Country Dances	21
	J.B. Milne	Reel 8 x 32 bars 3 couples, 4C set	Hugh Foss in: Angus Fitchett Album	33
	Nottingham Lace	Reel 96-bar squ set	Jenny Bradley	29
	Ramadan-ce	Reel 8 x 32 bars 3 couples, 4C set	John Drewry. Turkish Set	31
	Reel of the 51st Division	Reel 8 x 32 bars 3 couples, 4C set	J.E.M. Atkinson. RSCDS Book 13	26
	Reel of the Royal Scots	Reel 8 x 32 bars 3 couples ,4C set	Roy Goldring: in SCD Leaflets	23
	Reel for Rory	Reel 8 x 48 bars 3 couples ,4C set	Margaret Fell for Rory Poulton. Is Cottage Bk 6	22
	Shiftin' Bobbins	Reel 8 x 32 bars 3 couples, 4C set	Roy Clowes. Ormskirk 6	29
	Trip to Bavaria	Reel 4 x 32 bars all dance 4 couple set	James MacGregor-Brown Guide To SCD ex-Collins	30
STRATHSPEYS				
	Dance with your Soul	Strath 4 x 32 bars 4C set, all dance	M Boekner. Cameo Collection Vol 23	17
	Dragonflies (*Libellules*)	Strathspey 5 x 32 for 5 dancers	Jane Lataille. Santa Fe Always Enough to Dance	29
	Minister on the Loch	Strathspey 3 x 32 for 3C in 3C set	Roy Goldring: in 24 Graded and Social Dances	27
	Ruby Wilkinson's Farewell to Cranshaws	Strathspey 4 x 32 all dance, 4C set	Alasdair Brown.	20
	Sands of Morar	Strathspey 8 x 32 for 3C in a 4C set	Barry Priddey. RSCDS Book 45	27
	The Lannion Link	Strathspey 4 x 40 all dance, 4C set	Caroline Morgan-Smith of Bridport	28
	The Silver Thistle Ball	Strathspey 3 x 32 for 3C in 3C set	Moira Turner & Stella Fogg of Richmond	8
	The Wind on Loch Fyne	Strathspey 3 x 32 3 C triangular set	John Bowie. Dickson Dunedin Book 1	18

MEDLEY				
	MacDonald of Keppoch	Medley (S64+R64) 4C square set	Chris Ronald of New York. RSCDS Book 49	30
WALTZES				
	Fifty Years On	Waltz for longwise set of 4 couples	Moira Turner of Richmond, Virginia	7
	The Veleta Waltz	Waltz for 1 couple	Arthur Morris	9
	Waltz Country Dance	Waltz 40 bars for 2 couples facing	Traditional. Scottish moving round the room	3
CEILIDH DANCES				
	Canadian Barn Dance	Reel round-the-room in pairs	Traditional	31
	Circassian (Big) Circle	Reel 32 bars	Round the room couples	31
	Dashing White Sergeant	Reel round-the-room in 3s	Trad. RSCDS book 3	12
	Flying Scotsman	Jig for 4C or 5C	Hugh Thurston	9
	Gay Gordons	March in pairs	Traditional	12
	Nine Pins Dance	Reel for 9 people	Dance game	9
	Orcadian Strip the Willow	Reel unlimited	Traditional	17
	Virginia Reel	Reel 4 x 40 bars	Traditional	31
	Waves of Tory	Reel unlimited	Irish	13

Other dancing described in this book:

	African dance	African	Traditional	Intro, 4
	Ballet	Theatrical	Russian and French	1, 4
	Blue Bonnets step dance	Highland step	Traditional	20
	Ceilidh dances	Scottish	Traditional	9, 22, 31
	Contra dance	American dance	Irish-American	8, 13, 32
	Country	Line dance	American	29
	Eye contact	Scottish and Contra	Lessons for novices	2, 6, 27
	Grand March	Scottish	Traditional	15
	Hornpipe	Scottish / English	Royal Navy	17, 21
	Highland dancing	Scottish	Traditional	19
	Knot	Scottish	RSCDS	28
	Ladies' Chain	Scottish	RSCDS	31
	Leading and following	Waltz	Lessons for novices	5, 6, 7
	Minuet	Court dance	Traditional medieval	1, 2
	Noodles and firm arms	Scottish dance	Lessons for noodles	6
	Pas de basque	Scottish dance	Lessons for novices	19, 26
	Peace & Sufi dancing	Circular	Sufi dancing	32
	Poussette Diamond	Strathspey	RSCDS	6, 27
	Poussette Progressive	Reel	RSCDS	16, 31
	Rondel	Scottish	RSCDS	17
	Rufty Tufty	English country	Traditional medieval	3
	Scottish dance typology	List of dance styles	Scottish	17
	Schottish	Hebridean	Scandinavia	17
	Shepherd's Crook	Highland step	Traditional by McNab	12
	Tourbillon	Scottish	RSCDS	27

ANNEX II

HERE IS A FIRST SCOTTISH DANCE PROGRAMME FOR YOU

This programme—drawn from the dances described in this book— is heavy on Strathspeys, which are the dances that I most love. In the Spring edition of Scottish Country Dancer, Mervyn Short offered excellent advice about creating a dance programme, which included the plea not to make it too difficult for people to enjoy! I entirely agree with Mervyn. Some RSCDS teachers who love the challenge of complexity, forget that dance programmes should be put together for the pleasure of other people, for the people who are coming to the dance.

I challenge the idea that a dance programme needs to run in the traditional order Jig-Strathspey-Reel. I include in this first programme (there is a second offering below) some waltzes and extra strathspeys. As I get on in years I find that I have better control over my strathspey steps and my waltzing, which can also be less taxing on the ankles and knees than jigs and reels. However, even with my love of strathspey, I know nothing more exciting that flying up to the top of the set in the Reel of the Royal Scots, or soaring out through the bottom of the set of J. B. Milne, to curve around into that final setting on the side for all three couples with perfect phrasing. Ah, bliss! Naturally, I want to dance as much as possible: I have no desire to drive one or two hours to attend to an event that has only 14 or 16 dances. This programme has 18, and I prefer 20 dances. My grandchildren and RSCDS dance organisers can modify this programme as they like, or ignore me completely. Tricky dances are shown with asterisks* or ** or *** for the most difficult (beginners abstain) dances.

Order/diff	Dance name	Dance type	Source	Chapter
0	Grand March	March	Trad	19
1	St Andrews Fair	Jig 8 x 32 bars	Roy Goldring	15
2	Waltz Country Dance	Waltz 40 bars for 2 couples facing	Traditional. Scottish moving round the room	3
3 *	Shiftin' Bobbins	Reel 8 x 32 bars for 3 couples in 4C set	Roy Clowes Ormskirk 6	29
4	Dance with your Soul	Strath 4 x 32 bars 4C set, all dance	M Boekner Cameo Collection Vol 23	17
5 **	Ian Powrie's Farewell to Auchtaradar	Jig 128 bars all dance 4C squ set	Bill Hamilton	22
6 **	The Silver Thistle Ball	Strath 3 x 32 bars 3 couple set	Moira Turner & Stella Fogg	8
7 ***	Muirland Willie	Jig 8 x 32 bars for 3 couples in 4C set	Anon. RSCDS Book 21	16
8 **	Minister on the Loch	Strathspey 3 x 32 for 3C in 3C set	Roy Goldring: in 24 Graded & Social Dances	27
9 **	Reel of the Royal Scots	Reel 8 x 32 bars 3 couples ,4C set	Roy Goldring: in SCD Leaflets	23
	Pause for supper			
10	Blue Bonnets	Jig 8 x 32 bars for 2 couples in 4C set	Trad RSCDS Book 3	20
11 **	**J.B. Milne**	Reel 8 x 32 bars 3couples in 4C set	Hugh Foss in : Angus Fitchett Album	33
12 **	Ruby Wilkinson's Farewell to Cranshaws	Strathspey 4 x 32 all dance, 4C set	Alasdair Brown.	20
13 **	Irish Rover	Reel 8 x 32 bars 3 couples, 4C set	James B. Cosh in: 22 Scottish Country Dances	21
14 **	The Wind on Loch Fyne	Strathspey 3 x 32 3 C triangular set	John Bowie. Dickson Dunedin Book 1	18
15	Joie de vivre	Jig 8 x 32 bars for 3 Couples in 4C set	Irene van Maarseveen RSCDS Book 39	21
16 *	Trip to Bavaria	Reel 4 x 32 bars all dance in the 4 C set	James MacGregor-Brown Guide To SCD ex-Collins	30
17 **	The Lannion Link	Strathspey Four couple 40 bar	Caroline Morgan-Smith of Bridport	28
18	Reel of the 51st Division	Reel 8 x 32 bars 3 couples in 4C set	Roy Goldring SCD Leaflets	26
19 *	Fifty Years On	Waltz for a set of 4 couples	Moira Turner	7
20	All sing : Auld Lang Syne	Singing in Chorus	Robert Burns	See below

Of the 18 dances on this programme, 7 are easy if your partner knows the dance; 11 are enjoyable if you know the special figures; the one very difficult dance is best left to people who have learned it.

** means there are tricky one or two figures you should learn, in order to enjoy this dance.

*** means sit this one out unless you know Muirland Willie with the different movements for all dancers.

AULD LANG SYNE collected and arranged by Robert Burns in 1788
Traditionally sung at New Year / Hogmanay and after dances

Should auld acquaintance be forgot
And never brought to mind?
Should auld acquaintance be forgot
And days of auld lang syne?

Refrain
For auld lang syne, my dear
For auld lang syne
We'll take a cup o'kindness yet
For auld lang syne

And there's a hand, my trusty feire
And gie's a hand o' thine
And we'll tak a right gude-willie waught
For auld lang syne.

Refrain

Glossary:
Auld lang syne = for old times' sake; for the sake of good old times;
gude-willie waught = one for the road; a deep draft of ale;
feire = friend.

ANNEX III

HERE IS A SECOND SCOTTISH DANCE PROGRAMME FOR YOU

This second list of dances was the ball programme for the 2018 Scots Bonnet Ball in St Quay Perros, Brittany. It was so enjoyable that I am sharing it here. In previous years we have sometimes chosen dances that were too difficult, resulting in long walk-throughs, multiple problems and chaotic dance results. In 2018 there were simple dances, intermediate dances and a few challenges: the balance was perfect and everyone was ecstatic at the end of the dance—thanks to our exceptional musicians Ian Robinson and John Dudley and MCs Martine Guilbert Le Bideau and Sylvie Le Charpentier.

ORDER OF DANCE

Order/diffic	Dance	Type	Special feature
1	EH3 7AF	32 bar Jig 3C in 4C set	promenade
2	Summer on the Beach	32 bar Reel for all four couples at once	with 3 wheels
3	Delvin Side	32 bar Strath 3C/ 4C set	Slow from 1794
4 **	The Zoologist	32 bar Jig for 3 couples	3 ½ reels, 2 of them diagonal
5 **	Milton's Welcome	32 bar Reel for 3 Couples	Reel with a surprise turn & cast
6 *	Holyrood Strathspey	32 bar S for 3 C	C pass & turn
7 **	Glayva	2 couple Jig	3 distinct parts
8 **	MacDonald of Keppoch -	Medley - square set	6barR&L,center reel
9 **	Miss Eleanor	32 bar Strathspey	Bourrel
10 ***	Tempest in a Teacup	64 bar Reel, for 3 couples in set of 3C	2ᶜ C on opp side very fast Targe
11 *	Dundee Whaler	Strathspey	petronella and lacing figures
12 **	Ian Powrie	Jig 4 Couple Square set	a favorite ; reels and wheels
	Break for sit-down dinner		
13	Antarctica Bound	Jig for 4 couples	13 Kids fun dance
14 *	Craigleith	88 bar Reel - square set	R&L and ladies' chain ; long/easy
15 **	The Gentleman	Strathspey 3 Couples	3 ½ reels + diamond poussette
16 **	John Cass	88 bar 5-Couple Reel	Tandem reels
17 ***	Bratach Bana	32 bar Reel for 3 couples	½ reels and diagonal RT&L
18 **	Bonnie Stronshiray	3 couple strathspey	Diag ½ reels
19 **	J.B. Milne	32 bar Reel	Meanwhile figures

Of the 19 dances on this programme, 9 are easy if your partner knows the dance; 9 are enjoyable if you know the special figures; one very difficult tempestuous dance is best left to people who have learned it.

** means there are one or two tricky figures you should learn, in order to enjoy this dance.

*** means please sit out unless you know the Bratach, a fast Tempest and all the turns in the Teacup.

Made in the USA
Columbia, SC
10 November 2018